REDEVELOPING CHINA'S VILLAGES IN THE TWENTY-FIRST CENTURY

THE DILEMMAS OF POLICY IMPLEMENTATION

REDEVELOPING CHINA'S VILLAGES IN THE TWENTY-FIRST CENTURY

THE DILEMMAS OF POLICY IMPLEMENTATION

LIOR ROSENBERG

Australian
National
University

ANU PRESS

To Yaël, Yitai and Noa

Australian
National
University

ANU PRESS

Published by ANU Press
The Australian National University
Canberra ACT 2600, Australia
Email: anupress@anu.edu.au

Available to download for free at press.anu.edu.au

ISBN (print): 9781760466015
ISBN (online): 9781760466022

WorldCat (print): 1391124392
WorldCat (online): 1391124365

DOI: 10.22459/RCVTFC.2023

Cover design and layout by ANU Press. Cover photographs by Lior Rosenberg.

This book is published under the aegis of the Public Policy editorial board of ANU Press.

Contents

List of Illustrations

Charts

Figures

Tables

Acknowledgments

This book is a product of my PhD studies at The Australian National University (ANU) and post-doctoral work at the Hebrew University of Jerusalem. Many people have contributed to this research and it is my pleasure to convey my gratitude to them. Credit goes first and foremost to Professor Jonathan Unger for being an excellent and inspiring supervisor. I thank him for his patience, his constant encouragement and positive spirit, and his unconditioned belief in me and in this research project, as well as for all the knowledge I have acquired from him. I also thank him and Professor Anita Chan for opening their home to me and my family during our stay in Canberra and for being a family away from home.

Warm gratitude also goes to Professor Andrew B. Kipnis and Dr Ben Hillman for being outstanding PhD panel members. I thank them for reading all the chapters of this manuscript and for their many wise comments, questions and enlightening debates that constantly challenged me.

I also thank Professor Stig Thøgersen and Professor Li Lianjiang for reading my PhD dissertation and for their constructive comments and suggestions, which assisted me immensely in publishing this book.

I am indebted to the Australian Government and ANU for providing me with a generous scholarship that enabled me to conduct this research and enriched my academic experience. I am thankful to the School of Sociology, ANU, for selecting me as one of their few scholarship-recipient PhD candidates. My deep gratitude goes also to the Department of Political and Social Change and to the Contemporary China Centre, ANU, for carving out a great academic home to conduct doctoral research. Special gratitude goes to Professor Anita Chan, Professor Tamara Jacka, the late Dr Robert (Bob) Miller, Dr Sally Sargeson, Dr Luigi Tomba, Dr Graeme Smith and Dr Peter Van Ness for always having their doors open and for sharing their experience and wisdom with me. Warm gratitude goes to Janelle Caiger for her constant willingness to assist me with administrative and bureaucratic matters and to Darrell Dorrington for his useful help with bibliographic materials.

This research was also supported by the Hebrew University of Jerusalem. I thank the Harry S. Truman Institute for the Advancement of Peace, the Golda Meir Foundation, the Lady Davis Fellowship Trust and the Department of Asian Studies for their academic and financial support. Special gratitude goes to Professor Vered Vinitzky-Seroussi and Professor Menahem Blondheim, former heads of the Harry S. Truman Institute, Naama Shpeter, former executive manager of the Truman institute and Dr Orna Naftali, former head of the Department of Asian Studies at the Hebrew University of Jerusalem, for their support and belief in this research project.

Special thanks go to all the good people in mainland China who supported me and were willing to cooperate with me in academic institutions and especially in Chenggu and Beian counties—officials and villagers alike. While these people are too numerous to mention individually by name, their names are treasured by me.

I would also like to pay a special tribute to Yu Fengli, with whom I have already lost contact. Fengli was one of millions of young people emigrating from home, travelling in search of a job. I met him in Chenggu. He was working as a bellboy in the hotel I stayed at and he became a close friend who helped me in visiting and studying villages in the county. His friendship eased my loneliness during months of fieldwork away from home and family. When I left Chenggu he decided to leave as well, to seek a job in Shanghai. Maintaining contact turned out to be impossible. Mentioning him by name is the least I can do to thank him for his support.

My thanks also go to ANU Press for their belief in this manuscript. In particular, I thank Emily Tinker, the former deputy manager, and Dr Andrew Kennedy, the chair of the Public Policy editorial board, for their attentiveness and patience and for their pleasant guidance along the tedious road to publication. I also thank the two anonymous reviewers for their fair and constructive comments, which have improved the manuscript.

Last but certainly not least, I thank my family for their support and for believing in me. I will never be able to repay my wife, Yaël, who joined me for a crazy adventure in Australia and China and who has supported me unconditionally even when difficulties stood in the way. This book is dedicated to her and to our two children: Yitai, who was born during my PhD studies, and Noa, who was born a few years later, when I conducted postdoctoral work.

1

Introduction

Since the beginning of the new millennium, Chinese central authorities have invested unprecedented efforts in improving rural life and decreasing inequality and social disparities between China's rural and urban populaces. A key part of these efforts is the national Village Redevelopment Program (*cunzhuang zhengzhi jianshe* 村庄整治建设) that was launched in 2005 to improve the infrastructure of villages and the services available there. At a minimum, this program includes paving roads towards and within villages, installing running water, introducing sporting and cultural facilities, and introducing clean energy devices. In many locales, the program goes far beyond this, with the construction of entirely new, large, modern communities of city-like apartment buildings, into which the villagers of several nearby villages are relocated, while traditional family housing and whole villages are demolished. It is an extraordinary undertaking, at enormous cost, that is reshaping the very fabric of much of China's countryside.[1]

This book explores the implementation and outcomes of the Village Redevelopment Program in two very different locales: the industrialised county of Chenggu, in Shandong Province, and the predominantly agricultural county of Beian, in Anhui Province.[2] It undertakes comparative research of a policy that is at the top of the Chinese national agenda to reshape the countryside and rural lifestyle, and that involves all levels of

---

1   Bray, 'Urban Planning Goes Rural', 53–62; Gao, Yang and Wang, 'Shandong liang xian hecun bingju ji nongcun shequ jianshe qingkuang diaocha' [Investigation of merging villages and rural community building in two counties, Shandong Province], 53–60; Ong, 'State-Led Urbanization in China', 165–71; Rosenberg, 'Urbanizing the Rural', 63–71.
2   To ensure anonymity, both counties' names are pseudonyms.

government, social actors and local communities. In doing so, the book enhances our comprehension of the overall logic of the Chinese policy implementation process, shedding light on the possible fate of much of China's countryside and its inhabitants in the twenty-first century.

At the heart of this book is a puzzle. Far from replicating the common image of uniformity in national policy implementation ('cutting with a single knife', *yi dao qie* 一刀切), officials in Chenggu and Beian counties demonstrated a surprising degree of divergence in how they interpreted and implemented the redevelopment program. And yet, in both counties, many aspects of the outcomes were ultimately similar. Local officials were likely to subsidise major redevelopment and improve infrastructure and services in already industrialised and prosperous villages and leave behind the poorer and less developed ones. By channelling more resources and government attention to those who already had such resources, local implementers changed the nature of the redevelopment program from a policy aimed at diminishing inequality and social disparity into a governing tool that enlarged existing disparities between rural communities.

To understand such a peculiar outcome in both counties despite their diversified implementation of the Village Redevelopment Program, this book focuses on the concept of *discretion* in policy implementation. At the lowest ranks of the political hierarchy, implementers (i.e. grassroots officials) are in the inconvenient position of linking state and society. Their superiors expect them to implement state policies and yet be attentive to local communities and their needs. Often they find themselves subject to various pressures from above (e.g. to obey national policies and directives by superiors) and from below (communities) and need to wrestle with programs in terms of feasibility (e.g. lack of qualified manpower or required equipment), which they must reconcile or defy. By 'discretion' I mean the extent of *genuine* autonomy left to local officials to shape implementation after all pressures have been resolved.

In its most basic understanding, discretion has two facets. The first refers to the question of selective policy implementation. It explores local officials' decisions about whether or not to implement policies. The second refers to *how* policies are implemented—the genuine leeway that implementers have to decide on a modus operandi and strategies of implementation. While the question of selective policy implementation has been a subject for debate and has attracted scholarly attention,[3] the second facet has so far attracted much less attention and has not been subject to systematic research. This book fills this gap in the literature. As it shows, subjection to pressures can play a determining role in deciding the local modus operandi and subsequently a policy's outcomes and impact. Moreover, efforts to reconcile conflicting pressures may significantly shape local officials' overall attitudes towards (rural) society. Will local officials be attentive to rural communities' needs? How will they perceive the villagers: as trustworthy partners or untrustworthy others, as equal citizens or as subordinate subjects? Will local officials involve villagers in the implementation process and, if so, how?

In more general terms, while implementers are expected to carry out policies, it is only inside the parameters available to them that grassroots officials can exercise genuine discretion to shape implementation and its outcomes. This observation touches on one of the most basic questions in studies of policy implementation: Who should be held responsible for the successes and failures of policies? Too often, scholars tend to neglect this aspect when studying and judging the behaviour of grassroots officials.

A popular view among students of Chinese policy implementation is that the Chinese political system provides local officials (i.e. the implementers) with considerable discretion when deciding on specific methods and strategies of implementation.[4] This is also manifested in the core principle of *yindi zhiyi* (因地制宜, implementing national policies in accordance with local conditions), which Chinese central authorities have advocated in the post-Mao era.

The case of the Village Redevelopment Program reveals that the reality may be more complex than this. By researching its implementation from the perspective of the implementers, this book elaborates on the larger economic-political-social environment in which local officials operate and that shapes their 'own' decision-making and actions. As the following chapters show, in both counties, the village redevelopment's implementation was mainly shaped by local economic conditions on the one hand and the hierarchical nature of China's political system on the other. These

---

3   See, for example, Edin, 'State Capacity', 35–52; Whiting, *Power and Wealth*, ch. 3; O'Brien and Li, 'Selective Policy Implementation', 167–86; Fewsmith, 'The Elusive Search', 269–96.
4   Lieberthal, *Governing China*, 167; Ahlers and Schubert, 'Strategic Modelling', 832, 840; Zhou, 'The Institutional Logic of Collusion', 55–68; Ahlers, *Rural Policy Implementation*; Göbel, *The Politics of Rural Reform*, 52–53; Cai, 'Irresponsible State', 23.

significantly constricted the implementers' capacity to exercise *genuine* discretion to decide on implementation strategies and to adjust the policy to their local socio-economic circumstances.

In pointing towards economic conditions, I refer to the outcomes of three decades of economic development—wealth accumulation on the one hand and expanding disparities and inequality on the other.[5] In both counties, this axis of wealth accumulation vis-a-vis disparity and inequality played a major role in deciding on modes of implementation. By the same token, local officials were part of a hierarchical political system in which commandism (also referred to as 'politics of command') still plays a central role as a method of communication between upper and lower levels, and in circumstances in which supervisors control the careers of their immediate subordinates.[6]

Here a few words of caution and clarification are required. By locating the redevelopment program in terms of state policy and local economic conditions, I do not intend to claim that there were no other possible factors that may have influenced decision-making and the conduct of local officials. Accustomed tools of governance and economic legacies, for example, may significantly influence local officials' behaviour.[7] In addition, many scholars have mentioned clientelist ties, embezzlement of resources, collusion and corruption as motivating local officials' behaviour and potentially sabotaging policies.[8] Evidence has piled up of local cadres taking advantage of the village redevelopment policy to enrich themselves while disregarding villagers' needs and interests. These include, among other things, the illegal sale of villagers' land, ignoring villagers' basic legal rights, inadequate compensation for loss of land or housing, expelling villagers from their homes and forcing them into debt to buy new housing against their will (in the name of building 'new villages') and the illegal shifting of property from the villagers to companies in which local officials operate

---

5   For a discussion on sources of inequality during the Mao and post-Mao eras see, for example, Whyte, 'China's Post-Socialist Inequality', 229–34.

6   Fewsmith, 'The Elusive Search', 269–96; Edin, 'State Capacity', 35–52; Whiting, *Power and Wealth*, ch. 3; O'Brien and Li, 'Selective Policy Implementation', 167–86.

7   See, for example, Perry, 'From Mass Campaigns', 30–61; Heilmann, 'Policy-Making through Experimentation', 62–101; Fewsmith, 'The Elusive Search', 269–96; Whiting, *Power and Wealth*.

8   See, for example, Chen and Wu, *Will the Boat Sink the Water?*; Hillman, *Patronage and Power*; Lü, *Cadres and Corruption*; Zhou, 'The Institutional Logic of Collusion', 47–78.

and have financial interests.[9] Cases of local officials using physical violence against villagers who dared to oppose their corruption and misbehaviour have been documented as well.[10]

Although none of these problems were personally observed by me in Chenggu or Beian counties, I do not wish to claim that these were totally absent. The same applies to the argument that governance legacies play a role in shaping local officials' minds and conduct. I do wish to claim, however, that in both counties these factors paled in significance compared to the patterns of state involvement on the one hand and local economic conditions on the other, when explaining similarities and differences in implementation and outcomes.

Rethinking Policy Implementation and State Capacity in Contemporary China

Policy implementation is an indispensable part of state capacity, which, in its most basic meaning, can be understood as the 'ability of the state to transform its own preferences and goals into reality'[11] or, more subtly, as 'carry[ing] out effectively those functions which it [the state] claims to be able to perform'.[12] This was acknowledged by Sally N. Cummings and Ole Nørgaard, who coined the term 'implementational state capacity', meaning the ability of the state 'to carry out decisions that have been taken'.[13]

The aggregated conclusion that can be derived from scholarly works published about policy implementation in China (though this is also true elsewhere[14]) is that implementation embodies a complex world of interests,

---

9   See, for example, Marshall 99, 'Linzhou Henan: Village Officials Illegally Sold Land for Development; Villagers Were Beaten Up for Defending Their Rights', *Tianya Forum* (blog), 16 December 2011, bbs. tianya.cn/post-492-3733-1.shtml; Zhou Guang, 'The Construction of a New Countryside in Yunnan Makes Villagers Homeless', *Rights Defender* (blog), 6 December 2011, wqw2010.blogspot.com/2011/12/blog-post_9713.html (all links accessed 21 October 2021). See also Ong, 'State-Led Urbanization in China', especially 167–73; Guo, 'Nongcun shequ jianshe zhong cunzai de wenti ji qi duice' [Problems and countermeasures during the construction of rural communities]; Looney, 'China's Campaign', 925.

10   See, for example, Marshall 99, 'Linzhou Henan: Village Officials Illegally Sold Land for Development; Villagers Were Beaten Up for Defending Their Rights', *Tianya Forum* (blog), 16 December 2011, bbs. tianya.cn/post-492-3733-1.shtml; *Tianya Forum* (blog), 16 December 2011, bbs.tianya.cn/post-492-3733-1.shtml, accessed 20 October 2021.

11   Wang and Hu, *The Chinese Economy in Crisis*, 24.

12   Crouch, *Industrial Relations*, 298.

13   Cummings and Nørgaard, 'Conceptualizing State Capacity', 688.

14   See, for example, Grindle, 'Policy Content', 5–6; Sabatier, 'Top-Down and Bottom-Up', 31; Migdal, *Strong Societies*.

constraints and abilities, in which state capacity is better taken as a key variable rather than as a given.[15] Indeed, the problem of non-effective implementation has long been acknowledged by scholars. David Bray, for example, observed that 'even the best-planned policies can unravel when faced with realities of implementation'.[16] Christian Göbel claimed that: 'In no phase is the effect that the interplay of contexts, institutions, incentives and agency has on the outcome of a policy more uncertain than during its implementation'.[17] Some have even taken a radical position, claiming that distortions of original policies and intensions in such a complex system as the Chinese political system are inevitable. David Lampton, in the introduction to his edited book *Policy Implementation in Post-Mao China*, wrote: 'The following pages also lay bare a system in which central policies are *always* distorted in ways advantageous to implementers'.[18]

The reasons for policy distortion and mis-implementation are numerous and may touch all stages of implementation. For example, these may relate to the formulation and presentation of the policy itself. Stanley Rosen, in his account on key schools, wrote: 'Clear policy objectives do not assure smooth implementation, but goal conflict in policy does assure implementation problems'.[19] Similarly, disputes among policymakers and lack of clear support from above,[20] a lack of fit between the policy's content and the wider context,[21] clashes between policies[22] and lack of publicity[23] may all impede successful implementation.

A mismatch between policy intentions and the local means at the grassroots level may also hinder successful implementation. These may include a lack of technological knowledge or financial constraints, a lack of skilled workers and/or limited human resources, and difficulties in collecting and/or processing required data and so on.[24]

---

15   Jia and Lin, 'Changing Central-Local Relations', 7.
16   Bray, *Social Space*, 95.
17   Göbel, *The Politics of Rural Reform*, 94.
18   Lampton, 'The Implementation', 18 (emphasis added).
19   Rosen, 'Restoring Key Secondary Schools', 351.
20   Ibid.; O'Brien and Li, 'Accommodating "Democracy"', 478–81; Lieberthal, 'China's Governing System', 6–7.
21   Zweig, 'Context and Content', 255–83.
22   White, 'Implementing the "One-Child-Per-Couple"', 284–317; Edin, 'State Capacity', 36; Wright, 'State Capacity in Contemporary China', 176–80.
23   Kennedy, 'State Capacity and Support', 383–410; O'Brien and Li, 'Selective Policy Implementation', 179.
24   Zhao, 'The Debt Chaos', 36–44; Zhao, 'Hard-Pressed Township Finances', 45–54; Tao, Yang and Liu, 'State Capacity', 355–81; Swanson, Kuhn and Xu, 'Environmental Policy Implementation' 481–91; Liu, *China's Long March*, 35.

Opposition from local officials or communities is another popular impediment to successful implementation when local players experience policies as undesirable. This can be out of personal interests or due to structural contradictions between higher-level policies and the local government's interests, known in Chinese as *tiaotiao* (条条, namely top-down chain of command) versus *kuaikuai* (块块, namely local authority).[25] These are manifested in idioms such as *shangmian you zhengce, xiamian you duice* (上面有政策，下面有对策, the upper levels have policies, the lower levels have counter-policies) and *tian gao, huangdi yuan* (天高，皇帝远, heaven is high and the emperor is far away).

Lack of support by immediate local superiors,[26] as well as failing to link performances to a clear rewards-and-punishments system, may also play against the possibility that local officials will implement a policy, especially when they perceive it as endangering local interests.[27] On the other hand, overzealousness and overstretching the original scope and intentions of a policy may impede successful implementation as well.[28]

Difficulties in monitoring implementation and supervising the implementers are another source of potential impediments. First, even potential supervisors may be embedded in malpractices (e.g. structural corruption[29] or collusion[30]). But, even when this is not the case, monitoring, in a system that lacks the capacity for accountability, is a tedious task.[31] Finally, since implementation is the stage on which state and society meet, implementers

---

25   See, for example, Wright, 'State Capacity in Contemporary China', 180–82; O'Brien, 'Implementing Political Reform', 47–48; O'Brien and Li, 'Accommodating "Democracy"', 465–89. In the conflict of areas (local authority) v. branches (top-down chain of command), the areas often win. See Lieberthal, 'China's Governing System', 4; Unger, 'The Struggle to Dictate', 15–45; Swanson, Kuhn and Xu, 'Environmental Policy Implementation', 481–91.

26   A prominent attribute of communist organisations and command economic systems is that all levels of organisational hierarchies are responsible only to their immediate superiors. See Lü, *Cadres and Corruption*, 170.

27   O'Brien and Li, 'Accommodating "Democracy"', 480–81.

28   Manion, 'Policy Implementation', 269.

29   Hillman, 'Factions and Spoils', 1–18; Lü, *Cadres and Corruption*, especially ch. 6; Lieberthal, *Governing China*, 203.

30   Zhou, 'The Institutional Logic of Collusion', 47–78.

31   Zhao, 'Obligatory Interactions', 17–25; Liu et al., 'The Political Economy', 973–94; Tao, Yang and Liu, 'State Capacity', 355–81; Klotzbücher et al., 'What is New', 49; Göbel, *The Politics of Rural Reform*, 118; Cai, 'Between State and Peasant', 783–805; Han and Wang, 'Woguo gonggong zhengce zhixing de shifan fangshi shixiao fenxi: jiyu shifan cun jianshe ge'an de yanjiu' [Analysis of failures in the demonstration mode in China's public policy implementation: The case of constructing demonstration villages], 38–42.

may find themselves clashing with local political-social-cultural institutions such as *guanxi* relations among various local players, lineages, religion organisations etc. or constrained by local economic conditions.[32]

Acknowledging the complexity of the Chinese political system, several scholars have pointed towards the central government's ability to 'control and monitor lower-level agents'[33] and to maintain coherence among the rank and file[34] as the state's main Achilles' heel. Jia Hao and Lin Zhimin observed:

> Although uneven and perhaps not entirely irreversible, the trend toward a more fragmented state system and increasing autonomy among lower levels of the state agency has resulted in serious erosion of China's state capacity.[35]

Central–local relations have commonly been articulated along the lines of a principal–agent relations framework, which connotes successful policy implementation with policy designers (the principal) having a high degree of control over implementers (local agents).[36]

This book contributes to the debate on state capacity by focusing on an aspect that, to date, has received insufficient scholarly attention: the significant role that authorities at levels higher than the county, including those at the top of the political system, play in the implementation process—shaping programs, setting targets and monitoring implementation.

While not negating a positive correlation between the ability of superiors to control lower-level agents and state capacity, this book suggests that the prospects of a policy meeting its goals are dependent not only on the ability

---

32 See, for example, Kipnis, *Producing Guanxi*; Lieberthal, *Governing China*, 197–99. See also Boisot and Child, 'The Iron Law of Fiefs', 507–27. On the other hand, social institutions may support successful implementation by compelling the implementers to follow instructions and to be attentive to local needs. See, for example, Tsai, *Accountability without Democracy*. See also Lu, *Varieties of Governance*.

33 Edin, 'State Capacity', 35–36.

34 Lieberthal, *Governing China*, 7; Jia and Lin, 'Changing Central-Local Relations', 8.

35 Jia and Lin, 'Changing Central-Local Relations', 8.

36 To put it briefly, the principal–agent model locates the agent (policy implementers) and the principal (policy designers) in asymmetric relations. The principal's concern is how to ensure that the agent will act in the principal's best interests. For this, a system of incentives and sanctions is introduced that favours the agent for siding with the principal's interests and punishes him for diversions. The principal's ability to monitor the agent, however, is always limited and incomplete because the agent controls information with which the principal may not be familiar (unless informed by the agent). This provides the agent wide leeway for manipulation and subversion. For examples of applying this approach in the Chinese studies, see Göbel, *The Politics of Rural Reform*; Whiting, *Power and Wealth*; Huang, 'Central–Local Relations', 655–72; Edin, 'State Capacity', 35–52; O'Brien and Li, 'Selective Policy Implementation', 167–86.

of superiors to control their subordinates but also on the attributes and qualities of those relations. As the following chapters show, prioritising and subsidising the better off villages in both counties was not an outcome of superiors' lack of monitoring capacity, but exactly the opposite: it was the result of grassroots officials' obedience to their superiors, who issued directives that significantly reduced local officials' prospects of meeting the original goal of diminishing inequality.

The following chapters testify to the vitality of commandism—commonly translated at grassroots levels into the top-down imposition of performance and evaluation standards—in shaping local officials' decision-making and conduct. Notwithstanding wide consent among scholars that top-down impositions of performance and evaluation standards do influence local officials' decision-making and conduct, the exact extent and patterns of influence have been the subject of scholarly debate (see also Chapter 6). Recently, a group of scholars have claimed a constructive role for the Chinese 'evaluation regime' in achieving effective outcomes.[37] Anna L. Ahlers, for example, observed in her research on the Building a New Socialist Countryside (BNSC) program,[38] that evaluations at the county and township levels (e.g. the cadre evaluation system[39] and project evaluations) have served important roles as top-down instruments for monitoring and ensuring policy implementation, but also that local officials were still able to exercise considerable *strategic agency* to adjust the evaluation mechanisms and benchmarks to their local circumstances and capacities (e.g. bargaining for specific targets or adjusting a county's overall targets to the local townships' particular circumstances).[40] She suggested that evaluations can:

---

37 See, for example, Heberer and Senz, 'Streamlining Local Behaviour', 77–112; Thomas Heberer and René Trappel, 'Evaluation Process', 1048–66. See also Ahlers, *Rural Policy Implementation*.
38 The BNSC program was announced publicly in 2006 as an overall framework of rural development. The Village Redevelopment Program was announced as a central part of the BNSC. This is elaborated further in this and following chapters.
39 As part of this system, township leaders typically must sign annual performance contracts that specify targets for implementation and are held personally responsible for attaining them (known as the Cadre Responsibility System [*ganbu kaohe zhidu*]). Targets in these contracts, however, differ in terms of their de facto importance and are typically classified into three categories. 'Veto targets' (*yi piao foujue*) are considered most important and failures in attaining these may bring devastating consequences for the local leaders' professional careers; no matter how well they operate in other areas. 'Hard targets' are considered essential for the local leaders' positive evaluation (and typically convey larger bonuses for success and significant sanctions for failures). 'Soft targets' are considered least important in terms of influencing township leaders' careers. They tend to value a small share of the total evaluation score and local officials enjoy larger autonomy regarding their implementation. See, for example, Edin, 'State Capacity', 35–52; Whiting, *Power and Wealth*, ch. 3; O'Brien and Li, 'Selective Policy Implementation', 168–76.
40 Ahlers, *Rural Policy Implementation*, 184–85, 191–92.

> Be transformed into a crucial resource for local agency by county
> (and township) governments themselves, who can use it to coordinate
> and assess the implementation of BNSC in their spheres of influence
> and thus protect their interests.[41]

The empirical findings of this book consolidate a more 'traditional' understanding of the relationship between standards, evaluation and local bureaucrats' performance, which corresponds more to Susan H. Whiting's observation that 'we should think of local Chinese officials more as "politicos"—individuals who make their careers in the political system—than as risk-bearing entrepreneurs'.[42] As the following chapters demonstrate, the more the imposed standards for performance and evaluation were specific and measurable, and the more incentives and sanctions were attached to them, the more local (township and even county) officials in Beian and Chenggu tended to concentrate on obtaining these standards rather than attempting to negotiate with their superiors or exercise discretion to shape the implementation and adjust it to their communities' local needs.

Finally, by underscoring the limits of 'discretion' and by researching the implementation process from the viewpoint of the implementers, the empirical findings of this book contribute to a new conceptualisation of the Chinese policy implementation process. The heart of it shakes the commonly applied principal–agent relations model.

When national policies are announced, they often convey general targets and guidelines that Beijing expects local governments to further operationalise and adjust to each locale's specific circumstances.[43] In this process, each political level is expected to obey the instructions of its superiors, while further adjusting the policy and instructing its subordinates, serving as a principal and as an agent at the same time (apart from central and township governments). In this hierarchical system, adequate and responsible execution of commandism is necessary to facilitate successful implementation at the grassroots levels, while inadequate imposition of

---

41   Ibid., 174.
42   Whiting, *Power and Wealth*, 12. This view corresponds to Lipsky's research on the operation of the American street-level bureaucracies. Lipsky noted an enticement by street-level bureaucrats to concentrate on measured activities and to perform 'activities in ways that will improve their performance scores', even at the cost of neglecting other tasks, engaging in implementation shortcuts, seeking easy successes (e.g. 'picking lower lying fruits first') and goal displacement. See Lipsky, *Street-Level Bureaucracy*, 48–53, 165–70.
43   Zhou, 'The Institutional Logic of Collusion', 55–62.

targets, guiding principles and systems of incentives and sanctions may result in the mis-implementation and corruption of the policy's original goals, as occurred in the case of the Village Redevelopment Program.

The following chapters point to the dual role that authorities at levels higher than the county played in Chenggu and Beian as both policy enablers and thwarters, in a more complex and dynamic process of policy implementation than provided by a simple principal–agent model. Instead of a dichotomous view of principals and agents (often translated into policymakers *versus* implementers or superiors *versus* subordinates), which scholars often use when discussing policy implementation in contemporary China, the following chapters delineate a multi-principals–agents system in which the distinction between principals and agents is cross-cutting and blurred.

The Village Redevelopment Program: Background and Content

Prosperity and a Crisis

During the last four decades, China's economy has developed at an unprecedented pace. From an undeveloped, collectivised, poverty-stricken, centrally planned economy, with state control over almost the entire nation's means of production, a massive state-owned enterprise sector, and an economically, ideologically, politically and spatially controlled population, China has turned into one of the most vital economies, and one of the most important growth centres, in the world. The macro-economic figures are impressive. In the first several decades after 1979, China's GDP grew at an average of around 10 per cent annually and people's incomes continually increased.[44] Economic growth has significantly lowered the poverty rate, with about 700 million people (according to the official statistics) escaping extreme poverty.[45]

---

44 In 1978, average per capita disposal income of households was RMB171. In 2019 it reached RMB30,733.

45 Poverty in China is perceived mostly as a rural problem. According to official statistics, during the years 1978–2000 the poverty rate declined from 31 per cent of the rural population to 3 per cent. This trend has continued in the twenty-first century, with more than 90 million additional people escaping poverty between 2013 and 2019. According to official reports, at the end of 2019 about 5.5 million rural inhabitants still lived in extreme poverty. China declared its intent to completely eradicate extreme poverty (guaranteeing the population of the poorest rural areas enough food, clothing and safe housing, plus education and basic medical care) by the end of 2020.

Behind this rosy picture, however, a gloomy reality shows increasing disparities and inequalities between rural and urban populaces. The early years of the post-Mao reforms initially benefited the farmers. The transition from collective agriculture to household agriculture (known as the Household Responsibility System), the gradual lifting of the state monopoly on agricultural procurements and sales, and the development of mechanisms of a market economy brought a significant increase in villagers' incomes.[46] Yet, starting in the mid-1980s, and especially after the third plenary session of the Central Committee of the 12th National Congress of the Communist Party of China (NCCPC) in 1984, the rural areas' renaissance stalled. State attention shifted towards the development of cities and industries, and China's rural areas entered a period of negligence and deterioration. In the 1990s, China experienced a crisis in its rural areas, which central leaders perceived as a threat to social stability.[47]

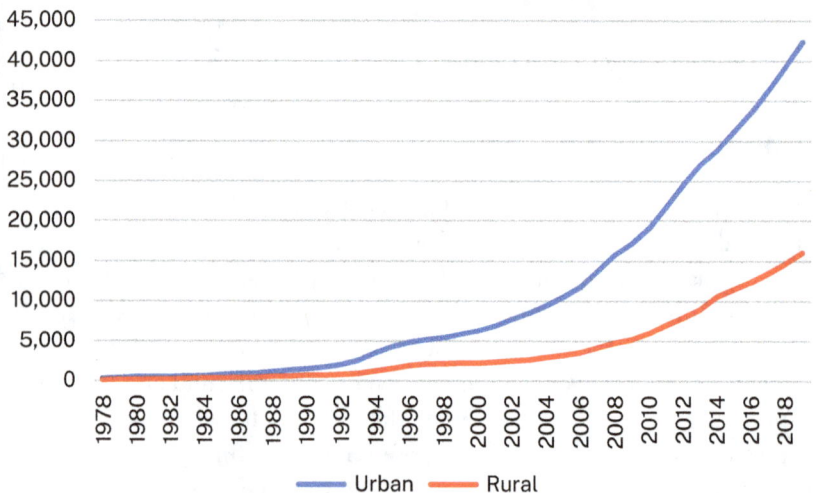

Chart 1.1: Average per capita annual income in rural and urban areas, 1978–2019 (in RMB)

Sources: All China Data Center — China Yearly Macro-Economic Statistics (National), www.china-data-online.com/member/macroy; *China Statistical Yearbook*, various years.

---

46   Whyte, 'The Paradoxes of Rural–Urban Inequality', 13–14.

47   Göbel, *The Politics of Rural Reform*, especially chs 2–4; Bernstein and Lü, *Taxation without Representation*; Bernstein, 'Unrest in Rural China'; Whyte, 'The Paradoxes of Rural–Urban Inequality', 20.

An obvious aspect of inequality is embodied in differences in levels of income between various groups of a society. It is easy to grasp from Chart 1.1 that, while incomes in both urban and rural populations have increased significantly since the early 1990s, the disparity between these populations' incomes soared as well. In 1978, the ratio between rural and urban average incomes was 1:2.57; however, by 2002 it was 1:3.11, increasing to an unprecedented rate of 1:3.33 in 2009. A decline has been noted since then, reaching a ratio of 1:2.64 in 2019.[48]

A rising disparity in incomes up to the early 2000s was just the tip of the glacier of the 'rural crisis'.[49] The average villager was also likely to pay significantly higher taxes than his urban counterparts. According to Chen Guidi and Wu Chuntao, during the years 1990–2000 the total of all the taxes extracted from the peasants increased by a factor of five. By 2000, the tax burden in rural areas averaged 146 yuan per head compared to only 37 yuan in the cities, a significant difference when considering that income in urban areas was several times higher than in rural areas.[50] Monopoly-like practices, such as the state's imposition of compulsory quotas of grain to be sold at a lower-than-market price and imposing limitations on villagers' discretion to decide to shift away from grain production to cash crops, curtailed villagers' incomes.[51]

Villagers felt themselves at the mercy of a powerful tax-collecting county and township bureaucracy, which grew larger in size over time, and whose officials often engaged in unrealistic economic projects that incurred increasing debts, with catastrophic results.[52] In prosperous areas, officials could extract funds from profitable, local, publicly owned industries.[53] In poorer areas, the local bureaucracy had to target the individual households

---

48 In 1978, the average per capita annual income of households in urban areas was RMB343; in rural areas it was RMB134. In 2019, the average per capita annual income in urban areas was RMB42,359; in rural areas it was RMB16,021.

49 The extent to which increased income inequality and distributive injustice presents a threat to social and political stability in China is indistinct. For example, Martin K. Whyte has found, based on two national surveys (2004, 2009), that distributive injustice has not been followed by increasing anger among the weaker strata of society over inequality issues; nor does this threaten China's political stability. In his words, 'the distributive justice social volcano remains dormant'. This is due to an overall improvement in the standards of living of the majority of the people. Whyte and Im, 'Is the Social Volcano Still Dormant?', 74. See also Whyte, 'China's Post-Socialist Inequality', 229–34; Whyte, *Myth of the Social Volcano*.

50 Chen and Wu, *Will the Boat Sink the Water?*, 151.

51 Xiong and Yang, 'Nongmin fudan' [Peasants' burden], 467–77.

52 Zhao, 'The Debt Chaos', 36–44; Zhao, 'Hard-Pressed Township Finances', 45–54; Göbel, *The Politics of Rural Reform*, ch. 2; Cai, 'Irresponsible State', 20–41.

53 Oi, *Rural China Takes off*.

to help cover the government's shortfalls. Like earlier eras in China's history, many villagers were groaning under excessive financial burdens. Arbitrary and illegal impositions of fees, fines, coercive 'contributions' and other extractions became part of everyday life in many of China's rural areas.[54] Especially for the poorer villagers, this economic burden was a major problem.[55]

Arbitrary impositions of fees were often followed by eruptions of violence between local officials and villagers who refused to pay or dared to challenge local officials. Chinese and Western literature has documented local officials bursting into villagers' homes, expropriating their possessions; detaining villagers illegally; misreporting and imposing injustices in court; and deploying local police to silence or occasionally even kill opponents who dared to demand their rights. Villagers' complaints piled up on desks at the highest levels and protests and violence acted out against local officials increased noticeably, as did suicides by villagers.[56] In many rural areas, China experienced a governance crisis.

The farmers' difficulties partly resulted from an explicit expectation that villagers would bear the burden of financing public services of a type that the central state supports in many other countries, such as militia training, roadworks and local officials' salaries.[57] These often entailed heavy expenses for rural households.[58]

In a paper on education in poor areas (*pinkun diqu* 贫困地区), Li Chuling claimed that shifting away from Mao-era collectives was especially detrimental to poor families. According to this research, education costs—which included school fees and stationery as well as other 'contributions' imposed on families to cover teachers' salaries and schools' operational costs—amounted to 20 per cent of a household's total income in families with two adults and two school-age children.[59] Despite the ruinous cost to poor families, in the early 2000s, 6.6 per cent of elementary and middle

---

54   Chen and Wu, *Will the Boat Sink the Water?*; Bernstein and Lü, *Taxation without Representation*; Gao, *Gao Village*.
55   Göbel, *The Politics of Rural Reform*, 31; Xiong and Yang, 'Nongmin fudan'; Liu, 'Xiaofei' [Consumption], 362–88; Bernstein and Lü, 'Taxation without Representation', 742–63.
56   See, for example, Chen and Wu, *Will the Boat Sink the Water?*; O'Brien and Li, *Rightful Resistance*; Bernstein and Lü, 'Taxation without Representation', 742–63; Guo, 'Land Expropriation', 422–39.
57   Sun, 'Zhufang cunzhuang jianshe' [Housing and village construction], 145.
58   Liu, 'Xiaofei', 379.
59   Li, 'Pinkun diqu jiaoyu' [Education in poverty-stricken areas], 228–37.

schools in rural areas were housed in dangerous buildings.[60] In poverty-stricken areas, students often attended school in decrepit buildings, barns or old temples with no basic utilities such as electricity, water and toilets, sometimes with leaking roofs or under the open sky. In some of these schools, teachers did not have chalk and blackboards and children could not afford to buy stationery, books and notebooks. Many children brought stools from home or studied while sitting on the floor. The quality of teaching was low, partly due to very low salaries.[61] But little help was offered by the national government. In the early 2000s, the state only spent 23 per cent of its compulsory education budget in rural areas, even though villagers comprised the majority of China's population.[62]

The situation in healthcare was no better. Government underfunding was a chronic problem, with 60 per cent of its investments in healthcare going to the cities.[63] Rural health clinics were often ramshackle, lacking basic resources and with low-quality manpower. Eighty per cent of township hospitals in central and western China were in need of new medical equipment.[64] As Charlotte Cailliez pointed out, underfunding meant that rural clinics and hospitals had to self-finance their operations through a policy of 'relying on patients' payments' (*bingzhe zifei* 病者自费). The result, according to Cailliez, was rampant over-prescribing and unnecessary medical procedures that the villagers had to pay for. For many villagers, seeing a doctor became a luxury that they could not afford; in poor counties, about half the population avoided medical treatment due to the cost. County hospitals, which offered better medical treatment, were out of financial reach for many villagers.[65] In the early 2000s, according to Wang Xianfeng, only about 15 per cent of the rural population had health insurance,[66] a result of the high costs embodied in buying the insurance in the first place. Without any safety net, falling into poverty due to serious illness was common.[67] A popular proverb depicted this well: 'With a small illness [you can] drag on, in a severe illness [you] wait for death' (*xiao bing*

---

60 Fock and Wong, 'China: Public Services', 31–32.
61 Li, Chunling, 'Pinkun diqu jiaoyu'.
62 Ibid., 32.
63 Cailliez, 'Nongcun weisheng zhidu de zhuangkuang' [The situation of the medical system in the villages], 240.
64 Wang, 'Xin nongcun jianshe de beijing he tiaojian' [The background and conditions of building the new countryside], 31.
65 Cailliez, 'Nongcun weisheng zhidu de zhuangkuang', 238–48.
66 Wang, 'Xin nongcun jianshe de beijing he tiaojian', 31.
67 Liu, 'Xiaofei', 379–80.

tuozhe, da bing deng si 小病拖着,大病等死).[68] Overall, in the early 2000s, life expectancy was 5.6 years higher in cities than in rural areas, and infant mortality was three times higher in rural areas.[69]

According to the Chinese Social Science Academy, in the early 2000s, 300 million people in rural China did not have permanent access to safe drinking water, more than 50 million villagers were exposed to drinking water with arsenic content, more than 40 million villagers had brackish drinking water, more than 90 million were subjected to seasonal drought and 130 million people drank water contaminated with microorganisms.[70] About 50 per cent of villages did not have access to running water at this time.

In addition, public roads did not provide access to 40,000 administrative villages, roads to 70 per cent of villages were not paved and 4 per cent of villages were not accessible by car. More than 50 per cent of villages used firewood and straw as a main energy source, 20 million people were not connected to electricity, 7 per cent of villages did not have access to telephones and 50 million villagers were not able to receive television or radio signals.[71] Thus, in the early 2000s, it was commonly stated that, while Chinese cities increasingly resembled Europe, rural infrastructure and services resembled Africa.

Inequality at the Sub-national Level

While the macro picture of the Chinese economy portrays a picture of rural–urban disparity and inequality, the reality is more complicated, as disparities have increased between rural communities as well. A general typology to analyse disparities within rural China tends to divide China into three main areas: the east, the centre and the west. A survey conducted in 2006 by the Development Research Centre of the State Council of the People's Republic of China (PRC) (*Guowuyuan fazhan yanjiu zhongxin* 国务院发展研究中心) depicts this well. The survey was conducted in 2,749 villages in 17 provinces and revealed large disparities between villages located in the prosperous east and villages in the rest of the country. It is worth citing its main findings. While almost half of the villages surveyed in east China reported an average annual per capita income of more than RMB6,000 (about 70 per cent higher

---

68 Jiang, 'Shehuizhuyi xin nongcun "xin" zai nali?' [What is new in the new socialist countryside?].
69 Fock and Wong, 'China: Public Services', 2.
70 These figures were officially cited by the Ministry of Water Resources, the People's Republic of China, www.mwr.gov.cn/english/sdw.html, accessed 20 October 2021.
71 Wang, 'Xin nongcun jianshe de beijing he tiaojian', 30–31.

than the nationwide annual average rural per capita income of that year), this was the average income in fewer than 1 per cent of the villages in west or central China; the other 99 per cent were lower. On the other side of the coin, an extremely low income of less than RMB1,000 was reported in only 3.2 per cent of villages in the east and 5.4 per cent of villages in central China compared to 23 per cent of villages in the west. The report defined 14.7 per cent of households in the west and 9.9 per cent of households in central China as poor households (*nongcun pinkun hu* 农村贫困户) compared to only 3.1 per cent of households in the east. Poor households in the east, however, enjoyed significantly higher government financial assistance (RMB106.7 per month per capita compared to RMB16.6 RMB per month per capita in central China and RMB27.4 per month per capita in western China).[72] Large differences were also found in villages' collective incomes (*jiti shouru* 集体收入) from publicly owned assets. While 60 per cent of villages in the east enjoyed a high collective income of RMB100,000 and above, this was the case in only 24.1 per cent of villages in central China and only 8.6 per cent of villages in the west. Village cadres (*cun ganbu* 村干部) were also likely to enjoy significantly higher salaries in the east. On average their salaries were more than six times higher than the village officials' salaries in central China and more than seven times higher than the salaries of their counterparts in the west.

The survey also revealed significant differences in the areas of infrastructure and public amenities. For example, villages in the east tended to pave more of their roads, and more villages provided running water to their inhabitants than elsewhere.[73] Computers were available in village government offices in 82 per cent of villages in the east compared to only about 10 per cent in central and west China. Significantly more villages in the east constructed central garbage collection stations; such villages were also likely to enjoy better medical cover thanks to additional support for serious diseases (in addition to the national rural cooperative medical scheme) paid by prosperous local governments.[74]

---

72   A paper at around that time on poverty and vulnerability similarly found that: 'While both poverty and vulnerability are close to zero in some regions or provinces (e.g. Beijing, Jiangsu, Guangdong), they are still high, for example, in Guizhou, Yunnan, Shaanxi or Gansu'. See Imai, Wang and Kang, 'Poverty and Vulnerability', 416.

73   According to the survey, in prosperous Jiangsu and Shanghai the average length of paved roads inside the villages was 8 kilometres per village, while it was only 1 kilometre in villages in poor Guangxi. While in places such as Shanghai, Jiangsu and Zhejiang, all villagers enjoyed safe drinking water, this was not the case in the poorer provinces of Qinghai, Sichuan and Gansu.

74   Guowuyuan fazhan yanjiu zhongxin [Development Research Centre of the State Council of the PRC], 'Xin nongcun diaocha: zou jin quan guo 2749 ge cunzhuang [Investigating the new countryside: Into 2,749 villages nationwide].

However, disparities were not confined to the east-central-west level only, as each of these mega-regions encompassed high levels of inequality and disparity as well. In the province of Anhui, for example, statistical data showed significant disparities among the province's prefectures in terms of production and industrialisation. In 2005, a difference of 7.75 times was found between the prefectures with the highest and lowest GDP, and 7.98 times in terms of the highest and lowest per capita GDP. More than a decade later, in 2018, differences in terms of highest and lowest GDP further increased to 12.8 times, while differences in terms of highest and lowest per capita GDP declined to 4.5 times.[75]

Descending a level, findings from a survey conducted in 2005 in Shandong Province, the location of the second of my fieldwork sites, revealed extreme disparities between the province's counties (discussed in Chapter 6).

Significant differences also existed at the sub-county level and these, as Chapter 2 demonstrates, could be dramatic. According to official data, in the first decade of the twenty-first century, the Chenggu government's total revenue was about nine times higher than Beian's, but the revenue in industrialised townships was more than 20 times higher than in rural townships within Chenggu. Chenggu's total GDP was five times higher than in Beian. Yet, the GDP of the most industrialised township in Chenggu was 10 times higher than in the least industrialised township, and the difference between townships in terms of rural incomes in Chenggu equalled the gap between rural Chenggu and Beian as a whole. Unfortunately, Beian did not publish its townships' GDP. Yet data from township income taxes revealed enormous differences of 30 times between the township with the highest income and that with the lowest. Differences in villages' collective income were sometimes even more dramatic, as demonstrated in the case of Chenggu (see Table 2.5). As Chapter 2 elaborates, in both Beian and Chenggu, the location of local settlements became one of the most significant institutional shapers of patterns of inequality at the sub-county level. To put it briefly, townships and villages that were located next to the counties' (or to neighbouring administrative units') main urban and industrial centres and/or adjacent to the main local roads were likely to

---

75 *Anhui Province Statistical Yearbook*, 2006, 2019.

enjoy more opportunities to extract wealth from local markets and to offer their inhabitants better livelihoods than their counterparts in the peripheral hinterland.[76]

Facing the Problem?

The Chinese Communist Party (CCP) and state played a very significant role in shaping and institutionalising rural–urban social and economic disparities through central and local authorities' discriminatory policies and governance institutions. This was true in the Maoist era, when rural inhabitants' ability to leave their communities to seek work was severely restricted and rural communities were expected to demonstrate self-reliance by being economically self-sustaining. During the current post-Mao era, the state has continued to rely on political-economic principles that were at the heart of the Maoist command economy. These precepts have proved inadequate to address the unequal allocation of the unprecedented wealth generated in China since its opening to the world, to such an extent that Martin King Whyte has referred to the urban–rural gap as a 'two-caste society'.[77]

Yet it was only in the late 1990s, when widespread discontent and rioting in rural areas became a significant concern for national authorities, that a gradual change in Beijing's attitudes towards rural areas became evident, culminating in 2006 in the public announcement of a broad program to 'build a new socialist countryside' (*shehuizhuyi xin nongcun jianshe* 社会主义新农村建设).

The year 1998 was a major turning point, with the revision of the 1986 Land Management Law, which now provided, for the first time, a legal basis for leasing land (for 30 years)[78] and full adoption of the Organic Law of the Villagers Committees, which furnished a legal base for village-level elections, after a 10-year trial period. In 2003, the Rural Land Contract Law, the most detailed law on land use arrangements, came into effect,

---

76 The role of location as a significant structural shaper of inequality and in creating core–periphery relations in China (though of larger geographical areas than counties) was observed several decades ago, particularly by students of the Regional Hierarchy Spaces Approach. See, for example, Qi et al., 'Evolving Core-Periphery Interactions', 376; Crissman, 'G. William Skinner's', 32; Skinner, 'Cities and the Hierarchy', 276–83; Skinner, 'Marketing and Social Structure', 9–32.

77 Whyte, 'The Paradoxes of Rural–Urban Inequality', 7–19.

78 Deininger et al., 'Implementing China's New Land Law'.

providing, at least from the official view, legal protection for farmers' land usage rights.[79] Generally, the years 1998–2003 marked an intensification of legislation to create a legal environment to secure villagers' interests.

In addition, a series of tax reforms and direct-subsidy programs were launched by the national government to solve some of the fundamental problems mentioned earlier. In 2001, the Rural Tax and Fee Reform was launched; by 2003, it was being implemented nationally. Many of the miscellaneous fees that were imposed on villagers by local officials were abolished, and the rest were subjected to strict regulation.[80] In 2002, subsidies for improved seeds and for grain production were launched by the Ministry of Agriculture and Rural Affairs (*nongye nongcun bu* 农业农村部) and the Finance Ministry (*caizheng bu* 财政部) to promote improved seed varieties and to increase the income of grain farmers. In 2003, the 'two exemptions and one subsidy' (*liang mian yi bu* 两免一补) reform in rural education was initiated, providing free textbooks and abolishing school tuition fees, and providing a subsidy to boarding students from poor families.[81] Also in that year, a New Rural Cooperative Medical Scheme was launched to gradually provide all villagers with basic subsidised medical insurance. In addition, subsidies for biogas digesters and a Medical Care Relief Fund to provide financial assistance to poor families in case of catastrophic healthcare costs were launched by the ministries of Agriculture and Civil Affairs, respectively. A year later, in 2004, a subsidy for the purchase of agricultural machinery was launched by the Ministry of Agriculture.[82]

Side by side with these reforms, the CCP also blew its ideological trumpet, bringing rural areas back onto the national agenda. In 2000, at the fifth plenum of the Central Committee of the 15th NCCPC, the problem of villagers' income was debated, and a call was conveyed to 'increase rural income by all efforts'. During the 16th NCCPC (2002), the concept of

---

79 On the other hand, several scholars have argued against the Chinese conception of 'farmers' usage rights' as representing states' interests more than farmers' interests. According to Sherry Tao Kong and Jonathan Unger in their research on land redistribution in Anhui, most farmers have continued to illegally redistribute their collectively owned land to re-equalise per capita landholdings. See Kong and Unger, 'Egalitarian Redistributions', 1–19. From this view, the Rural Land Contract Law is against the wishes of most farmers.

80 Göbel, *The Politics of Rural Reform*; Li, 'Working for the Peasants?', 89–106.

81 This policy was preceded by the 'tuition control' reform, which was announced in 2001. Under this policy, annual tuition fees for attending public primary schools in rural areas were limited to a maximum of RMB160 per student, and RMB260 for attending a junior high school. Xiao, Li and Zhao, 'Education on the Cheap', 546–47.

82 Lin and Wong, 'Are Beijing's Equalization Policies', 28.

coordinated rural–urban economic and social development (*tongchou chengxiang jingji shehui fazhan* 统筹城乡经济社会发展) was raised for the first time. In 2003, during a national government conference on rural affairs (*zhongyang nongcun gongzuo huiyi* 中央农村工作会议), the policy of 'give more, take less, and invigorate private endeavours' (*duoyu, shaoqu, fanghuo* 多予, 少取, 放活) was introduced. At the fourth plenum of the Central Committee of the 16th NCCPC (2004), Party Secretary Hu Jintao claimed that China had entered the stage of 'industry nurtures agriculture and cities support rural areas' (*yi gong cu nong, yi cheng dai xiang* 以工促农, 以城带乡). A year later, in 2005, during the fifth plenum of the 16th NCCPC, a call was officially issued to build a 'new socialist countryside'.[83] For the first time in 18 years, the CCP had begun dedicating its entire first annual national directive (*zhongfa yi hao* 中发一号) to rural issues.

What Is New in the 'New Socialist Countryside'?

The appeal to build a 'new socialist countryside' was an important step in tackling rural problems (known in Chinese as 'the three rurals' [*san nong* 三农]).[84] At least from the political centre's view, China was ready to walk a new stage of economic development and state–society relations.

The concept of new villages in a new countryside is not new to China.[85] Since its announcement, many publications inside the PRC have been dedicated to the question of what is new in the BNSC scheme. While various authors have emphasised different aspects of the 'new', these discussions can be summarised in four general points. First, the background for the attempt was now different. After decades in which efforts were deliberately undertaken to develop cities and industries at the expense of villages, China had now entered a new stage where changes in priorities

---

83 A few months later, this policy became public knowledge with the appearance of the party's first national directive of 2006, which was dedicated entirely to introducing the New Socialist Countryside policy.

84 The 'three rurals' is an abbreviation for agriculture (*nongye*), villages (*nongcun*) and villagers (*nongmin*).

85 In Chinese accounts, BNSC is often referred to as the third attempt to reconstruct villages and the countryside. The first attempt was made in the 1930s with village reconstruction during the republic era led by intellectuals such as Liang Shuming, who operated in Shandong Province, mainly in the county of Zouping, and Yan Yangchu (James [Jimmy] Yen), who operated in Ding County, Hubei Province. The second attempt is attributed to the 1950s and collectivisation. From another perspective, BNSC is sometimes referred to as the third revolution during the reform era, the transition from collective economy to the Household Responsibility System being the first, and the Rural Tax for Fee Reform (2003) being the second. See, for example, Jiang, 'Shehuizhuyi xin nongcun "xin" zai nali?'.

and governance principles were needed.[86] This is not to say that the party/government was lamenting its own role in creating social disparities. On the contrary. Hu Jintao in 2004 declared that, at the initial stages of industrialisation, there had been a general trend for agriculture to support industry. However, after a considerable level of industrialisation had been achieved, these relations should be reversed, with agriculture supported by industry and urban areas supporting villages.[87] By the same token, by theorising economic development as consisting of two distinguishable stages of economic development, the call to establish a *new* countryside served as an ideological vindication for necessary changes in the priorities that had guided the state during the first stage of discrimination against rural areas.

Although BNSC proclamations did not criticise previous malpractices, the theme of long-term development gained a sense of urgency in the need to support rural areas, which was conveyed by BNSC announcements. After decades of supporting the urban economy and urban residents, China had finally reached the stage of development when it could afford to support its rural areas. This moment was depicted by central policymakers as China's 'grand historical task' (*zhongda lishi renwu* 重大历史任务), for if this opportunity failed, disparities would increase, social conflicts would multiply and China might endure growing unrest.[88] The BNSC was supposed to meet a national vision of a 'moderately prosperous society' (*xiaokang shehui* 小康社会) and a 'harmonious society' (*hexie shehui* 和谐社会) that supported its weakest and most sensitive links.[89] Rural areas were no longer to be used simply as sources of cheap resources to enable the prosperity of the urban sector. National prosperity was now subject to, and conditional on, rural prosperity:

> If there is no agricultural stability, there will be no stability in the national economy; if there is no development of the villages, there will be no genuine national development; if there aren't affluent villagers, there will be no lasting prosperity for the country.[90]

---

86   Ibid.
87   Ibid. See also Li, 'Xin nongcun jianshe 'xin' zai nali?' [What is new in Building the New Countryside].
88   Jiang, 'Shehuizhuyi xin nongcun "xin" zai nali?'.
89   Ibid.
90   *Jingji Ribao* [Economic daily], 29 September 2009.

Second, BNSC was announced as a holistic policy seeking to introduce a comprehensive solution to rural problems in their widest sense—as manifested in a slogan of 20 characters that constituted the heart of the new socialist countryside scheme: 'advanced production, well-off livelihoods, civilised communities, clean and tidy villages, and democratic management' (*shengchan fazhan, shenghuo kuanyu, xiangfeng wenming, cunrong zhengjie, guanli minzhu* 生产发展, 生活宽裕, 乡风文明, 村容整洁, 管理民主). BNSC broadened the concept of 'rural problems' beyond the immediate narrow understanding of economic output and income to include infrastructure, services, social security, civil conduct and governance.[91] Acknowledging the comprehensive scope of BNSC's targets, Stig Thøgersen perceived it as 'presently the closest match to the master plans of earlier periods'.[92]

Third, BNSC was supposed to entail a new conceptualisation of rural society–state relations. Since the establishment of the PRC, the state had taken very different approaches towards its rural and urban populaces. Generally, while it took on the responsibility of providing urban inhabitants all their basic needs (e.g. education, housing, employment, medical care, pensions after retirement, etc.), rural communities were expected to pursue the principle of self-reliance. Except for very unusual circumstances, such as severe natural disasters, applying for state support was beyond the capacity of local officials and potentially harmful to their professional careers.[93]

Government underfunding during the 1980s–90s period of fiscal decentralisation meant that rural communities had to continue relying on self-financing of public amenities and services. BNSC symbolised a significant change in the legacy of self-reliance. Under the policy, central and local governments were expected to take a major part in the project of building a new socialist countryside, including financial expenses.

Last, although BNSC's title contains the word *nongcun* (农村), which refers literally to villages, BNSC exceeded the scope of the village, acknowledging that a real solution to rural problems could not be confined to villages only, but instead required fundamental changes in the larger environment in which villagers were embedded, as well as fundamental changes in the dual structure of the Chinese economy established under Mao's rule. As China

---

91 Jiang, 'Shehuizhuyi xin nongcun "xin" zai nali?'; Dang, 'Zhongguo de xin nongcun yinggai shi zheyang de' [China's new countryside must be this way].

92 Thøgersen, 'Building a New Socialist Countryside', 175.

93 Oi, *State and Peasant*, especially ch. 6.

entered its 'second stage' of economic development, the dual structure was perceived as an obstacle, potentially endangering China's economic achievements and its long project of modernisation and efforts to develop a harmonised society.[94] Thus, while the revolutionary era sanctified social divisions (e.g. urban *versus* rural, revolutionary *versus* counter-revolutionary etc.), BNSC was based on the exact opposite—the need to blur social gaps and divisions towards better coordination and unification between rural and urban systems, decreasing inequality and increasing the opportunities of rural inhabitants to enjoy the fruits of economic development.[95] A leading figure from Shandong conceptualised it thus: if BNSC is an eagle, then urbanisation and industrialisation serve as its two wings.[96]

To sum up, BNSC offered a new vision for twenty-first-century China: a vision of a better-balanced national economy in which resources are allocated more equally, cities and industries better absorb surplus rural labour, and villages are offered better infrastructure.[97] In this vision, villages offer their inhabitants modern facilities and high-quality accessible services, and the villagers are better equipped to cope in a modern economy and to compete for resources and wealth in developing markets. It also presented a new subjectification of the rural population, from inferior and almost unseen to an equal status and participation in national prosperity and a harmonious society.

Increasing Government Investments in the Countryside

The announcement of the BNSC program marked an intensification of the government's fiscal investment in rural areas and a determination on the part of central and local authorities that 'public financing was necessary to achieve coverage and incentivize (popular) participation'.[98] The reforms that were launched were expanded in scope and consolidated, in several cases beyond policymakers' original intentions. Direct subsidies were increased

---

94 Jiang, 'Shehuizhuyi xin nongcun "xin" zai nali?'; Li, 'Xin nongcun jianshe 'xin' zai nali?'.

95 Li, 'Xin nongcun jianshe 'xin' zai nali?'.

96 *Jingji Ribao* [Economic daily], 29 September 2009. Others have questioned the adequacy of urbanisation as a nationwide uniform development strategy. See, for example, Tong, 'Xin nongcun jianshe bing bu biran zhuiqiu nongcun chengshihua' [Building a new countryside is not necessarily urbanising the villages]. See also Song, 'Xin nongcun jianshe yao zhuzhong ruan jianshe' [Building a new countryside must pay attention to soft construction].

97 Li, 'Xin nongcun jianshe 'xin' zai nali?'; Song, 'Xin nongcun jianshe yao zhuzhong ruan jianshe'.

98 Vilela, 'Pension Coverage', 6.

and new channels for financial investments were established. The following describes some of the central facets of governmental investments in the rural areas since 2006.

In education, in September 2006, the standing committee of the 10th National People's Congress approved a revised compulsory education law that called for nationwide implementation of free nine-year compulsory education and the rescinding of tuition fees. Covering all rural areas, 150 million children were exempted from tuition fees and 'other miscellaneous fees' and provided with free textbooks. Millions of children from poor families were also provided with living allowances to subsidise boarding expenses at schools.[99] In healthcare, trials of a new type of rural cooperative medical care system were expanded rapidly. According to official reports, in 2008, 92 per cent of the rural population already participated in the new rural cooperative medical care program.[100] In welfare, a basic cost-of-living allowance (*dibao* 低保) for impoverished rural residents was established in 2007 and the government increased its involvement to guarantee basic needs: food, clothing, medical care, housing and burial expenses of the weakest strata of the rural society (known as *wubao hu* 五保户).[101]

An important step towards reducing the tax burden of rural households was taken in 2006. Agriculture and livestock taxes were rescinded nationwide and subsidies for the purchase of high-quality seeds were expanded to include wheat, rice and corn.[102] The rescindment of rural taxes also enabled institutional reframing of the functions and image of local officials from tax collectors to developmental agents and from resource extractors to service providers, a change that, according to Anna L. Ahlers, facilitated effective implementation of the BNSC.[103]

---

99 Lin and Wong, 'Are Beijing's Equalization Policies', 31–32; Opertti and Wang, 'China: Regional Preparatory Workshop', www.ibe.unesco.org/fileadmin/user_upload/COPs/News_documents/2007/0711Hanghzou/Final_Report_of_ICE_Workshop_East_Asia.pdf. See also 'Report on the Work of the Government', 2008, www.chinadaily.com.cn/china/2008npc/2008-03/19/content_6549177.htm.

100 National People's Congress of the People's Republic of China, 'Report on the Work of the Government', 2009, npc.gov.cn/englishnpc/c2762/200903/4b76ad6093f44ded8ce92fbc7b134f16.shtml, accessed 21 October 2021.

101 National People's Congress of the People's Republic of China, 'Report on the Work of the Government, 2007, npc.gov.cn/zgrdw/englishnpc/Special_11_5/2010-03/03/content_1690626.htm, accessed 21 October 2021.

102 Lin and Wong, 'Are Beijing's Equalization Policies', 28.

103 Ahlers, *Rural Policy Implementation*, 39–45. Not everyone agrees with this observation. See, for example, Smith, 'The Hollow State', 601–18.

A further significant step towards ensuring people's livelihood was the launch in 2009 of the New Rural Social Pension Insurance Scheme, with an aim to reach full coverage by 2015.[104] To facilitate rural economic development, a major infrastructure project was launched to upgrade rural roads. The initial target for the 11th Five-Year Plan period (2006–10) was to build or rebuild 1.2 million kilometres of rural roads, of which 300,000 new kilometres of roads were planned to be mainly built in 'old revolutionary bases, border areas, poor areas and major grain producing areas'.[105] The road-building goals escalated during the 11th Five-Year plan, and, in 2011, paving additional rural roads was announced as an important goal of the 12th Five-Year Plan, which began that year.[106] According to official estimates, by the end of 2015, total coverage of rural roads reached 3.95 million kilometres, encompassing 99 per cent of the country's towns and 93 per cent of the administrative villages.[107]

Providing safe drinking water was another major BNSC project. In 2011, the Chinese government set an ambitious goal to solve the problem of unsafe drinking water by 2015. However, despite efforts, this difficult task has not yet been achieved.[108] The government also invested significant efforts in other aspects of rural infrastructure, such as building and upgrading electric power lines,[109] reinforcing reservoirs, building and renovating county and township hospitals and community health service centres, improving national capacities to prevent and mitigate natural disasters, and more.[110]

---

104 Lin and Wong, 'Are Beijing's Equalization Policies', 28; 'Report on the Work of the Government', 2011, china.org.cn/china/NPC_CPPCC_2011/2011-03/15/content_22143099.htm, accessed 21 October 2021. In the early 2000s, only about 11 per cent of the villagers had pensions. See, for example, Li, *Zhongguo xin nongcun jianshe baogao* [A report on the Building of a New Countryside in China], 30–32. According to official statistics, by the end of 2015 participation in basic pension plans exceeded 80 per cent of the whole population. See State Council, People's Republic of China, 'Report on the Work of the Government', 2016, english.www.gov.cn/premier/news/2016/03/17/content_281475309417987. htm, accessed 21 October 2021. A new target was announced as part of China's 13th Five-Year Plan to reach a coverage of 90 per cent of urban and rural residents by 2020. See 'Sustainability Vital for China's Pension Funds', *China Daily*, 9 March 2017, africa.chinadaily.com.cn/business/2017-03/09/content_ 28487641.htm, accessed 21 October 2021.

105 '1.2 Mln KM Rural Roads to be Built', *Xinhua News Agency*, 8 February 2006, china.org.cn/ english/government/157310.htm, accessed 21 October 2021.

106 'China to Expand Rural Road Network', *Xinhua News Agency*, 10 February 2010, www.china.org. cn/china/2011-02/11/content_21898403.htm, accessed 26 October 2022.

107 'China's Rural Road Network to Reach 3.95 Mln Km by 2015', *Xinhua News Agency*, 21 September 2015, en.people.cn/n/2015/0921/c90882-8953064.html, accessed 21 October 2021.

108 Liu, *China's Long March*.

109 According to official data, in 2009 alone, 266,000 kilometres of electric power lines were built or upgraded in rural areas. See 'Report on the Work of the Government', 2010, www.npc.gov.cn/zgrdw/ englishnpc/Special_11_5/2010-03/19/content_1690630.htm, accessed 2 January 2023.

110 'Report on the Work of the Government', 2011.

The Village Redevelopment Program, the subject of this book, was also announced as a key part of the BNSC policy to improve infrastructure and social services within villages. In 2006, the CCP went further and, at the sixth plenary session of the Central Committee of the 16th National Party Congress, called for changes that went beyond the simple improvement of infrastructure and actively promoted 'the building of rural communities' (*nongcun shequ* 农村社区). Most notably, in China's industrialised rural areas, it began to become common for local governments to impose urban residential planning on rural communities,[111] while merging several villages together into large residential communities and moving the villagers into apartment buildings (see Chapter 3).

Such large-scale reforms and direct subsidies required significant government financial outlays. Since 2005, a new category of fiscal reporting appeared in official financial reports entitled 'the three rurals' (*san nong*). For the first time, all public expenditure on the rural sector was brought together under one category.[112] Official reports reveal significant increases in central fiscal allocations to rural areas since 2005. In that year, total expenditure in rural areas equalled RMB297.5 billion. This increased to RMB339.7 billion in 2006, RMB431.8 billion in 2007, RMB595.5 billion in 2008, RMB725.3 billion in 2009 and RMB858 billion in 2010. Central allocations to rural areas increased to RMB1.04 trillion in 2011 and 1.25 trillion in 2012.[113] Unfortunately, since 2013, official statistics have stopped reporting the '*san nong*' category. However, the goal of improving rural services and infrastructure has remained a top priority, with significant earmarked allocations under the leadership of Xi Jinping and Li Keqiang, as can be seen in official annual reports on the central government's work and national budget. In a few cases, this also included taking large international loans.[114]

The Village Redevelopment Program

In both Chenggu and Beian counties, the Village Redevelopment Program has been one of the most prominent areas of government activity in the BNSC agenda. From the beginning of my research, it became clear that village redevelopment had seized much of the officials' attention. The newly established leading groups (*lingdao xiaozu* 领导小组) and offices

---

111 Bray, 'Urban Planning Goes Rural', 53–62.
112 Lin and Wong, 'Are Beijing's Equalization Policies', 23.
113 This embodies an average annual increase of about 23 per cent. Figures are calculated from various years of China's 'Report on the Work of the Government'.
114 World Bank, *China: World Bank*; World Bank, *China to Improve*.

(*xin nongcun jianshe bangongshi* 新农村建设办公室) that were established in both counties to facilitate BNSC were focused mainly on facilitating village redevelopment (see Chapter 4).

In both counties, there was no designated budget for BNSC as a whole, and the many new subsidies made available following the announcement of BNSC were allocated as designated financial allocations for specific uses. There was, however, a special budget to support the redevelopment of villages. Therefore, village redevelopment could stand on its own—an independent program detached from its larger context as part of the new socialist countryside program.

Involving all government levels and various social actors in its implementation, the Village Redevelopment Program is a dynamic arena in which various political and economic interests, as well as administrative and societal constituencies, are in play. Importantly, conducting research on it helps to overcome a significant bias in the literature on policy implementation in post-Mao China. It has long been observed that scholars who research policy implementation tend to focus on failures and conflicts and less on success.[115] Yet, even critical voices must admit that, despite the many difficulties that implementers face and the shortcomings of the Chinese political system, national authorities have been able to demonstrate a high capacity 'to deliver', even if not always efficiently.[116]

Village redevelopment presents a type of policy that has escaped rigorous attention and whose implementation does not involve inherent conflicts of interest. As the following chapters show, the political-economic environment in which village redevelopment was implemented in Chenggu and Beian provided an opportunity to establish win-win relations between local communities, local governments and central authorities.

Locations and Methodology

Chenggu and Beian counties share several similarities. Located relatively close to provincial capitals (Jinan in Shandong and Hefei in Anhui), both are considered the most industrialised counties in their prefectural city's jurisdiction, are populated entirely by Han people and contain about 700,000 inhabitants. Yet they differ significantly from each other in terms

---

115 Zweig, 'Context and Content', 256.
116 Ahlers, *Rural Policy Implementation*, 2.

of economic development. As Chapter 2 elaborates, Chenggu is located in a prosperous part of Shandong Province and is significantly more industrialised and urbanised than Beian.

Both counties were selected based on the author's personal contacts. The research follows Mill's method of agreement methodology, which advocates a comparison between two (or more) instances of a phenomenon (e.g. prioritising the better off rural communities) to find possible common causal circumstances.[117] To gain a deeper understanding of the implementation process, I conducted semi-structured interviews and conversations with officials and villagers during the years 2009–11, the heyday of the implementation of the BNSC policy.

In the years that followed, I lost my contacts in both counties, as the officials I knew were transferred, so I was not able to conduct further research. However, in 2016, I returned to China to carry out research in other parts of the country. I engaged in shorter fieldwork trips to South Field, a village near industrialised Qingdao City, Shandong Province, and Middle Hill, a remote, county-level, rural township governed by the province-level metropolis of Chongqing in China's west, where I studied four villages. As in Chenggu and Beian, I purposely selected prosperous and non-prosperous rural areas to study. The new information I gathered in South Field and Middle Hill confirmed that the findings and analyses of Beian and Chenggu counties are valid for other parts of China.

Two comparative axes guide this research. The first refers to the county level. It asks about implementation and outcomes in two different counties that belong to two different provinces in two different regions of China, with supplemental material from South Field and Middle Hill. As subsequent chapters show, while the local state has succeeded, at least partly, in adjusting implementation of the Village Redevelopment Program to the different economic realities of locales such as Beian and Chenggu, the program has failed to meet the goal of decreasing inter-regional inequality and disparity, as significantly more villages and rural inhabitants in prosperous Chenggu have joined the redevelopment program and enjoyed its material benefits than in less prosperous Beian. The second axis refers to the sub-county level. It shifts attention from the county as a solitary unit towards perceiving the county as a complex set of political-economic-administrative jurisdictions that include a wide variety of townships and villages, each with distinctive characteristics, needs and economic capacities, as shown in Figure 1.1.

---

117 Ragin, *The Comparative Method*, 36.

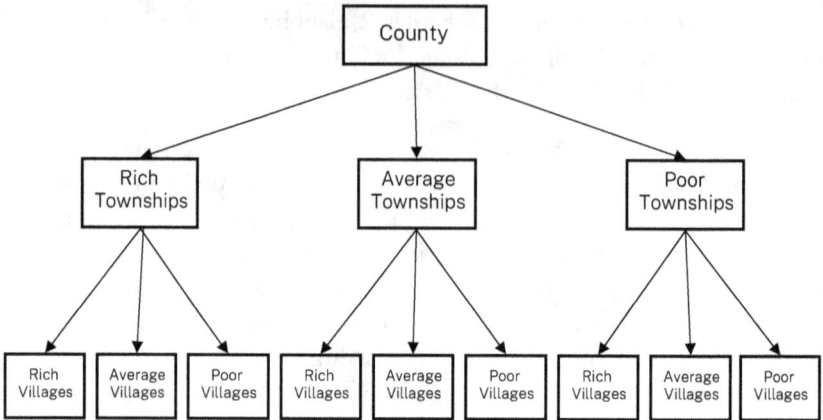

Figure 1.1: County layout
Source: Created by author.

The importance of acknowledging the complexity of counties is that, ultimately, this is the reality that local officials must face. This is especially true when implementing policies that seek to change local economic development conditions such as the Village Redevelopment Program. As subsequent chapters show, in both counties, officials failed to adjust the policy to accommodate the needs of the least advantaged sub-county locales, and most officials' efforts were channelled towards the more prosperous townships and the most prosperous rural communities inside each township.

I conducted two rounds of fieldwork in Chenggu (in 2009 and 2011, a total of five months) and engaged in one month of intensive fieldwork in Beian in 2010. In Chenggu, my research was more formal and I was asked to submit a list of interviewees (government offices and departments) and village and township fieldwork sites, which was approved by the county government before my arrival. In Beian, my research was more intuitive and interviewees and fieldwork sites were decided 'on-the-spot' at my request. In most cases, local officials in both counties approved my requests and I enjoyed full cooperation to arrange interviews. No formal restrictions were imposed on the research agenda.

To grasp the complexity of both counties, I broadened my research to as many townships and villages as possible. In total, I researched more than 20 villages in eight townships in Chenggu and eight villages in six townships in Beian. About half of the villages that I studied in Chenggu, and seven out of the eight villages in Beian, had already started their redevelopment. In both counties, I studied industrialised townships, average townships and rural townships, providing a good sample of each county's reality.

In both counties, the need to obtain research permits did not allow me formal access to villages without official 'companions' from my hosts (the county government Office for Outside Relations [*waishiban* 外事办] in Chenggu and the Agricultural Bureau [*nongwei* 农委] in Beian). Fieldwork trips to villages were on a daily basis and my requests to spend a few days residing in villages were declined due to 'safety' reasons. In most cases, however, my feeling was that interviewees were open and sincere about their activities and the redevelopment policy's outcomes.

I conducted semi-structured interviews in both counties and, when possible, held informal conversations with local officials at the county and township levels (mainly at party and government offices/units that were involved directly in the implementation of the program) as well as with village leaders (mostly village party secretaries and village heads), to learn about their perceptions of the redevelopment program and its implementation. In Chenggu, I conducted eight interviews with county officials, 14 interviews with township officials and 16 interviews with village officials. In Beian, I conducted six interviews with county officials (excluding officials from the county Agricultural Bureau, who accompanied me during my whole stay in Beian and served as constant informal interlocutors), four township heads and five village leaders.

While in villages, I also engaged in conversations with villagers. In most cases, village officials enabled me to interview members of the villages' leading bodies or villagers who, as I learned during the interviews, were supportive of their village's redevelopment program (mainly wealthy families). It was 'suggested' by my hosts that I should refrain from visiting very poor villages since, according to local officials, they had not yet started redevelopment and hence had no value for my research.

However, in Chenggu, where I spent more time and where transportation facilities to villages were significantly better, I used personal contacts fostered with local people to research villages that were not included in my official research plan. Some of these were in the county's remote and undeveloped areas. This included clandestine visits to villages and conversations with inhabitants and leaders to learn about their knowledge and their attitudes towards the BNSC and the government's Village Redevelopment Program.

Surveying rural households systematically was beyond the ambit of my research permit and budget. Therefore, while I conducted numerous conversations with villagers, I was not able to obtain statistical data based on a survey of households. While I have inserted villagers' testimony in several chapters, I suggest that these be taken as anecdotal only—that is, as referring to their own experiences in their own villages but not necessarily to others.

Internal local government documents and secondary Chinese and Western literature were useful supplementary sources. These contributed significantly to my understanding of national and local goals, procedures and the progress of the Village Redevelopment Program, and helped me to locate Beian and Chenggu in a larger context. I also interviewed several academics in Shandong, Anhui and Beijing who specialise in rural Chinese development.

The Book's Layout

The remainder of this book is organised as follows. Chapter 2 introduces Beian and Chenggu counties. It starts with a discussion of the significant economic differences between them, examines the emergence of inequality inside each county—between townships, rural communities and households—then explores the main reasons for this. The chapter ends with a discussion of the poor infrastructure and social services in most of the villages, which the redevelopment program was expected to improve.

Chapter 3 discusses the profound changes that the redevelopment program brought to villages in Beian and Chenggu. Both counties undertook very different approaches to implementation. Chenggu promoted construction of new city-like apartment housing and even entirely new villages. In poorer Beian, by contrast, local officials supported redevelopment of the villages' public areas while the villagers continued to live in their original houses and villages. The chapter points towards each county's economic conditions and local officials' perceptions of these conditions as the main explanatory variables to such different approaches. The chapter evaluates the positive aspects of the redevelopment scheme and analyses its pitfalls and drawbacks, especially where construction of new villages was involved.

Chapter 4 introduces the institutional setup surrounding the redevelopment program and its main actors. It starts by discussing the institutional environment established in Beian and Chenggu to facilitate implementation of the program. It then investigates the main governance strategies and practices applied by the local bureaucracy. It shows that each county walked a different path, presenting two distinct approaches to implementation. Chenggu took a government-oriented approach that focused on hierarchical relations between supervisors and subordinates and mechanical duplication of policy targets without much adaptation to local conditions. Beian, on the other hand, took a more village-oriented approach and was more welcoming to local initiatives and attentive to local needs. It placed less emphasis on the hierarchical nature of the local political system and was less formal and standardised than Chenggu. It was also less transparent than Chenggu. This was an outcome of very different constellations of local economic conditions and higher-level intervention ('commandism') in each of the counties.

Chapter 5 explains the local officials' tendency to mainly redevelop and finance prosperous villages. At the heart of this chapter is a discussion of two popular governing principles in contemporary policymaking: the construction of 'demonstration villages' (*shifan cun* 示范村) and the establishment of experimental areas (*shidian qu* 试点区). The chapter shows how local economic conditions and the hierarchical nature of politics have formed a very different interpretation and implementation of these institutions in each of the counties.

Chapter 6 explains why both counties ended up supporting the more prosperous villages, a dubious strategy for social development. It points towards a number of institutional obstacles in China's political tradition and bureaucratic practices, as well as the interests of crucial actors, that blocked the possibility of choosing other villages to enjoy the program. It concludes that higher levels of the political bureaucracy inadvertently forced local officials to select prosperous villages, irrespective of their individual wills and beliefs.

Chapter 7 summarises the main findings and arguments of the book. It integrates the question of selective policy implementation (i.e. why local officials implement certain policies but not others) and my research on the modus operandi (i.e. how policies are implemented) into a comprehensive model of Chinese policy implementation. At the heart of this theoretical model is an elaboration of the concept of 'discretion', which helps to explain the special position of Chinese implementers and offers a new paradigmatic view of the entire process of policy implementation in contemporary China.

2

An Overview of Chenggu and Beian Counties

It is a pleasant drive to Chenggu County. The ride is smooth due to the well-paved, double-lane, asphalt highway that brings you directly to the county seat and its modern bus station. Along both sides of the highway, tall trees have been planted. During summer, their thick green leaves almost hide the small villages and corn fields extending on both sides of the road. At the entrance to the county capital is a beautiful artificial lake built by the county government for recreational purposes; on the other side of the road is the county government's modern compound. Continue along the road a few minutes and 'Welcome to Harmonious Chenggu' greets you in large Chinese characters.[1]

The county enjoys a preferable location in Shandong, one of China's rich coastal provinces, only an hour's drive from two of the province's largest cities and a few hours drive from some of China's largest economic centres. Its location enabled Chenggu to industrialise rapidly over the last three decades. From an average or 'typical' Chinese county during the 1980s, it has become not only the most industrialised county in the prefecture but also one of the most successful counties in the province.

---

1   'Constructing a Socialist Harmonious Society' (*goujian shehuizhuyi hexie shehui*) was a key political agenda under the leadership of Hu Jintao, the general secretary of the CCP at the time of my fieldwork in Chenggu.

My second research site, Beian County, is located in Anhui Province in central China. Similar to Chenggu County, it is intersected by a highway, leading from Anhui's provincial capital city of Hefei to the industrialised city of Wuhan, the capital of Hubei Province, about 500 kilometres from Beian. After a 20-minute drive, leaving behind Hefei's new extensive built-up area with its numerous skyscrapers, the urban scenery is suddenly replaced by the tranquillity of the countryside. Paddy rice (*shuidao* 水稻) and canola (*youcai* 油菜) are the dominant crops in this area and small reservoirs are dispersed in and between villages on both sides of the highway. After exiting the highway, a cement road leads to the county's bus station in the old, busy and dirty part of Township I,[2] the current location of the county's government. Unlike Chenggu County, there is no sign to welcome you to Beian.

Beian is far from the coast and from large commercial and industrial centres. Even its relative closeness to the province's largest city (1.5 hour's drive from Hefei) brings few benefits, as Anhui is not a highly industrialised province. Despite being a prosperous county in local terms, its economic development over the last three decades has been significantly slower than in Chenggu.

Both counties have a similar population of about 700,000 inhabitants. Yet the ratio between rural and urban inhabitants differs, a clear indication of the significant differences in economic development between the counties. According to official data, in 2007, 26 per cent of Chenggu's population held a non-agricultural household registration (*fei nongye renkou* 非农业人口),[3] compared to only 10 per cent in Beian.[4] However, the urban population is not scattered equally or randomly throughout either county. At the time of my fieldwork, 80 per cent of Chenggu's non-agricultural (i.e. urban) population, which consisted of 20 per cent of the county's total population, resided in the county seat and its three main districts (*jiedao banshi chu* 街道

---

2   For reasons of anonymity, township names were coded into letters according to alphabetical order. Townships in Chenggu were coded from A to H. Townships in Beian were coded from I to N. Within each of the townships, villages that were included in this research were coded by number. For example, Village A1 refers to the first village in Township A, Village A2 refers to a second village in Township A, Village B1 refers to the first village in Township B, etc.

3   *Chenggu County Statistical Yearbook*, 2008.

4   *Beian County Statistical Yearbook*, 2009.

办事处). In the rural townships, the proportion of the population holding a non-agricultural household registration was still meagre, consisting of less than 10 per cent of the populace.[5]

In Beian, more than 60 per cent of the county's non-agricultural population, which consists of 7 per cent of the county's entire population, is concentrated in two townships—Township K (the previous location of the county government, where 24 per cent of the population held a non-agricultural household registration), and Township I (the county government's current location, where 43 per cent of the population held a non-agricultural household registration).[6] In the rest of the rural townships, the non-agricultural population consisted of a meagre percentage of the townships' total population (from 2 to 6 per cent only).[7]

It should be noted that the distinction between agricultural and non-agricultural household registration refers only to the counties' inhabitants' formal household registration status, which serves as a good indicator of economic development but is a fairly poor indicator of the inhabitants' habits and patterns of life. As is elaborated further in this chapter, the rural population—and this is more notable in industrialised Chenggu—was, in many aspects, embedded in the urban life of the county. Most of Chenggu's rural households' income was generated from working in non-agricultural sectors, largely in or near the rural township or the county seats, as were many of the services they consumed in their everyday lives. Many of the rural inhabitants (particularly young people) dwelt in the county's urban areas, returning to their villages once in a while. According to official data,

---

5   Author's calculations, *Chenggu County Statistical Yearbook*, 2008. In only one rural township did the population holding a non-agricultural household registration surpass 10 per cent, at 12 per cent. According to Chinese definitions, a distinction is made between a rural township (*xiang*)—an administrative unit with typically less than 10 per cent of the population holding non-agricultural registration and where agriculture occupies a significant part of the local economy—and a rural town (*zhen*), where the population with non-agricultural registration typically exceeds 10 per cent and where non-agricultural sectors are more developed. In both Chenggu and Beian, however, these definitions were not followed, and the counties referred to most of their townships as *zhen*, despite a low rate of non-agricultural households and significant differences in townships' economic structure and economic performances (as is explained further in this chapter). Since the original Chinese in the counties did not follow the *zhen–xiang* definitions, I am referring to both *zhen* and *xiang* as 'townships' but distinguish between their level of economic development.

6   The county had one more relatively urbanised township, where slightly less than 25 per cent held non-agricultural registration. This township enjoyed relatively good financial conditions due to profitable mines. Yet its population was significantly smaller than in the townships of I and K and its urban population was only a quarter to a third of the urban population in these townships, respectively. This township was not included in my study.

7   Author's calculations, *Beian County Statistical Yearbook*, 2009.

as of a decade ago, about half of Chenggu's total population lived in the county and township seats.[8] Recalling that only 26 per cent of the county's population held a non-agricultural household registration, we can conclude that villagers constituted about half of the county's urban areas population. Thus, although officially holding an agricultural household registration, villagers were, in many respects, an integral part of the county's urban cultural, social, administrative and economic life and were by no means confined to their villages.

In total, there were more than 850 administrative villages (*xingzheng cun* 行政村) in Chenggu and about 240 administrative villages in Beian, but the administrative villages in Beian were significantly larger and could reach up to a few thousand people. Each of the administrative villages in Beian contained hamlets (*cunzhuang* 村庄) that are governed together. Most of the administrative villages that I studied averaged around 20 such hamlets, although a few of them had more than 30. Some of them were very small in size, with only several households, while others were quite large, holding several hundred people. Some hamlets were close to neighbouring ones, while others were quite dispersed. In total, there were more than 3,000 hamlets in the county.

Chenggu's county seat has expanded significantly over the last three decades, incorporating many nearby villages and more than doubling its area. Land around the county seat has been mostly converted into industrial, commercial and governmental uses, and agriculture has vanished almost entirely. The earlier mentioned modern government compound, for example, was built on agricultural land that was bought by the government from local villages. In front and behind the compound, beautiful parks were built, with lawns, fountains and water channels, and the county's modern movie theatre was built next door. To save land, and as part of its modernisation, the county seat had undergone significant reconstruction over the previous decades; by 2010, most of its inhabitants, including the incorporated villages, lived in modern apartment buildings, mostly of six floors or higher, and the process of residential concentration was still under way.

The county seat of Chenggu served not only as a government centre but also as a central industrial zone, hosting a massive economic development zone that, in mid-2003, was recognised by the provincial government as a provincial-level development zone (*sheng ji jingji kaifa qu* 省级经济开

---

8   *Chenggu County Statistical Yearbook*, 2008. Unfortunately, comparable data were not provided publicly in Beian.

发区). The county seat also served as the county's main commercial area, boasting numerous shops, restaurants and hotels, including a few three- to four-star hotels and a modern shopping mall offering leading international brands. Local restaurants offered an impressive array of international food, including excellent Western bakeries and two KFC fast-food outlets. The roads inside the county seat were wide and well paved. Tall trees were planted on both sides of the main roads, easing the hot summer days with shade and creating green boulevards.

As a flourishing county, there were many Chinese visitors arriving for business purposes, professional conferences or simply to enjoy the county's facilities: hotels, restaurants, and Karaoke bars. An official from the county's Tourist Bureau estimated the number of outside visitors to be 2 million annually (most of whom arrived for one-day visits). The wealth of Chenggu County, which hosted a couple of the largest business groups and factories in the province, was a direct result of its massive industrialisation. According to official data, by 2007–8 industries provided employment for more than half of the workforce in the county while agriculture and the tertiary sector provided 22 per cent each. The industrial sector contributed 76.5 per cent of the county's GDP while the tertiary sector contributed 18 per cent and agriculture only 5.5 per cent.[9]

Chenggu's economic development has enhanced the wellbeing of its inhabitants. By 2007, the average annual per capita income of *rural* inhabitants was slightly over RMB6,000, 46 per cent higher than the national average that year (RMB4,140). The average income of its urban inhabitants was RMB14,000, slightly higher than the national average of that year (RMB13,786) and more than twice the average *rural* income.

In contrast to Chenggu County, there was no designated county seat in Beian. In the past, the county government was in Township K, on the county's south side. But, at the beginning of this century, it moved to its current location in Township I, on the other side of the county, due to its closer proximity to the Hefei–Wuhan highway. Subsequently, Township I—small, undeveloped and the same as every other township in the county until then—experienced a golden age. It expanded significantly, incorporating many nearby villages. Apart from a small old portion (the 'original Township I'), the entire town was built in the first two decades

---

9   *Chenggu County Statistical Yearbook,* 2008; Chenggu County, internal document, 2007, copy in author's possession.

of the twenty-first century. As in Chenggu, modern multistorey apartment buildings were the dominant residential pattern and roads were wide and well paved.

Unlike Chenggu, the new government compound in Beian was simple and modest. Yet, as in Chenggu, the county had invested in the environmental development of the new parts of the township, especially the areas around the government compound (although standards were not comparable with Chenggu). Two large canals were built along both sides of the main road adjoining the government compound and walking paths were constructed for recreational purposes. Public squares were dispersed in the area, with many statues and thick green vegetation. Across the road was the city's modern pedestrian shopping zone. On the north-east side, behind the governmental compound, a large park with expansive lawns, walking paths and a lake commemorated a well-known, local historical figure.

The county government had tried to develop Township I to become the county's main urban, commercial and industrial centre and a magnet to attract people, especially young adults. The hope was that people would voluntarily leave their overpopulated villages and move into the township's new residential areas. By 2010, Township I was already second in size only to Township K, the former seat of the county government. Township I was spearheading urbanisation in the county. As mentioned earlier, at the time of my fieldwork in Beian, over 40 per cent of Township I's population held a non-agricultural household registration; this was about four times higher than the county's urban population ratio and almost twice the ratio of Township K. In sharp contrast to Beian's mostly chaotic, dirty, old-fashioned townships and their very poor infrastructure, Township I seemed modern.

Beian developed more slowly than Chenggu. According to official data, in 2007, the industrial sector contributed only 44 per cent of the county's GDP. The tertiary sector contributed 33 per cent and agriculture 23 per cent, significantly higher than in Chenggu. Total GDP was only a fifth of Chenggu's,[10] a clear indication of the underdevelopment of the county's industrial and commercial sectors. As a result, the county government's revenue was also lower in Beian (reaching only a ninth of the Chenggu government's revenue). Inhabitants' incomes, although rising consistently, were also significantly lower than in Chenggu. In 2007, the average rural

---

10   GDP in Chenggu in 2007 was RMB34.4 billion. In Beian, total GDP in 2007 was RMB6.4 billion. GDP per capita in Chenggu was RMB47,560 compared to only RMB9,340 in Beian.

annual per capita income was RMB4,600, about 11 per cent higher than the average national income of that year, but only 76 per cent of the average rural income in Chenggu. Unfortunately (and unlike Chenggu), Beian did not report its urban average income. However, according to an official from the Statistics Bureau, the urban average income in 2008 (the latest data available when I lived in the county) was about RMB12,000, more than twice the average rural income in the county but significantly lower than the national urban income average of that year, which was RMB15,781.

In both counties (as in many parts of China), land was scarce and insufficient to sustain farmers. Therefore, villagers depended on non-agricultural work as the main source of household income.[11] In Chenggu, 70 per cent of the villagers' income derived from non-agricultural resources.[12] In a survey conducted among more than 500 former production teams (*xiaozu* 小组) in the province of Anhui in 2008, in all seven teams surveyed from Beian County, manual labour outside the village (*chuqu dagong* 出去打工) was reported as the most important source of household income.[13]

Since most villages did not offer enough employment opportunities, the majority of villagers in both counties relied on work *outside* the villages to sustain themselves. But 'outside the villages' had a totally different meaning in each of the counties. In industrialised Chenggu, the local labour market was developed enough not only to provide employment to all local inhabitants but also to offer work opportunities to thousands of immigrants arriving in the county from all over the country. Villagers in Chenggu who worked outside the villages were likely to be employed by the county's many factories or the commercial and services sector and were most likely to return to their villages at the end of the working day. Two prominent exceptions were villagers from relatively remote townships and villages who dwelt outside their villages in dorms offered by the employers, saving the trouble of commuting to work every day, and young people who decided to move to the county's towns to experience living in urban environments. The important thing to note, though, is that, in most cases, leaving the villages in Chenggu was a result of a choice more than any kind of lack of

---

11   In Chenggu, average agricultural land per capita was 1.5 mu (1 mu = 0.667 dunam or 666.667 square metres). In Beian, the average was even smaller and villagers, on average, cultivated only 1.45 mu per capita (data calculated from counties' statistical yearbooks [2008 in Chenggu, 2009 in Beian]). Various villagers indicated the number of 5 mu per capita as the minimum amount of land required if a person wished to sustain themselves only from agriculture.

12   Chenggu County, internal document, 2007.

13   I am indebted to Professor Jonathan Unger for sharing this survey's findings with me.

choice. This is a significant difference between the two counties' labour markets, as Beian was not yet developed enough to sustain all the county's residents. According to local officials, 200,000 people (mostly young rural adults), slightly less than 30 per cent of the county's total population, were working outside the county—in the province or, most likely, in other more industrialised provinces, mainly along the south-east coast. They returned to their villages once or twice a year, leaving their villages half deserted during most of the year, inhabited mainly by older people and children.[14]

Out-migration has become a real concern for local authorities in Beian and a significant consideration in their local economic development agenda. Expansion of the county labour market became very important to Beian County's leadership. To keep the county's able-bodied young adults close to home, county leaders tried to develop a new industrial zone located at the outskirts of Township I and sought to attract investors.[15] In the officials' view, this would facilitate further expansion of Township I, as the economic and residential epicentre of the county.

Agriculture in both counties was barely profitable, and some villagers preferred to lease out their land. Leasing out the land enabled them to work in non-agricultural jobs full-time, receiving leasing rents, while the lessees were able to engage in larger-scale and more efficient agriculture. It was also quite common in Beian that local villagers let other family members or friends cultivate their land without asking for rent or other material benefits (I did not encounter such cases in Chenggu). The most important thing, according to interviewees, was that the land not become barren, as would have happened had it not been cultivated. All in all, larger-scale agriculture was more common in Beian, where agriculture was more important as a source of livelihood, than in Chenggu.

Promoting larger-scale agriculture was an important goal for the local government of Beian. This increased significantly in the early 2000s due to the support of the central government for a transition from small-scale

---

14   Loosening migration restrictions is one of the most important institutional changes during the post-Mao era. Like many other developing countries in the world, cityward migration has become a common channel for young villagers to shift away from agricultural occupations towards more profitable jobs in towns and cities, and an important means of increasing rural households' income. In 2018, the number of migrant workers was estimated as slightly less than 290 million and their average monthly income reached RMB3,721. See, for example, Whyte, 'The Paradoxes of Rural–Urban Inequality', 13; *China Labour Bulletin*, 'Migrant Workers'.

15   One result of the process of strengthening Township I was a sharp rise in housing prices from RMB500 per square metre in 2005 to RMB3,000 in 2010.

agriculture, after the return to household farming in the early 1980s, to large-scale (and more efficient) agriculture.[16] Chen Biding, a leading scholar from Anhui Province (the birthplace of land decollectivisation), named this transition as being from *dabaogan* (大包干) to *zaibaogan* (再包干)—that is, renting out the rights to cultivate the land without changing ownership patterns.[17] In Township I, for example, household plots of 10–20 mu were already very common in 2011 and 10 households cultivated plots larger than 100 mu. In total, 12 households in the entire county cultivated 1,000 mu and above.

In both counties, grain was still dominant. The main crops in Beian were rice and canola. The main crops in Chenggu were wheat, corn and cotton (which, in some places, I was told, was becoming less important due to climate change and the need to invest a lot of effort to gain a modest income). In both cases, county governments invested to improve agriculture, including moving away from traditional grain agriculture into more diversified and profitable crops. Yet both places faced difficulties. Agricultural work was mainly being conducted by older people, who often lacked the skills and readiness to change existing patterns. This is why, a high official in Beian County explained, they were trying to find ways to bring young migrant women workers into the villages, as it was hoped they would be willing to act as agricultural change agents. Officials also hoped that more young people would be ready to engage in agriculture if plots were larger and more profitable—the desired outcome of the *zaibaogan* system.

Another obstacle to changing the nature of local agriculture, I was told by many villagers in industrialised Chenggu, was the minimal care that grain crops demand. Except for the sowing and harvesting periods, in which work was very intensive, the work in maintaining the crops was minimal. This enabled most of the people in the household to work in more profitable undertakings in industry and commerce. Had they planted cash crops, they would have needed to go to the fields on a daily basis, since these crops need intensive care. Thus, industrialisation was encouraging the continuity of traditional grain agriculture.

---

16   According to officials from the county Agricultural Bureau, to encourage people to cultivate larger plots of land, agricultural subsidies were higher (RMB110 per mu instead of RMB100) if the plot cultivated was larger than 100 mu. Data refer to 2010.

17   Chen, 'Tuijin "dabaogan" xiang "zaibaogan" de xin fazhan' [The new development of shifting from a 'household responsibility system' to a 'new responsibility system'].

Officials in both counties were proud of their economic progress over recent decades and perceived further economic development as the main channel to further improve their inhabitants' livelihoods. In 2010, officials in Beian County proudly stated that Beian was the most developed county in the prefecture but, at the same time, fully acknowledged the economic inferiority of Beian vis-a-vis industrialised parts of China. In Chenggu, as several internal documents indicated, aspirations were to become a leading county not only in the province but also nationally. For county officials, 'being number one' was a leading governing principle.

However, economic development had brought some unfortunate outcomes to the counties as well. As in many other industrialised places in China, the rapid industrialisation of Chenggu County was followed by serious environmental pollution. In most of the townships, the local water had become contaminated and undrinkable. People bought drinking water from the few non-industrialised townships in the county where water reserves were still drinkable or from water resources outside the county.[18] In many industrialised townships, industrial chimney smoke was becoming an inescapable part of life; I was told by local inhabitants in one of these townships that a thick white smoke would sometimes cover the township, making it hard to breathe.

The second unfortunate outcome was an expansion of inequality, manifested not only in income levels but also in the physical conditions of residential environments. Since improving rural residential environments was the main goal of the redevelopment program, and inasmuch as income inequality substantially shaped the implementation of the Village Redevelopment Program (as will be elaborated in the next chapters), the rest of this chapter is devoted to an elaboration of inequality in Beian and Chenggu.

Economic Inequality

Two conclusions may be drawn thus far regarding villagers' income in Chenggu and Beian. First, villagers in Chenggu enjoyed higher incomes than villagers in Beian. Second, in both counties, the average rural income was significantly lower than in the counties' urban areas. Comparing average incomes to average expenses provides an indication of people's savings ability,

---

18   The price of water was very cheap and by no means imposed any economic burden on the people. Twenty-five litres of drinking water cost only RMB1.

an important indicator of the magnitude of existing inequality. In 2007, the average person's expenditure in Chenggu's rural areas was RMB5,660, some RMB400 lower than the average rural income, while the average person in the county's urban areas spent RMB11,000, about RMB3,000 lower than his or her average income. In other words, the average urbanite in the county saved annually about RMB2,500 more than his or her counterpart in the villages. Unfortunately, these types of data are not publicly available for Beian County.

Inequality is evident not only at the urban–rural level but also between rural communities within the same county. These imbalances have expanded significantly since the beginning of the economic reforms in 1979,[19] and Chenggu and Beian are no exceptions.

Inequality in Chenggu County

Despite the economic centrality of the county seat, many of the economic activities in Chenggu County took place outside the county seat, in the rural townships. Although the county as a whole was considered industrialised, the townships differed significantly from each other in their level of industrialisation and economic development. While some of the townships were highly industrialised, industrialisation had not yet blossomed in others. These differences can be seen in Table 2.1, which presents the total GDP in each of the townships that I studied in Chenggu County.

Table 2.1: GDP of different townships of Chenggu County, 2007 (in 10,000 RMB)

	A	B	C	D	E	F	G	H
Total GDP of the township	389,579	190,420	95,746	68,459	50,058	47,799	41,940	38,465

Source: *Chenggu County Statistical Yearbook*, 2008.

It is important to note that differences between the townships' GDP refer only to differences in the *overall* economic output of the townships, which, in the case of industrialised townships, included the contribution of migrant workers who worked in secondary and tertiary industries in the townships (many arrived from other townships in the county as well as from other counties and provinces). As can be seen in Table 2.1, total

---

19 Xu, '"Rich Brothers"', 801–17; Zhang, 'Retreat from Equality', 535–57; Zhou, Han and Harrell, 'From Labour to Capital', 515–34; Sicular, 'The Challenge of High Inequality', 1–5.

GDP in Township A, the most industrialised township in the county, reached almost RMB3.9 billion while GDP in Township H, the lowest in the county, reached only RMB384 million. In other words, the difference between Chenggu's most and least industrialised townships in terms of GDP reached more than 10 times, about twice as large as the difference between the overall GDP of Chenggu and Beian counties.

Other important factors to consider when discussing inequality at the township level are revenue and the ratio between revenue and expenditure. These are presented in Table 2.2.

Table 2.2: Total revenue and expenditure of different townships of Chenggu County, 2007 (in 10,000 RMB)

	A	B	C	D	E	F	G	H
Total revenue	11,275	6,462	2,494	2,404	1,148	1,363	632	658
Total expenditure	7,748	5,138	2,394	2,810	1,706	2,579	1,106	1,273

Source: *Chenggu County Statistical Yearbook*, 2008.

Two points in Table 2.2 warrant mention. First, industrialised townships enjoyed significantly higher revenue than rural ones (the difference between Township A's and Townships G's and H's revenue is more than 17 times). The second point is that only industrialised townships enjoyed higher revenue than expenditure and that rural townships tended to have serious financial deficits. As the following chapters show, a township's financial capacity played a significant role in deciding the extent of its financial support for village redevelopment.

Generally, there was a positive correlation between the proximity of a township to the county seat and its level of industrialisation. Townships that were further from the county seat of Chenggu were more likely to be less industrialised and poorer. One notable exception was Township H, which is located on the edge of the county seat and yet was relatively poor. Its designation as a tourist township prevented it from hosting any environment-polluting industries. In 2009, after considerable effort and financing by the county and the township governments, it was successfully recognised as a tourist site by the province. Officials hoped that with better infrastructure, fostered tourist sites and provincial recognition, tourism would be boosted even further. This in turn would be followed by significant development of commerce in the township: for example, transportation, accommodation, eateries and restaurants along the township's main transportation routes and, no less important, in the township's mountainous areas, the location of the poorest villages in the township. Moreover, to further link Township H with the county seat, a new six-lane (three for each direction) asphalt highway was completed at the time of my fieldwork (2011) between the county seat and Township H, reducing the time between them to few minutes drive.

Inequality in Villagers' Incomes

Inequality was manifested not only in the townships' total GDP and revenue—which indicated large differences between the townships in terms of their governments' financial capacities—but also in the villagers' incomes, as can be seen in Charts 2.1 and 2.2. Chart 2.1 presents the average income of villagers in *each* of the townships that I studied in the county.

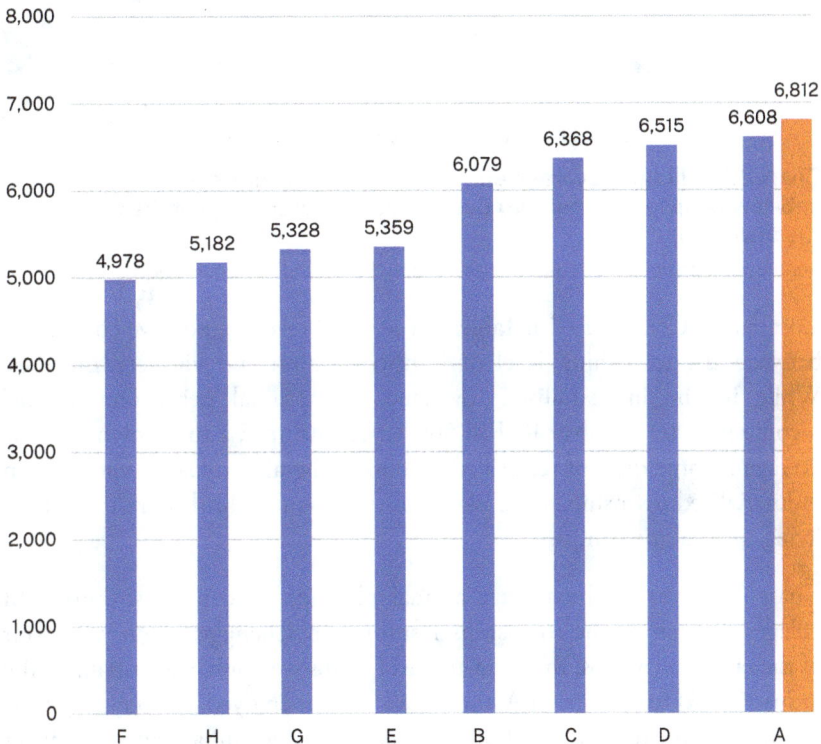

Chart 2.1: Average annual per capita income of rural inhabitants in different townships, Chenggu County, 2007 (in RMB)

Note: In Township A, the average income in one village was exceptionally high (RMB16,000). Therefore, the chart also presents the average without this village (of RMB6,608).

Source: Author's calculations, *Chenggu County Statistical Yearbook*, 2008.

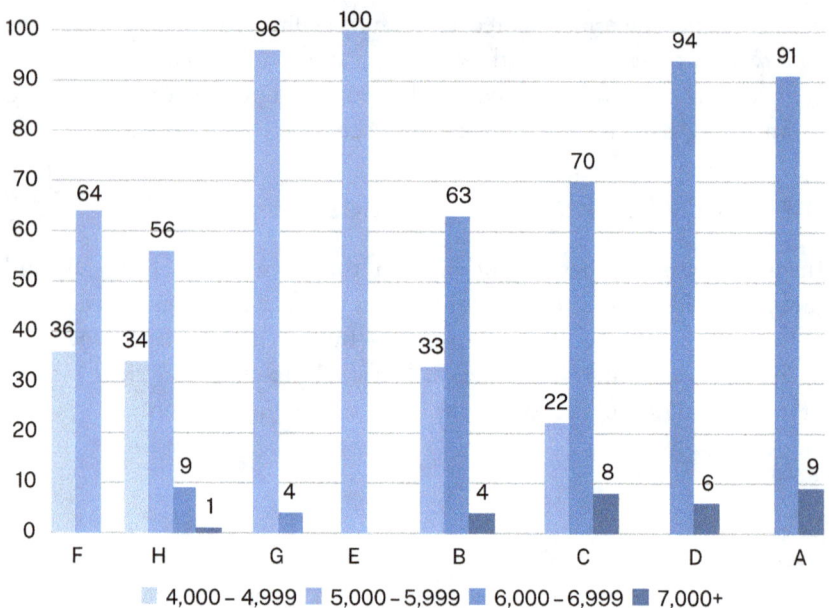

Chart 2.2: Villages' average annual per capita income distribution at the sub-township level, Chenggu County, 2007 (percentage of the villages in the township)

Source: Author's calculations, *Chenggu County Statistical Yearbook*, 2008.

Comparing Chart 2.1 with Tables 2.1 and 2.2 reveals a positive correlation between the townships' level of industrialisation and villagers' incomes. While in the industrialised townships the annual per capita average income in 2007 was over RMB6,500, in Township F, a rural township, the average income did not reach RMB5,000. Generally, villagers who lived in industrialised townships were likely to earn about a third more than those living in rural townships.

Chart 2.2 presents the average annual per capita income distribution of villages in each of the townships I studied in Chenggu County. In four of the eight townships, the intra-township gaps were relatively small. In the industrialised townships of A and D, all villages enjoyed an average annual income of more than RMB6,000 per person, of which inhabitants in 6–9 per cent of the villages enjoyed an income higher than RMB7,000. In Township E and Township G, two of the county's less industrialised townships, the average annual income of inhabitants in 96–100 per cent of the villages was RMB5,000–5,999. In the rest of the townships, however, diversity was clearly visible. For example, in 34 per cent of the villages in Township H, the average annual income was RMB4,000–4,999 per person; in 56 per cent of the villages it was higher, reaching RMB5,000–5,999; in 9 per cent of the township's villages, the average income was RMB6,000–6,999; and in 1 per cent, the income was 7,000 or more.

What can explain differences in income between urban and rural communities as well as between rural communities in such a small geographical unit as a county? An appropriate answer requires systematic socio-economic research, which exceeds the scope of this book. However, a few points are worth noting. The first relates to the assumption that household composition may bear responsibility. According to this assumption, families with more dependents (e.g. children under the age of 18 and old people aged 60+) would report smaller average individual incomes, as the household's income is divided between more members. This assumption is reinforced when remembering that the policy of family planning (*jihua shengyu* 计划生育) allowed more births to families in rural areas than in urban settlements. Unfortunately, Chenggu County, which normally provides very comprehensive statistical data, did not distinguish between rural and urban households relating to inhabitants' ages. Yet, Chenggu did report separately for the county seat and its three districts as well as for every rural township, and a simple mathematical calculation may provide the missing link to test this assumption.

According to official data, all inhabitants in the county seat were urban by household registration definition. As previously noted, the county seat held 80 per cent of the entire urban population in the county. In the rural townships, more than 90 per cent of the population held agricultural household registration. Therefore, comparing these two groups—the county seat versus the townships—may be a good enough indicator of the existence or absence of significant differences in household composition between rural and urban populations.

Calculating the average size of urban and rural households (by dividing the total population by the number of households) reveals only minor differences between the two populaces. The average size of rural households was 3.6 persons compared to 3.4 in urban households. Calculating the percentage of inhabitants under the age of 18 reveals very minor differences as well: 20 per cent of the total population in the county seat compared to 19.7 per cent in the townships. Calculating the percentage of elderly people (60+) in both populations reveals larger differences between these groups: 12.9 per cent of the county seat's population compared to 15.4 per cent in the townships. In all calculations, no significant differences were found in household composition between the townships. To conclude, differences in population composition were only manifested in a higher percentage of older people in rural areas. This, however, cannot explain the significant gap between the two groups' incomes.

The income gap may be an outcome of many variables simultaneously: for example, level of education, personal contacts and whether a person is employed temporarily or permanently. I wish to highlight two factors that repeatedly appeared in my interviews as important contributors to inequality between communities, and that can explain, even if only partially, significant income differences between social groups in the county: 1) the extent of access of household members to local labour markets (i.e. proximity to urban and industrial centres); 2) the availability of enough agricultural land to compensate for a lack of integration of one or more of the household members into the labour market. In the rural towns, accessibility to labour markets was not an issue, as the towns constituted the core of all industrial, commercial and service activities. Location, however, was much more of an issue when it came to the village communities.

Extracting income from markets is easier when one dwells near large commercial and/or industrial centres and can integrate with existing markets on a daily basis than if one lives in remote townships or villages. Proximity to developed markets may also provide additional income-extraction channels beyond being an employee or entrepreneur: for example, owing stocks in local enterprises, renting out houses to migrant workers and/or getting dividends from assets run collectively by the village. Location is also important to facilitate or hinder the integration of the weakest strata of rural households (e.g. older people, young mothers and people with health issues) in labour markets outside the villages. Table 2.3 exemplifies the importance of location in households' potential income. It presents the ratio of agricultural labourers out of the total labour force in each of the townships I studied in Chenggu.

Table 2.3: Ratio of agricultural labourers in selected townships in Chenggu County, 2007

	D	A	C	B	G	F	H	E
Ratio	1:13	1:7	1:5	1:3.5	1:3.5	1:3	1:3	1:2

Source: Author's calculations, *Chenggu County Statistical Yearbook*, 2008.

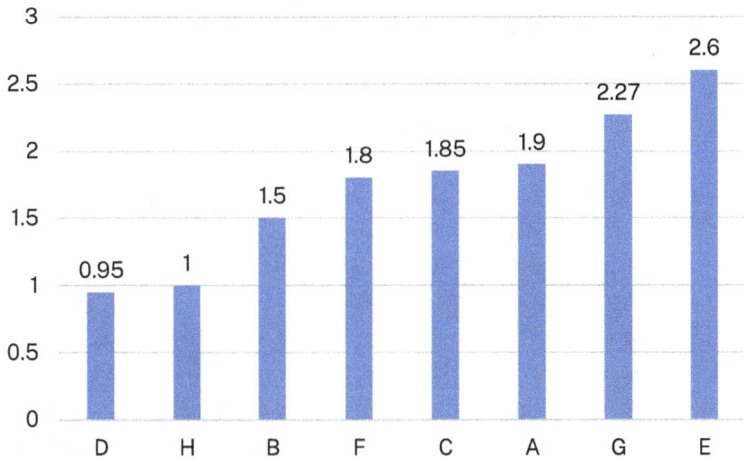

Chart 2.3: Average amount of agricultural land per capita in various townships, Chenggu County, 2007 (in mu)

Source: Author's calculations, *Chenggu County Statistical Yearbook*, 2008.

Even in industrialised Chenggu, agriculture was still a dominant 'employer'. According to official data, about a third of the county's total rural workforce was engaged in agriculture. Yet, as can be seen in Table 2.3, considerable differences existed between the townships in terms of the ratio of agricultural labourers. While in industrialised townships only a minor portion of the total labour force engaged in agriculture (e.g. 1:13, 1:7), this ratio increased significantly in rural townships, involving a third and even half of these townships' labour force.

Generally, the more remote a village/township was, the larger the likelihood that more household members were excluded from non-rural employment and reliant on agriculture or small-scale undertakings inside the villages. The importance of the division between agricultural and non-agricultural occupations lies in the fact that grain agriculture is more likely to generate lower incomes than working in factories or services due to insufficient agricultural land to ensure a sufficient income to rural households. According to villagers, the average annual income from 1 mu of grain land hardly equalled one month of salary in the secondary or tertiary sectors as low-level employees (RMB1,000–1,500 per year at the time of my fieldwork). This means that for one household member to gain an income equal to that earned in the non-agricultural sectors, he/she had to cultivate a minimum of 10 mu of land, or, in other words, a minimum of 2.5 mu per person. Chart 2.3 presents the average amount of agricultural land per capita in the townships where I conducted research.

Chart 2.3 reveals significant differences in the availability of agricultural land between the townships. Only one township in the county—Township E—reached the standard of 2.5 mu per household member. This rural township had only a limited industrial sector; however, 2.5 mu per person meant that the average household could compensate for one household member being outside the labour market.[20] In the rest of the townships, land plots were significantly smaller. An extreme example was Township H, one of the poorest townships in the county. With average plots of 1 mu per person, leaving one household member behind to cultivate household plots invoked an immediate loss of eight months salary had this person worked in the non-agricultural sector. At the other end of the scale were Township A, the most industrialised township in the county, and Township C, a rapidly industrialising township where villagers enjoyed relatively large plots of land (1.9 mu and 1.85 mu, respectively). In these townships, not only did many of the villagers enjoy better access to non-rural employment, but their safety net from agriculture was also larger. Clearly, if two household members were left behind in a village with small landholdings to cultivate the land (not a rare case in remote townships and villages), the financial impact on household income was dire. This was why village officials, in collaboration with the county's Agricultural Bureau, had tried to shift away from traditional agriculture towards more profitable agriculture (e.g. greenhouses, fruits and vegetables, and organic agriculture) and the county had pushed to make agriculture specific to local conditions, a policy known as 'one village one product, many villages one product, one village many products' (*yi cun yi pin, duo cun yi pin, yi cun duo pin* 一村一品，多村一品，一村多品).[21] However, despite the inequality between rural communities, in all of Chenggu's rural townships—industrialised and non-industrialised alike—most of the villagers enjoyed higher incomes than the national average. Even in Township F, a remote rural township, the average income in 2007 was still 20 per cent higher than the national average. This was a direct result of the county's ability to establish an economy in which its urban centres and adjacent villages provided employment and its rural areas served as the main source of employees. This coincided with the central government's vision of the ideal rural–urban relationship. In the case of Chenggu, this was due to three main reasons. First, as noted, there was enough work in the county for everyone. In all the villages I researched in Chenggu, including some of the

---

20   Nevertheless, average rural households' income in this township was significantly lower than in the county's industrialised townships (see Chart 2.1), clear evidence of the lesser importance of agriculture and the greater importance of the county's secondary and tertiary sectors as sources of villagers' income.
21   Interviews with township and village officials, Township F, Chenggu County, 1 July 2009.

county's most remote ones, I was told that young people normally worked in industries either in their township, in neighbouring townships or in the county's industrial zones. Thus, the economic success of an industrialised township spread outward to the whole county's population, contributing to the welfare of others, even if not equally.

The second enabling factor was the county's very good road network, which facilitated transport from the villages to the industrial and commercial zones.[22] Many of the roads inside the county had been paved in the early 1990s. In response to a national policy of paving roads between administrative villages to establish a sub-county transportation network in which villages were interconnected, *cuncun tong gonglu* (村村通公路), the county launched a second wave of road paving in 2003. According to the county's statistical yearbook, in 2007, all villages, except for 10 located in the county's poorest township, had roads accessible to cars. Although cars were still rare in most villages, small motorcycles were becoming common and served as a popular mode of transportation inside the county. All the main roads to the township seats I visited were multi-lane and well paved, and buses ran regularly all day long from the county seat to the townships. In 2004, all the villages were connected to the bus network, known as *cuncun tong keche* (村村通客车), offering villagers bus services to townships' urban centres and the county seat. In 2010, the county announced a new policy to facilitate further transportation inside the county, called *cuncun tong gongjiao* (村村通公交). Under this policy, buses were to go through every village in the county (and not only to within 1 km of a village, as was the case until then) and to offer subsidised transportation services, for which the county allocated RMB10 million annually. [23] According to local documents, the policy was implemented by the end of 2011, providing comprehensive public transport within the county.

The third important factor that facilitated rural–urban labour integration was that industries in the county were not concentrated in one central area but were dispersed over several parts of the county. This increased the possibilities of finding work close to home, enabling more household members to find work outside agriculture.

---

22 Travelling from the county seat to its most remote border took about one hour by car.

23 Interview with officials from the Transportation Bureau, Chenggu County, 17 May 2011.

Inequality in Beian County

Although Beian County was much less developed than Chenggu, inequality between townships and rural communities existed there as well. Unfortunately, unlike Chenggu, Beian did not publicly report the GDP of individual townships. However, the county did report each township's revenue and expenditure. Table 2.4 presents total revenue and expenditure in each of the townships that I researched.

Table 2.4: Total revenue and expenditure of townships in Beian County, 2007 (in RMB10,000)

	I	J	K	L	M	N
Total revenue	2,606	1,687	1,011	355	152	103
Total expenditure	1,132	647	1,000	506	414	285

Source: *Chenggu County Statistical Yearbook*, 2008.

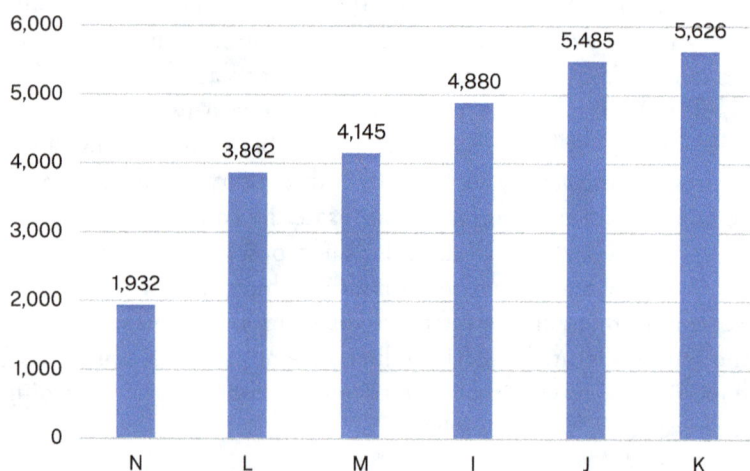

Chart 2.4: Average annual per capita income of rural inhabitants in different townships, Beian County, 2007 (in RMB)
Source: *Beian County Statistical Yearbook*, 2009.

As in Chenggu, industrialised townships enjoyed significantly higher revenue than non-industrialised ones (the difference between Township I's and Township N's revenue was more than 25 times) and their revenue outweighed their expenditure, while rural townships tended to be in serious financial deficit. As in Chenggu, there was also a positive correlation between the location of a village (in an industrial or alternatively a rural township) and villagers' level of income. Chart 2.4 presents the average annual per capita income of villagers in each of the townships I studied in Beian.

Generally, villagers living in the northern part of the county—around the rapidly developing Township I and its industrial area, and near the main roads in the county—were more likely to enjoy higher incomes than those in the south. One exception was Township K in the county's south, where, according to official data, the average income of villagers was the highest in the county. According to local officials, this was due to two main reasons. First, as already noted, Township K was the previous host of the county's government and was the county's main industrial and commercial centre before the government moved to Township I. Although the political centre had moved, much of the previous industrial and commercial infrastructure still existed, and the township still offered a better labour market than most of the other townships. Second, villagers in this township specialised in growing vegetables, which yield higher incomes than grain. Township K stood out as a rich island surrounded by the county's poorest townships, with reported rural average annual per capita incomes of less than RMB3,000.

Interestingly, the official data in Beian indicated the existence of significantly larger inequalities in income between rural communities than in Chenggu. While in Chenggu the gap in average per capita income between rural and industrialised townships was 33 per cent, in Beian, according to official statistics, the gap reached 290 per cent! Inequality in Chenggu is understandable, taking into account the significant differences in the level of industrialisation in townships and, consequently, the differences in opportunity to accumulate wealth. High inequality in Beian, where industrialisation was much more limited and most villagers counted on manual work as migrant workers outside the county, is less explicable.

As in Chenggu, one reason lay in the significant differences in the availability of agricultural land and its ability to serve as a safety net for the household. Chart 2.5 presents the average amount of agricultural land per capita in the townships in which I conducted research.

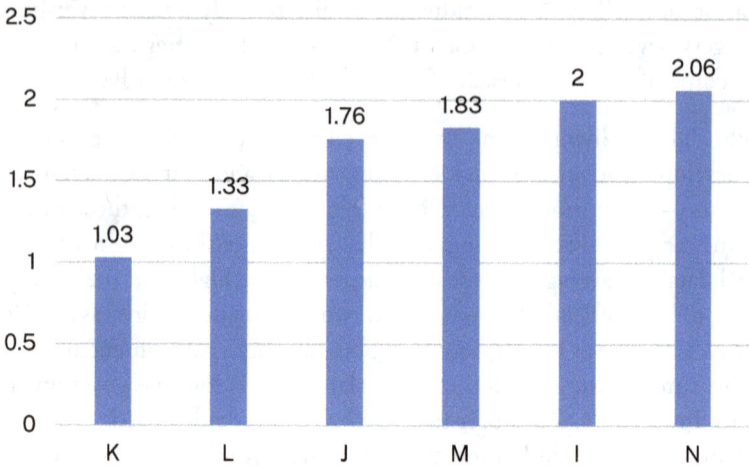

Chart 2.5: Average amount of agricultural land per capita in various townships, Beian County, 2008 (in mu)

Source: Author's calculations, *Beian County Statistical Yearbook*, 2009.

In most townships, the per capita agricultural land was not sufficient, and the income the household could generate from grain crops (the most common crops in the county) was scant.[24] Moreover, while average agricultural plots were not much different in size than in Chenggu, villagers in Chenggu enjoyed better access to developed labour markets and to other economic undertakings, which Beian, as a less developed county, failed to offer its inhabitants.

Discussing the issue of inequality in villagers' income with local officials revealed another possible reason for high income inequality in Beian: deliberate misreporting. In the past, townships in the south were indeed very poor and were recognised by the central government as poverty zones, entitling them to special financial support from the central government. However, as the economic situation improved, the differences between these villagers and others in the county grew less significant. Nevertheless, since these townships were poorly located, it was difficult for them to attract investors, meaning that industrialisation was more limited than in northern

---

24   This is discerned also by comparing Charts 2.4 and 2.5. As can be seen, household income tended to be smaller in townships with larger household agricultural plots.

parts of the county. Therefore, one way for these townships to increase their revenue was to misreport the villagers' income and to keep receiving financial help from the central government.[25]

Yet, even if smaller than officially reported, the disparities between rural communities and within administrative villages in Beian were large. The earlier mentioned survey conducted in 2008 among former production teams revealed substantial income inequality between rural communities. The seven teams that were surveyed in Beian County all resided in the same township, which may be considered 'average' in terms of economic development, and six of them came from the same administrative village. Two reported an average annual per capita income of RMB4,000–6,000, three reported an average per capita income of RMB3,000–4,000 and two reported an income of less than RMB3,000.

Inequality in Villages' Collective Income

Another important aspect of economic inequality relates to villages' collective income (*jiti shouru* 集体收入). This can be earned by village governments or by hamlets (former production teams) by leasing out collective land for non-agricultural economic activities, collecting fees (*guanli fei* 管理费) received from enterprises operating on village land, operating village government–owned enterprises and/or leasing out collective assets such as apartments or shops owned by the village, etc. This type of inequality was more important in Chenggu than in Beian, where most villages had very limited collective incomes, if any. As will be elaborated in the next chapters, collective income played an important role in the way the Village Redevelopment Program was implemented in Chenggu County. Unfortunately, official data on villages' collective income is not available publicly, but my personal interviews revealed immense differences in revenue between villages. Table 2.5 summarises the collective income of selected villages, as reported by village leaders.

---

25   On misreporting by local government(s) see also Cai, 'Between State and Peasant', 783–805; Göbel, *The Politics of Rural Reform*, 21; 'Poverty Elucidation Day', *Economist*, 20 October 2014, economist. com/free-exchange/2014/10/20/poverty-elucidation-day, accessed 21 October 2021.

Table 2.5: Collective income in selected villages, Chenggu County, 2009 (in RMB)

Village name	Average annual collective income
A1	400,000
A2	500,000
A3	100,000
B1	8,000,000
C1	80,000
C2	30,000
C3	80,000
C4	70,000
C5	60,000
D1	1,600,000
D2	280,000
E1	500,000
F1	60,000
F2	None
G1	None
H1	80,000
H2	800,000 +

Source: Author's interviews.

Table 2.5 clearly illustrates dramatic differences in collective incomes between villages in Chenggu. While some villages drew very high collective incomes of several hundreds of thousands and even millions of RMB annually, others generated very modest incomes of a few tens of thousands of RMB, or none at all. As expected, the differences between villages lay mostly in the extent of the village's commercialisation and/or industrialisation. Leasing land to industry or for commercial use produced a significantly higher income than leasing land for agricultural use. In some of the rich villages, all or most of the previous agricultural land was leased out to industries and commercial ventures. Generally, the closer the village was to the county seat or a township seat, and the closer the township was to the county seat, the more attractive it was to investors. Thus, while villages that were poorly located had no or only a few small-scale workshops and enterprises operating in them, well-located villages served as bustling economic arenas. For example, in Village D1, one of the most thriving villages I studied, located in a prosperous township adjacent to a main road that connects Chenggu with a large neighbouring city, there were no less than 180 different economic enterprises operating.

To conclude, in both Chenggu and Beian, market-forces-based wealth accumulation and distribution accelerated fiscal inequality between the local urban and rural communities. In Chenggu, inhabitants of the county's urban centres (township seats and most notably the modern county capital) were more likely to enjoy better access to labour markets, higher incomes, and better infrastructure and social services. Yet villages located in proximity to urban centres and along the county's main roads tended to enjoy more economic opportunities and better livelihoods than those in the county's hinterland. Similarly, villagers in Beian around the county's two main urban centres—the previous and the current locations of the county government—were likely to enjoy higher incomes than villagers in the county's hinterland, who tended to be more confined to their villages, due to the county's poor transportation network and underdevelopment of most of the township seats.

Nonetheless, market forces were not the only factors accelerating the institutionalisation of inequality between local urban and rural communities, as, in both counties, concentration of the location of industry was a leading policy. The province of Shandong valued the concentration of industry as a manifestation of a developed countryside.[26] Coinciding with this perception, most of the industrial areas in Chenggu were concentrated near the county and township seats and the nearby villages. In Beian, every township had its own small-scale industrial area and, as noted, the county government invested in developing the county's main industrial park on the outskirts of Township I. The head of a non-industrialised village in one of the industrialising townships in Chenggu complained about the lack of any factories in his village, implying that the township government would not let investors put money into his village even if they wanted to. According to him, the township concentrated all investments near the township seat, where 'it is easy to be seen by officials who arrive at the township'. Factories would flow to other villages only when there was no more available land in the most highly 'visible' villages. He was pessimistic about the possibility of investors locating their activities at his village even then, since it was located

---

26 Fu et al., 'Guanyu dui Shandong sheng shehuizhuyi xin nongcun jianshe jiaqiang fenlei zhidao de zonghe yanjiu baogao' [Integrated research about strengthening guidance in Building a New Socialist Countryside in Shandong Province], 3–34.

on the outskirts of the township away from main roads.[27] A township official supported his view. In remote villages, the township designated land mainly for agriculture and investors were not allowed to locate industrial activities without approval from the township government, which was 'very hard to get', according to him.[28] Equally, it is difficult to envision why a rational investor would choose to locate his or her business far from the good infrastructure that can be enjoyed near the urban areas of the county. Thus, locating investments near the county or the industrialised township seats served the interests of both investors and officials.

Inequality in the Living Environments

The discussion so far has focused on fiscal aspects of inequality—between rural and urban communities as well as between rural communities within the same county and even townships. This section discusses another aspect of inequality that existed in both counties prior to the announcement of the BNSC program in 2006: inequality in the physical living environments in villages vis-a-vis urban centres. As discussed in the introductory chapter, this is the main aspect of inequality that the Village Redevelopment Program sought to eliminate. Since many of the villages that I researched had already been influenced significantly by the redevelopment program, the following describes the villages in both counties as they were on the *eve* of BNSC. It is applicable to most of the villages in both counties—poor, average and rich.

In both counties, the urban population has gone through significant changes in its living environment over the last two to three decades. Modern high-storied buildings have replaced traditional residences, and many of the facilities that were being sought as part of the BNSC program, such as gas for cooking, hygienic toilets, running water and a good electrical network, had already been provided to the counties' urban dwellers. Generally, the urban neighbourhoods (*shequ* 社区) already contained infrastructure such as outdoor recreational spaces and sports facilities, health clinics and drugstores, shops, primary schools and preschools. Since rural towns are not large, such services in most cases were very accessible even if not provided in the immediate residential area.

---

27 Interview with a village official, Chenggu County, 2 July 2009.
28 Interview with a township official, Chenggu County, 20 May 2011.

In contrast to the counties' urban centres, the dominant living pattern in the rural areas comprised traditional private houses. In both counties, adobe houses were no longer prevalent, although they were more common in Beian than in Chenggu. There was no distinct pattern to houses in Beian; however, in Chenggu, traditional rural houses were most often a square compound with an internal courtyard. Typically, the houses were quite large and occupied a sizeable amount of land. In many cases, they were still shared by three generations living together. Occasionally, the size and shape of the land was a legacy of the 1980s or even earlier, and houses were often built in a haphazard pattern with narrow alleys curving between them.

Basic infrastructure tended to be very poor in the villages. All roads and alleys inside the villages (except for the villages' main roads in Chenggu) were likely to be dirt, and villages would become very muddy after a rain. In Beian, arterial roads between villages were dirt as well, and transport was almost impossible after heavy rains or snow.

Figure 2.1: Dirt roads in a village, Chenggu County
Source: Author's photograph.

Figure 2.2: Dirt roads in a village, Beian County
Source: Author's photograph.

Villages in both counties tended to lack cultural and leisure facilities. Public yards and sports facilities were old and dilapidated, if they existed at all, and more 'sophisticated' facilities such as reading rooms did not exist. The main facilities likely to be found in villages in Chenggu were the office of the village leadership (although not necessarily up to standard), an accessible health clinic, a small grocery shop (selling mainly dry goods) and a local agricultural supplies shop. In Beian, where the administrative villages had significantly larger populations, each administrative village had its own primary school[29] and some had a small hospital in addition to the village clinic. Small-scale commerce was also more common in villages in Beian, such as small eateries and shops selling basic daily goods. For all other services and needs, people normally would travel to the township seat or even to the county seat (in Chenggu County).

Most villages had poor environments in terms of hygiene. In many villages, there was no separation between residences and livestock-raising areas. It was not uncommon to see people raising a few chickens or even a cow or

---

29 In the past, every village in Chenggu County had its own primary school as well, but most of them had already been merged into large modern schools located in the township seats or in large villages.

two in their internal yard in Chenggu County, though it was much more common in Beian, where livestock wandered freely between houses in many of the villages.

In most cases, villagers used soft coal for heating. There was no heating in many rural houses in Beian and winter nights were very cold. Firewood was often used for cooking. Flush toilets were infrequent in many villages, and people often cleaned the waste by themselves. According to official data in Chenggu County, in 2006, 'hygienic toilets' (*weisheng cesuo* 卫生厕所) only existed in slightly more than half of the villages.[30]

Dirtiness was another characteristic of the villages that village redevelopment was supposed to eradicate. As much a result of villagers' lack of concern, there was a lack of suitable means to gather and dispose of garbage. Entering many of the villages in both counties, the first thing one noticed was garbage thrown everywhere—on the main roads, in small alleys, in drainage ditches as well as in improvised dumps on the outskirts of the village. In many villages, arable land served as 'empty-trash sites'.

Figure 2.3: Lack of separation between human and livestock areas in a village, Beian County
Source: Author's photograph.

---

30 *Chenggu County Statistical Yearbook*, 2008.

Figure 2.4: Garbage along a village path, Chenggu County
Source: Author's photograph.

Living in a Poor Environment — Lack of Finances or Lack of Concern?

The above characteristics were shared not only by poor villages but also by some of the richest villages in the counties. All the officials and villagers I talked to strongly supported the policy of village redevelopment (and BNSC in its wider sense), claiming it answered *real* problems and needs. And yet, out of the 20 or so villages I studied in Chenggu, only two had taken significant initiatives on their own to introduce changes in their living environment and none had done so in Beian. If local officials and villagers acknowledged the existence of needs and shortcomings in the villages, why had they not redeveloped their villages before BNSC was announced? Lack of finance was a main obstacle impeding poor villages from improving their own living environment. As will be elaborated in the next chapter, redevelopment required significant expense and subsidies only became available after 2006 to reduce the financial burden. However, as the next chapter also demonstrates, for many of the better off villages, redevelopment did not impose such a heavy financial burden that they could not have financed it prior to 2006 (without government subsidies) had they wanted to.

It is also true that, in many of the villages in both counties, the younger generation was engaged in non-agricultural employment outside the villages, and many were moving away from the villages, so this group had less interest in redeveloping their village.[31] But, while young villagers in Beian were migrating away from the villages, they were still part of the rural landscape in Chenggu. Moreover, in several conversations I had with older villagers in redeveloped villages, my impression was that, overall, the redevelopment program was perceived very positively by them and new cultural facilities, such as croquet courts in Chenggu and culture yards, were often packed with older villagers during my visits.

Why, then, weren't villages developed before the announcement of BNSC? The answer of village leaders and township officials was very simple: they did not have targets then. The following example is an excerpt from an interview with a township official in an industrialising township in Chenggu County:

Q: Why did you start to redevelop your villages only in 2006?

A: The objectives for the new villages were announced in 2006 with the announcement of the 20 characters.[32] Since 2006 the objectives have been relatively clear. Before 2006 the macro-policy embraced by the central government was to develop cities and industries. After 2006, the Premier Wen Jiabao gave a speech; it is a metaphor, saying that 'to know whether a naval force is sailing fast or slow it is not enough to watch the lead ship, but (it is necessary) to watch the main force of the fleet. If there is no wellbeing for the entire population of China, there will be no wellbeing for China'. Hence the centre started to pay attention to the villages, villagers and agriculture. Originally the villages gave support to the cities, but since 2006 the cities and industries support villages and agriculture. This is a strategic adjustment of the central government.[33]

---

31   Several scholars have observed a negative correlation between a village rate of outward work migration and its inhabitants' (those live outside and those left in the village) willingness to contribute to local public goods investments. See, for example, Zhang et al., 'Investing in Rural China', 69–73; Lu, Varieties of Governance, 109–20.

32   This refers to 'advanced production, well-off livelihoods, civilised communities, clean and tidy villages and democratic management', as is explained in Chapter 1.

33   Interview with a township official, Township C, Chenggu County, 17 February 2009.

While many factors contributed to earlier decisions not to redevelop the villages, living in a poor environment was, at least in the case of better off villages, a matter of choice and inertia, in which local officials and villagers were embedded. From this perspective, the BNSC's Village Redevelopment Program provided a necessary catalyst.

Conclusion

One of the unfortunate outcomes of Chinese economic reforms was a meteoric increase in inequality. Chenggu, an industrialised county in an industrialised province located in the east of China, and Beian, an above-average county in the moderately industrialised province of Anhui, located in the centre of China, demonstrate the east–centre gap: villagers in Chenggu were likely to enjoy higher incomes than in Beian; villages in Chenggu were likely to enjoy significantly higher collective incomes, due to increased opportunities to extract revenue from developed markets; and local governments in Chenggu enjoyed significantly higher revenue. Yet both counties demonstrated larger degrees of inequality at the sub-county level between better off and worse-off townships and villages. In fact, the case of Chenggu and Beian shows that inequality at the micro-level within a county may be significantly more prominent than between east–central counties, and this is true not only in highly industrialised counties such as Chenggu.

Consequently, the Village Redevelopment Program, as a national policy that aspired to affect the entire Chinese countryside, was expected not only to adjust itself to different economic environments at the county level but also to tackle inequality at the sub-county level (as is illustrated in Figure 1.1). The extent to which the Village Redevelopment Program succeeded in meeting this expectation is answered in the following chapters.

3

Redeveloping the Villages

As the previous chapter described in detail, inequality was part of economic-political life in both Chenggu and Beian counties. Disparities were manifest not only in different levels of income but also in the physical living environment, which tended to be more modern, hygienic and service-oriented in the counties' urban centres than in the villages. This chapter discusses the main changes that the Village Redevelopment Program brought to the villages. As we will see, while in both counties these changes were substantive and profound, local understandings of what redevelopment meant differed significantly between the counties. As the centre did not impose a specific interpretation of the 'new socialist countryside', this was left to the provincial and local state to decide.[1] In both counties, local economic conditions and local officials' perceptions of their county's economic conditions played a decisive role in how the redevelopment program was interpreted.

Both Anhui and Shandong governments instructed their counties to draw up a 'scientific' plan before redevelopment could start.[2] Thereafter, any redevelopment project was expected to be in accordance with that plan. The concept of a 'plan' was new to villages in Beian. Prior to 2006, village plans

---

1   It is common for the central government to announce national policies without specifying the exact methods of implementation. Beijing expects localities to find the most suitable practices to ensure successful implementation. Lieberthal, *Governing China,* 167; Zhou, 'The Institutional Logic of Collusion', 65–68. Nonetheless, China's experience teaches that for local players it is not always easy to achieve flexibility. See, for example, O'Brien, 'Implementing Political Reform', 33–59; Rosenberg, 'Why Do Local Officials', 18–42.

2   In October 2007, the requirement to draw up detailed plans in rural areas as a precursor for any redevelopment gained legal validity with the adoption of the Law on Urban and Rural Planning (*Chengxiang guihua fa*).

did not exist at all, and villages developed piecemeal mainly in accordance with geographic conditions and people's individual financial capacities and wishes, as long they did not violate local construction regulations. More striking, even the townships did not have an overall plan for their jurisdiction and their pre-2006 plans were likely to include only the township seat and nearby villages.

From this perspective, the request to draw up an overall and detailed master plan for every township and administrative village was new to Beian. Typically, township plans consider the main features, such as the location and size of administrative villages, industrial zones, nature reserves, main roads, reservoirs, etc. Typical village plans include residential areas and style of housing, infrastructure (such as roads, electricity networks and underground pipes, water channels and reservoirs), public squares, green areas, public facilities, etc. In 2010, Anhui Province extended its demand for plans not only for every administrative village but also for every hamlet, of which there were more than 3,000 in the county. This demand put the county Construction Bureau (*jianshe ju* 建设局), the unit in charge of drawing up the plans, under pressure due to a lack of human resources. By early 2010, they had only just finished drawing up plans for all the townships and 175 administrative villages (not including individual plans for these villages' hamlets). Drawing a map for each village took at least two weeks, not including approval procedures.

In contrast to Beian County, villages in Chenggu County had plans in place long before the Building a New Socialist Countryside (BNSC) policy was announced. However, these plans were very general in nature, normally including only residential areas, and were not strictly enforced. Consequently, having a comprehensive compulsory plan for the villages, to which any future redevelopment must adhere, was an innovation in this county as well. Unlike in Beian, where the responsibility for drawing up the plans was borne by the county's Construction Bureau, in Chenggu, professional designers from the prefectural or provincial Housing and Urban–Rural Development Office (*zhufang he chengxiang jianshe ju / ting* 住房和城乡建设局/厅) were invited to draw up the plans for the villages to ensure the highest quality.

二00九年四月

Figure 3.1: A village map at the entrance of a village, Beian County
Source: Author's photograph.

In both counties, the village plans were made accessible to all villagers and served as a source of pride to village officials, who always seemed happy to present them to outsiders, explaining the many benefits of the 'new' village over the 'old'. In many of the villages, though much more frequently in Beian due to the county's direct demand, maps presenting the new villages' appearance were displayed publicly on the main streets and entrances and/ or in other public areas. In Chenggu, maps were mounted mainly inside the village offices. However, to spread knowledge about the redevelopment program, large bulletin boards along the county seat's main road presented selected village redevelopment plans, with a few paragraphs explaining the expected benefits for the inhabitants of each village. Publicity is a clear indication of the seriousness and desirability of a policy.[3]

---

3   Kennedy, 'State Capacity and Support', 383–410; O'Brien and Li, 'Selective Policy Implementation', 179.

Village plans announced two types of redevelopments. The first were villages in which the residents were most likely to stay in their original housing while efforts were invested in improving the villages' original public environment. This model was popular in Beian County. In the second group were villages where the whole, or a significant portion, of the village's population were expected to move to entirely new residential areas known as *nongcun shequ* (农村社区) or 'rural communities'. This model was more typical of Chenggu and entailed two distinctive residential patterns. The first were villages where residents moved into new housing inside their original village jurisdiction. The second (and more popular) were villages where residents moved to a new nearby location and merged with other villages to form a large new community. In both models, the transition was mainly to multistorey apartment buildings, which were becoming a common part of the county's rural landscape.

Village redevelopment in Chenggu has gone through two distinct stages. In the early years of implementation there were no unified standards in the county regarding rural housing. With the exception of Township D, which the Chenggu government selected as an experimental site for piloting the policy of constructing rural communities, and a few industrialised villages that county officials designated the heart of future rural communities (and in which villagers had to move to multistorey apartment buildings), villages under redevelopment could decide for themselves whether to construct new housing and could choose their desired housing preferences in line with local financial capacities and wishes (e.g. multistorey buildings, townhouses or villa-like housing).

Table 3.1 presents residential patterns in selected villages in Chenggu, as reported by village leaders in 2009. It includes villages that had already started their redevelopment, as well as villages in which redevelopment was still at the planning stage. The table excludes villages in which construction of multistorey apartment buildings was imposed by the local government. It clearly demonstrates that, when villagers could decide for themselves, multistorey apartment buildings were not necessarily their choice. This was true for industrialised villages as well as rural ones.

Table 3.1: Residential patterns in selected villages, Chenggu County, 2009

Village name	Housing	Unit size in square metres
A1	Private one-storey buildings	132
A2	Mostly private two-storey buildings, plus a few four-to five-storey apartment buildings	320 (for houses); 100, 120, 140 (for apartments)
B1	Five-storey buildings	130, 168
C1	Most people would stay in their original housing; a few private two-storey buildings, plus one building of five stories	160–70
C2	Five-storey buildings	140–50
C3	People would stay in original housing	
C6	Five-storey buildings	126
H1	Private one-storey buildings, private two-storey buildings and some four-to five-storey buildings	*
F1	Most people would stay in their original housing, except for houses that were in the way of straightening the roads	
G1	Five-storey buildings	120, 140
H1	Private two-storey buildings	300+
H2	Private two-and five-storey buildings	128 (for apartments) 300 (for houses)

Source: Author's interviews. *Figures not available.

In 2009, the county government intensified its involvement and drew up a grandiose plan in which all villages would be concentrated in 173 residential communities. Most of these communities were expected to host several villages living together, mostly in multistorey apartment buildings. To support this plan, several townships had changed their construction policy by the time of my second round of fieldwork, and construction approvals for family housing were no longer available. By mid-2011, construction had already started in 67 communities.[4]

---

4   Interview with officials from the Construction Bureau, Chenggu County, 18 May 2011.

Figure 3.2: A new residential community, Chenggu County
Source: Author's photograph.

Figure 3.3: A new residential community, Chenggu County
Source: Author's photograph.

Construction of new rural communities was one of the most profound developments of the early twenty-first century in rural China. It was advocated by the Chinese Communist Party (CCP) as an indispensable part of the BNSC at the sixth plenary session of the Central Committee of the 16th Party Congress, held in October 2006. Central authorities have strongly supported it up to the present day, and new high-rise rural communities have continued to be planned and erected.[5]

Construction of rural communities manifested the authorities' belief that solving rural problems required not only channelling more finances into rural areas but also significantly restructuring the countryside to 'rectify' some of its most basic characteristics, which authorities perceived as impeding modernity and perpetuating social disparities. These include poor infrastructure and public amenities; lack of village planning; waste of land (e.g. rural housing patterns that tend to seize large plots of land and the existence of empty villages due to people migrating to cities for work); dispersal of villages (resulting in difficulties in adequately providing for the needs of each locality); rural economic patterns (e.g. fragmented land and the prevalence of small-scale family economic ventures, decentralisation in decision-making and old-fashioned business philosophy) that create difficulties in adjusting to the developing market; and low capacity of local investment due to lack of finances, a weakening of collective consciousness and an unwillingness to invest in non-profitable public undertakings.[6]

Construction of large-scale rural communities was supposed to remove these impediments and boost rural (and subsequently national) development in ways that could not have been achieved under previous conditions. First, it was expected that, after transition, villagers would enjoy a modern living environment—new housing equipped with modern facilities, better infrastructure and accessible public amenities and services. These, according to China's Ministry of Civil Affairs (*Minzheng bu* 民政部), were expected to include at least the following: social assistance to those in need, maintenance of public order, health care, family planning, and sports and

5   General Office of the CCP Central Committee and General Office of the State Council, *Guanyu shenru tuijin nongcun shequ jianshe shidian gongzuo de zhidao yijian* [Instructions on further promoting the pilot work of constructing rural communities]; Zhang, Zeng and Ruan, 'Miaozhun yiliu biaozhun gongjian xingfu jiayuan-Xianningshi zhashi tuijin nongcun shequ jianshe' [Work together to build high standards happy homesteads: The city of Xianning soundly promotes construction of rural communities]; Yep, 'Local Alliances', 169–86; Meyer-Clement, 'Rural Urbanization', 187–207.
6   Yang, 'Dui xin nongcun shequ jianshe de tansuo' [Exploring the construction of new rural communities], 36.

cultural facilities. A direct instruction of the ministry was that all rural services should be provided within a radius of no more than 2–3 kilometres and no more than 20 minutes walking distance.[7] When the communities were located adjacent to rural towns/urban centres, local governments were expected to integrate rural and urban services and infrastructure.[8]

Second, transition from rural housing and small-scale villages into large residential compounds was expected to save land. Central authorities have acknowledged the need to optimise land allocation and use, and to more effectively link urban and rural land systems, as an essential part of national development and solving 'rural problems'. A major means has been the policy of 'linking increases and decreases of urban and rural construction land' (*chengxiang jianshe yongdi zengjian guagou* 城乡建设用地增减挂钩), with which the Ministry of Land and Resources (*Guotu ziyuan bu* 国土资源部) has experimented since 2005. According to this policy, quotas of farmland and construction land can be mutually exchanged between rural areas and nearby urban centres on the condition that the same amount of construction land is converted to farmland in the rural areas. Quotas, however, are fixed and this process is highly regulated.[9]

Construction of rural communities provided another means to save land at the local level. After villagers had moved to their new location, the land occupied by the former homesteads (*zhaiji di* 宅基地) was freed up and could be used for further industrialisation, commercial undertakings or agricultural extension, without the need (as long as agricultural land was not involved) to involve officials in the conversion of arable land or violating land seizure laws.[10]

Third, construction of large-scale communities was expected to strengthen the state's capacity for managing rural society. Construction of rural communities was not only about new housing for the villagers to reside in. From the authorities' viewpoint, rural communities were expected to replace administrative villages as a new type of rural grassroots unit. As such, they were expected to pool their local political, social and economic resources

---

7   Ministry of Civil Affairs, *Minzheng bu guanyu kaizhan 'nongcun shequ jianshe shiyan quan fugai' chuangjian huodong de tongzhi* [A notice by the Ministry of Civil Affairs on 'full coverage of experimenting construction of rural communities'].

8   General Office of the CCP Central Committee and General Office of the State Council, *Guanyu shenru tuijin nongcun shequ jianshe shidian gongzuo de zhidao yijian*.

9   Ong, 'State-Led Urbanization in China', 165–66.

10   Su, *China's Rural Development Policy,* 244–45. See also, Meyer-Clement, 'Rural Urbanization', 187–207.

and to engage in activities such as community policing, encouraging volunteering, 'educating people to act according to the law' and civil mediation.[11]

Last, the new rural communities were perceived as an essential part of China's process of urbanisation. According to the plan, the level of urbanisation was to reach 60 per cent by the year 2020 (a goal that, according to official data, had already been met by the end of 2019 when China's urbanisation rate hit 60.6 per cent).[12] Construction of rural communities was perceived as necessary for ensuring the wellbeing of the many hundreds of millions of villagers who would remain in rural areas.[13] Also, construction of a modern rural living environment and improving local labour markets was intended to reduce villagers' motivation for migrating to China's large cities, and to motivate highly skilled migrant workers to return from the cities back to their communities and families.[14] In that spirit, central authorities expected industrialised rural communities to promote the social integration of migrant workers who worked in these communities, and to facilitate their access to local public services.[15]

The province of Shandong was a great supporter of the transition from traditional villages to large-scale communities and multistorey buildings, and the transition was very fast. In 2007, the Ministry of Civil Affairs selected 251 counties nationwide to serve as experimental sites for the creation of new rural communities (*quanguo nongcun shequ jianshe shiyan xian* [*shi, qu*] 全国农村社区建设实验县 [市，区]). The two leading provinces on this list were Shandong, where 34 counties were selected as experimental sites, and Jiangsu, with 33 counties selected. Together, these two provinces served as a vanguard, leaving the rest of the provinces far

---

11   General Office of the CCP Central Committee and General Office of the State Council, *Guanyu shenru tuijin nongcun shequ jianshe shidian gongzuo de zhidao yijian*.

12   'China's Urbanization Rate Hits 60.6 pct', *Xinhua*, 19 January 2020, xinhuanet.com/english/2020-01/19/c_138718450.htm, accessed 21 October 2021.

13   'Jiedu: weisheme yao jiaqiang nongcun shequ jianshe' [Reading: Why strengthen the construction of rural communities?], *Xinhua*, 17 January 2009, news.sohu.com/20090117/n261802831.shtml, accessed 21 October 2021.

14   'Xin nongcun shequ diaocha: cunmin ju shang lou, wu ren juzhu cheng "guilou"' [A survey on new rural communities: Villagers refuse to move upstairs, creating uninhabited ghost houses], *China News*, 7 July 2016, chinanews.com/gn/2015/07-07/7389910.shtml, accessed 21 October 2021; Yang, 'Dui xin nongcun shequ jianshe de tansuo'. On the role of village conglomerates as a key to rural development, as focal points to future controlled urbanisation and as a buffer against excessive migration to big cities, see Chen, 'Politics and Paths', 25–39.

15   General Office of the CCP Central Committee and General Office of the State Council, *Guanyu shenru tuijin nongcun shequ jianshe shidian gongzuo de zhidao yijian*.

behind. By the end of 2011, out of 106 counties anointed by the Ministry of Civil Affairs as national 'demonstration units' (*shifan danwei* 示范单位) in the project of constructing rural communities, the most prominent province was Shandong, with 27 demonstration counties.[16] Chenggu County was included in the 2007 Ministry of Civil Affairs' list of 251 experimental sites (though not in the subsequent list of 106 national demonstration units), due to its excellent economic conditions. However, as several township and county officials testified to me, the construction of rural communities and transition from traditional housing to multistorey apartment buildings, although highly valued by high-level authorities, was not translated into government-sanctioned quotas or incorporated into the cadre evaluation system as hard numerical targets (*shuzi mubiao* 数字目标) that local officials had to meet.[17] 'Establishing rural communities is a soft target, not a hard one' (*shequ fazhan bushi yingxing de, shi ruan de* 社区发展不是硬性的, 是软的), an official from the county Civil Affairs Bureau explained.[18] It was, however, an important part of the general annual evaluation of the township's work (*zongti kaohe* 总体考核) and from this aspect could, even if indirectly, influence leaders' future careers if not taken seriously. And yet, it would be wrong to explain grassroots implementation only in terms of soft requirements. It became very clear in my interviews that the policy of transitioning from traditional rural housing to communities was warmly welcomed by grassroots officials in Chenggu, who shared common perceptions with their superiors regarding rural development and modernisation. They pointed to four main reasons to explain their high level of support. First, in most of the villages I studied, redevelopment of public areas did not burden the villagers with compulsory payments, as it was paid totally out of income from the villages' collectively owned assets, local governmental subsidies, local business groups and voluntary contributions, in some cases from the villagers themselves. However, no subsidies were available for housing construction and the villagers were expected to pay for their new residences. As land for new houses was provided free of charge by the village and villagers were only required to pay construction costs, a new rural house/apartment was only about 20 per cent of the cost of housing in the county's rural towns. (On average the total expenditure for new housing was RMB100,000–150,000 per unit [RMB600–800 per square metre].) Local officials in most townships and villages did not perceive this expense as unaffordable for villagers. What

---

16   Second in the list was Jiangsu with 17 national 'model units'.
17   For elaboration on the cadre evaluation system, see Chapter 1, footnote 39.
18   Interview with an official from the Civil Affairs Bureau, Chenggu County, 17 May 2011.

mainly counted for them was that housing in the villages was significantly cheaper than in the local towns. 'This is a developed county', one said, 'and the villagers these days have money in their hands'. Moreover, villagers were expected to receive compensation fees, which were meant to cover part of their housing costs after their old houses were demolished.

Second was the desire to save land. All officials claimed that increasing rural income was the most important goal under the BNSC policy, and they perceived that freeing up land was a precondition to meeting this goal. In each of the villages under redevelopment that I studied, the new villages occupied significantly smaller plots of land than the old ones: in some cases, only 20–30 per cent of the original village size. Even in cases in which villagers moved to new private housing, saving land was a result of concentrating the villagers in a circumscribed residential area. In several cases, this was the result of the transition from one-storey buildings to two-storey structures, which enabled the villagers to maintain large houses on smaller plots of land and/or was due to smaller yards being attached to the houses. According to officials from the Construction Bureau, when the plan to construct 173 residential communities was completed, the county would save 88,000 mu (about 5,870 hectares) of land to boost further economic development.[19] In all townships, officials contended that, after the transition, the land would remain collective and would be used by the villages/communities to increase their collective income (e.g. by leasing out the collective land for industrial/commercial use or by operating collective undertakings), as well as rural household income (by increasing accessibility to non-agricultural employment or through expanding the amount of agricultural land).[20]

Third, concentrating thousands of villagers who were previously scattered in various villages into higher density residential areas was intended to improve the provision of public amenities and services to the villagers, a main target under the BNSC policy. Many local officials perceived construction of rural communities as a rare opportunity to design new modern environments from scratch—a prospect that offered more opportunities to modernise villages and was much easier than installing modern facilities in the chaotic old ones.

---

19 Interview with officials from the Construction Bureau, Chenggu County, 18 May 2011.
20 Land grabbing by local governments is a major problem in today's China, and a main reason for rural protests. It remains to be seen whether local officials in Chenggu will attempt to grab villagers' land (in contrast with their statements) when the transition is completed.

Last, for many officials, the transition from traditional rural houses to modern apartments symbolised the transition from backwardness to modernity; it meant that people's lives in villages could be equated not only to those in cities and rural towns (the ultimate goal of the BNSC) but also to those in developed Western countries. Local officials seemed to truly believe that leaving the old villages, no matter how difficult, was the only possible solution to rural problems and answered a real need. They assumed the move would ultimately be welcomed by villagers, even if gradually.

Beian was not selected for the national list of experimental counties to construct rural communities. Without pressure from above, officials leaned on local economic factors to decide a village's redevelopment and tended to redevelop public areas only. Officials in Beian assumed that requiring villagers to move to new homes would invoke serious resentment, possibly even social unrest, an outcome they sought to avoid as much as possible.[21] There were two main groups of residents that local officials suspected would resist buying new housing and leaving their old villages. First, those who had recently constructed a new house. As a less industrialised and less economically developed county, Beian had a slower rate of wealth accumulation than in Chenggu, and many of the county's villagers had built new houses in the 1990s. In most cases, these houses were quite large (most of them were two storeys). They were still in good condition and these villagers did not feel the need to move. If officials wanted to ask (let alone demand) them to move, they needed to provide these villagers with a very good reason to do so. Moreover, unlike officials in Chenggu, officials in Beian perceived that buying new housing (which cost the same as in Chenggu, although incomes in Beian were lower) was a gigantic economic expense for households. Thus, they estimated that villagers were unlikely to agree to move without adequate compensation, which the county could not afford to pay.

The second group that officials suspected would be potentially problematic were the young villagers. As noted in the previous chapter, about a third of the county's population were migrant workers who were absent from their villages for most of the year. Officials assumed that they were likely to refuse to buy new houses that they would not use. Also, and again unlike in Chenggu where saved land could be translated in many villages into further wealth accumulation, in most of the villages in Beian, the

---

21 Social unrest is typically classified as a 'veto target' in the cadre evaluation system and, as such, gains special concern by local officials. The cadre evaluation system is elaborated in Chapter 1, footnote 39.

more likely scenario was an extension of unprofitable agricultural land—not a strong incentive. Finally, many of Beian's villages did not enjoy any significant collective income and, therefore, did not have collective revenue to support redevelopment of public village facilities. The success of any redevelopment was heavily dependent on the willingness of the villagers to contribute to the cost of new infrastructure.[22] Officials in Beian were sensitive not to overburden villagers by demanding, in addition, that they move to new residences.

Noting these reasons, officials in Beian assumed that attempts to move the villagers would probably fail and could invoke mass anger and resentment. Therefore, while warmly supporting the upgrading of villages' living environments by introducing 'city-like' public amenities and services into the original villages, officials said that the time had not yet come to move.

Although each of the counties had its own preferred interpretation of the redevelopment program, in neither of the counties was redevelopment imposed blindly on all the townships and villages. In Beian, for example, there were a few villages in which people had moved, or were expected to move, to new housing as part of redevelopment. One example is Village J1, the most industrialised village in the county. It borders the county government's current location and enjoys a very convenient location, hosting part of the county's main industrial area, the county train station and a few wood-processing factories. In this village, both household and collective incomes were very high in local terms (RMB8,000 per capita and more than RMB1,000,000, respectively, in 2009) and, in contrast to most of the county's villages (and similar to many in Chenggu), land was valuable. According to the village plan, its entire population of 3,350 villagers were to be concentrated in three to four main residential areas, mostly in two-storey townhouses, in the hope that the saved land would further boost the local economy.

At the other end of the spectrum were those who still lived in poor conditions and in remote locations. In these cases, transition could be an outcome of villagers' desire to move to new (nearby) residential areas with higher standards of living. There were also a few hamlets in which houses were widely dispersed due to poor geographical conditions. In these cases, the county and the township governments decided that redevelopment was too expensive and not worthwhile, and the inhabitants were expected to move

---

22 For further detail on the financial aspects of villages' redevelopment see Chapters 4 and 6.

to nearby villages (the hamlets they belonged to kept their administrative position as independent hamlets). Yet, even when villagers were moving, they were most likely to move to new rural-style family housing and not to multistorey apartment buildings as in Chenggu.

All the officials I interviewed in Chenggu supported transition to multistorey buildings and concentration of villagers. Yet, the construction of rural communities was not occurring as a campaign-style policy affecting all villages simultaneously and in the same way. Since 2007, the year Chenggu was selected as an experimental county, the transition to new rural communities had affected mainly the industrialised townships and villages, where officials assumed more villagers could afford to buy new apartments and where land was a valuable resource for further boosting the local economy. In rural and less prosperous townships and villages, even where officials were very enthusiastic about this idea, construction of rural communities remained an unreachable dream and villages were developed separately to improve their access to infrastructure and social services. As local officials explained, the first priority under the BNSC was raising villagers' incomes, only then could multistorey buildings be built.

The pioneer of merging villages together and transitioning to apartment buildings was Township D, an industrialised township that the county government designated as an experimental site. By 2011, 3,000 rural households had moved into four- to five-storey housing and the township expected its entire rural population (approximately 8,000 households) to move by 2014.[23] Its 39 administrative villages were to be merged into 10 residential areas (the populations of three to four villages on average in each), of which eight were to be located close to the township seat, serving as its de facto suburb. After transition, it was planned that the villages in each residential area would be merged politically then, at a later stage, economically. By then the villages would have lost their status as 'administrative villages' (*xingzheng cun* 行政村) and would be referred to as 'rural communities' (*nongcun shequ* 农村社区).

---

23 In 2011, however, the pace of transition had slowed down due to unforeseen land problems, as many of the communities did not have enough land left for further construction. The next stage, therefore, was to demolish the old houses of those who had already moved to clear new land to continue construction of the communities. The prospects of completing the transition by 2014 seemed less likely. And yet, whether Township D had been able to meticulously meet its 2014 goal or not, recent local documents and online publications leave no doubt that the township had maintained its leading position in the construction of rural communities in the county.

What prompted Township D to push the transition so fast? First and foremost were views of the township's leaders, who perceived their township as 'number one' in the county. They were extremely competitive and desired to lead villages' redevelopment and appear more advanced than any of the county's townships. In 2008, for example, the township's goal was to ensure that every village had a croquet court—to become the 'croquet number-one township in the prefectural city' (*quanshi di yi ge menqiu zhen* 全市第一个门球镇); in 2009, its goal was to finish paving all footpaths in the villages before anywhere else had achieved this. The construction of rural communities was no different, and a quick transition was to serve as solid 'evidence' of the excellent economic conditions of the villagers and the superiority of the township officials over others. The township was proud of this impending change and the township leaders considered themselves to be the vanguard of the road to development.

The second driver was land. Township D, while one of the most industrialised in the county, was the smallest township both in terms of total land size and land size per capita, and land was constantly needed for further economic development. Concentrating the villagers in 10 large residential communities was expected to save 6,800 mu of land (about 450 hectares), which officials hoped would further boost their local economy. The third motivation was the deputy governor of Shandong Province's inspection in 2009, in which he praised the township for its construction of rural communities and urged officials to continue the transition as an example for the entire province.

Following this path was Township B, the largest township in the county, containing 73,000 inhabitants and more than 100 administrative villages. Its plan stated that rural households would concentrate in three main residential areas with 16,000–30,000 rural residences in each. Each of these areas would consist of several smaller communities of some 10 villages each. Officials in this township, which was not only significantly larger than Township D but also less industrialised (although still considered industrialised in local terms), fully acknowledged that, in some villages, the inhabitants would not be able to move soon due to economic constraints. To enable them to enjoy the benefits of the redevelopment program, their original village would be redeveloped while they stayed in their old houses. Yet the township would monitor and supervise redevelopment closely to ensure that investments (especially in permanent infrastructure) would support the master plan of the community construction project.

Township D's and B's experiences were of interest to other townships in the county, especially the rapidly industrialising Township C. According to its plan, all 36 administrative villages would be merged into seven communities. Yet, unlike in townships D and B, Township C's plan was still in its initial stage of drafting and far from realisation in 2011. At that time, this township was implementing village redevelopment by redeveloping every village from within (*yi cunzhuang wei danwei* 以村庄为单位)—that is, without moving residents into new communities. However, since two of the township's villages had enjoyed good economic conditions before 2006, the county and the township governments decided that these two villages would form the heart of two future communities. In these villages, multistorey buildings comprised the only permitted residential pattern, and government investments in the old part of the villages ceased.[24]

Township A, the most industrialised township in the county, demonstrates the gradual consolidation of constructing communities in the county. In the early years of the Village Redevelopment Program, the township's main interest was in improving the accessibility of services and the provision of public goods. The township was the only one in the county to subsidise villagers' fees for the new cooperative medical insurance (RMB20 per year per person in 2009), and rural residents were not required to pay. It also subsidised the cost of travelling by bus between villages and provided free public transport inside the township. Focusing on service orientation, the township established service centres (*renmin fuwu zhongxin* 人民服务中心) in each of its villages. Villages managed these centres and provided services that previously could be accessed only in the township seat, such as facilities for submitting applications relating to birth control and land and residential approvals.[25]

According to township and village officials, villages at that time were given full discretion to choose their preferential residential model. In 2009, I interviewed the party secretary of Village A1. This was one of very few villages in the county that had taken significant steps on their own to improve the living environment before the BNSC policy was announced. A new residential area of one-storey houses was planned there in 1989 and construction started three years later. The last families moved into their new residences in 2009. When asked about their hopes for the future, the secretary answered:

---

24 Interview with an official, Township C, Chenggu County, 20 May 2011.
25 The villages sent their own runners to the township seat to collectively submit the applications.

Our hopes are to live in small townhouses (*xiao yanglou* 小洋楼),[26] not multistorey buildings (*da de loufang* 大的楼房). We want to live in villa-like (*bieshu* 别墅) buildings. We want every household to have a private car. Our village now has only one style of building. You understand the New Socialist Countryside as a national policy, but I say every village should have its own style. In our village, the final aim is to develop infrastructure while living in villa-like housing.[27]

Village A3 had a similar perspective. Many of the residents had recently built new houses and did not feel any need to move. Their decision, therefore, was to construct public areas only. Nevertheless, by 2011, the idea of compressing residential areas had gained momentum in Township A. Like Township C, Township A had stopped providing construction approvals inside villages, apart from villages adjacent to the township seat, and these were all moving to multistorey buildings. According to the long-term plan, all villages were to be concentrated in a few large residential areas of 10,000 people each. However, officials in Township A were prudent about this transition and willing to acknowledge publicly its many embedded difficulties. Unlike in Township D, transition to rural communities was expected to take a long time and was more thought out. What mainly preoccupied officials was how to merge the villages—a very difficult problem that none of the townships had managed to solve. Moving the villages was easy, they explained, but merging them politically and economically was another story.

Although the townships differed significantly from each other in terms of how fast they transitioned, it was agreed that under no circumstances would people be forced to leave their original houses or to buy new ones due to the BNSC. In the many conversations I had with rural inhabitants from various townships and villages, I could not find any evidence of coercion. In fact, forcing villagers to move was more likely to result in exhaustion of the local cadres and other counterproductive outcomes. As one might expect, and as several villagers confirmed, even in prosperous villages, not every household could invest RMB100,000–150,000 at short notice. Moreover, buying new housing was not necessarily a top priority for those who did have the required sum. As mentioned earlier, it took 17 years for Village A1 to complete its residential transition *without* external pressure. This is an

---

26 Houses in this village were constructed in rows. Each row consisted of four single-storey houses (four households) attached to each other. Houses retained their traditional structure and were constructed as a quadrilateral around an internal yard. I also witnessed this type of residential structure in a few other villages in Chenggu.

27 Interview with a village party secretary, Village A1, Chenggu County, 19 February 2009.

above-average village in terms of collective and household incomes and is located in the county's most industrialised township; therefore, it may serve as a good indicator that residential transition may take longer than officials predict, especially in less prosperous areas.

Forcing people to invest heavily against their will might have resulted in mass discontent and social instability, a very sensitive issue with potentially devastating consequences on local officials' future careers. Understandably, officials in Chenggu, like their counterparts in Beian, tried to avoid this, not only because of the cadres' performance evaluations but also because of the prefectural city's special attention to this issue in the context of village redevelopment. As Chapter 4 explains, the prefecture inspected every village under redevelopment in Chenggu. Successful inspection meant that the village had met several conditions imposed by the prefecture, one of which was the absence of social unrest. Increasing the economic burden on rural households violated a central government direct instruction not to do so under the BNSC. Higher government levels were more forgiving of delays in implementing the redevelopment program than they were vis-a-vis social instability.

Even if officials decided to press the villagers, the likelihood of them obtaining mortgages was limited. To obtain a mortgage from a bank one must provide an adequate guarantee to support the application. Villagers do not possess ownership of the land on which their houses sit; it belongs to the collective (today called a 'villager small group'). Nor do they have premises permits (*fangchan zheng* 房产证), a required certification to convert houses into a commodity sold freely on the market,[28] that can serve, when and if needed, as a guarantee for mortgage applications.[29] Other possible channels entailed borrowing money from family members or friends or taking out loans from the village coffers. However, as many villagers observed, most

---

28   This contrasts with houses in rural towns, where the buyer pays full market price and gets full ownership of the asset.

29   The central authorities have recently recognised the difficulty farmers face in obtaining bank loans due to a lack of adequate collateral as a significant impediment to modernising the countryside and improving rural life. Since 2015 authorities have been experimenting with a new policy to allow farmers in selected areas (mainly within the jurisdictions of Beijing and Tianjin metropolises) to mortgage land use and housing property rights as collateral for bank loans. In 2017, the policy was officially evaluated as yielding 'strong outcomes' in improving rural financial services and in increasing farmers' income, and experiments were extended beyond the original deadline. See, for example, Patton and Yao, 'UPDATE 1'; Xu, 'China's Rural Land Reform'; 'China Extends Pilot Plan to Mortgage Rural Land Rights, *China Daily*, 27 December 2017, global.chinadaily.com.cn/a/201712/27/WS5a439592a31008cf16da3d43. html, accessed 31 October 2022.

of them would not attempt any of these paths even if they were available. The reason for this was not economic but cultural. Taking out a loan to buy a house was considered a 'habit of the cities' and not part of rural culture. If needed, they would save, persistently waiting for the day their economic situation would enable them to afford to buy or renovate their house.

At the same time, the process of residential transition was not totally free of local government pressures. As already mentioned, townships changed their construction approval regulations and stopped providing approvals for the construction of new traditional rural housing. Thus, although not forced to buy a new apartment, if people wanted to improve their residence or if parents wanted to buy housing for their children—a common practice in rural China, especially when children get married—the only option was a new apartment. To expedite the pace of transition, when a village was designated to make the transition, government investments in the old village would stop completely. The hope was that, upon such termination of investments, people would move 'voluntarily' to the new communities or to neighbouring villages that, after redevelopment, offered a better living environment to their dwellers.

At least during the early years of implementation, officials did not need to even ponder exercising coercion as villagers were moving voluntarily, as the following examples from my fieldwork clearly show. As of mid-2009, 80 per cent of the villagers in Village D1 had already moved into new apartments; in Village B1, about half of the households had already moved; in Village H2, about a third of the households had moved, many to new apartments;[30] and in Village C7, a few dozen households had already shifted. In total, by the end of 2009, almost 7,000 rural households had moved to new rural communities in the county.

Moving to an apartment entailed significant changes in a villager's living habits and customs. In most cases, apartments were smaller than traditional rural housing. Social networks could be interrupted since, in most cases, people would find themselves with new neighbours. Villagers in apartments lacked internal yards, which had had many instrumental uses, such as raising livestock, planting vegetables for self-consumption and/or as a storage place. When villagers moved to a new geographical area, they could find it less convenient, especially if they lived far from their agricultural land. Finally,

---

30 In this village, new apartment buildings and private houses were built side by side. The majority of residents, though, were expected to move to apartment buildings.

in most of the villages I researched in Chenggu, people were expected to move before getting compensation for their old houses. Officials explained that compensation would be paid after the demolition of the old houses, but, in most villages, old houses were not demolished until all the villagers had moved to new apartments. Therefore, villagers were expected to pay for their apartments up-front. In light of these factors, one may wonder why any villagers agreed to move.

The following is based on the many conversations I had with villagers both in villages under redevelopment and in those where redevelopment had not yet started. First and foremost, villagers moved because they perceived the shift from the 'old' and backward villages to living in a modern and hygienic environment as a 'fair deal', even if that meant living in smaller housing units.

In addition, villagers acknowledged the importance of saving land. Although this was especially true in the industrialised townships and villages, where saved land could be translated directly into further industrialisation and wealth accumulation, inhabitants in many other villages also supported the idea of concentration and saving land for agricultural expansion and future industrialisation or simply because 'China is big and land is [too] scarce' (*Zhongguo da, tudi shao* 中国大土地少). This phrase was cited by many in Chenggu, almost as a religious mantra. The case of Village H1, in rural Township H, is worth mentioning. This village lost a significant amount of land in the 1990s to the construction of an arterial road. According to village officials, this resulted in a significant decrease in inhabitants' income. Their hope was that, after villagers moved to new residences and the old houses were demolished, the land would be converted to agriculture. In their view, redeveloping the village was an opportunity not only to improve residential conditions but also to regain what had been taken from them.

A third factor refers to idealised perceptions of an urban lifestyle. For many villagers, the transition from rural houses to apartments symbolised the transition from backwardness to modernity. Living in apartments was likened to living in the cities, a notion warmly embraced by many villagers. This coincided with views held by officials at the province and local level.

Another factor supporting the transition was the availability of units of various prices. Houses were more expensive than apartments as they were larger.[31] The larger the apartment, the more expensive it was, and apartments on upper levels (fourth or fifth floor) tended to be cheaper than those on lower levels, as apartment buildings lacked elevators. This enabled families to buy the most appropriate unit in terms of size and price. Also, although smaller than traditional rural houses (especially when taking the internal yard into account), the new apartments were still quite large in size, certainly by Western urban standards (see Table 3.1).[32] However, villagers perceived the apartments as less convenient than traditional rural housing for accommodating three generations—a still common practice in Chenggu's rural areas. As a result, apartments often contained only two generations, leaving older people to move to their own apartments or, most notably in prosperous villages, to local retirement homes, with the collective taking full economic responsibility for them.

Last, in all the villages I researched, the new villages were built fairly close to the original 'old' villages; therefore, the new location was not perceived by the villagers as an issue. They were still living close to their land and, even though previous neighbours did not necessarily share the same building, villagers still lived together in the same residential compound, making it easy to maintain social networks. In new communities where several villages were expected to reside together, the new residential buildings were allocated per village to ensure that those from the same village continued to reside together. In many of the new multistorey buildings, warehouses and enclosed parking lots were attached to the apartments (or could be bought separately), providing better storage than before (see Figure 3.4). In several communities, villagers planted vegetables and even grain crops in parts of the community's public area for self-consumption and as part of its greenification.

---

31 Construction of private houses was confined mainly to the first few years of the BNSC policy. As noted earlier, in several of the townships where I conducted research, building new rural houses was not an option in 2011; multistorey buildings had become the only residential pattern available for new construction.

32 Shandong Province stipulated that a standard of 30 square metres per person was a desired ratio. See Shandong Sheng Fazhan he Gaige Weiyuanhui [Committee of Development and Reform of Shandong Province], 'Shandong sheng jianshe shehuizhuyi xin nongcun jianshe zongti guihua, 2006–2020' [Building a New Socialist Countryside—an overall planning of the province of Shandong, 2006–2020].

Yet some villagers harboured suspicions about the new lifestyle. Some considered it more convenient to stay in their old ramshackle ground-level house than to live in a modern clean apartment on the fifth floor without an elevator (if they could not afford to buy a more expensive unit on a lower floor). Several villagers were worried about living without an internal yard, which they used for storing agricultural tools. Some had livestock living in the yard and could not imagine leaving their animals in a separated area far from their watchful eye. Others were simply used to life in the 'old' village. However, my overall impression was that, at least in industrial villages in which households did not depend on agriculture as a main source of income, few people were reluctant to move and such cases occurred mostly before and during the early stages of transition. In all the villages, I was told that transition occurred gradually. The first to move were usually the village officials (if they did not possess a nice house already) and young people; others moved after learning from the experience of those who had left before them.

Villages after Redevelopment

What did redeveloped villages look like? An unfortunate outcome of economic reforms and decentralisation from the late 1970s onwards was severe neglect of the provision of public goods in villages by local governments, which were more focused on investing in profitable undertakings than providing unprofitable public goods.[33] The Village Redevelopment Program brought significant changes in this area.

Paving Roads

Paving roads was a prominent aspect of village redevelopment. The prefectural city demanded that all access roads to the villages and all the main roads within the villages be paved as part of the redevelopment project. As recounted in the previous chapter, by 2006, Chenggu County already had a well-established road system. Most of the county's roads had been paved since the early 1990s, and a new wave of road paving had started in 2003 with the announcement of the central government's *cuncun tong gonglu* policy.

---

33   Edin, 'State Capacity', 37–42; Tsai, *Accountability without Democracy*, especially chs 2–3, 8; Whiting, *Power and Wealth*, ch. 3.

Figure 3.4: Paved roads in a new residential community, Chenggu County
Source: Author's photograph.

While higher levels demanded that access and main roads be paved, it was up to villages to decide on, and to finance, the paving of footpaths and alleys. In 2009, I found that where villagers had stayed in their original housing, most of the roads were still dirt. Officials claimed that paving these roads was done gradually due to the large investment required. I revisited two of these villages in 2011 and found that a significant amount of paving had been conducted in the last two years; many of the previously dirt roads were now paved. Yet, in cases where villagers were moving to new residential areas (alone or with other villages), the whole of the new residential compound was being paved, including all paths leading to and between the houses, a sharp contrast to the muddy-after-rain appearance of the old villages.

In contrast to Chenggu, in Beian all roads in and between the villages were dirt before 2006. The BNSC policy brought with it the provincial demand that all administrative villages have at least one paved access road. Unlike in Chenggu, where officials from the Transportation Bureau (*jiaotong ju* 交通局) insisted that the county should decide its overall paved roads policy, Anhui Province provided Beian with a deadline of five years to pave 711 kilometres of roads (based on provincial measurements). It took the county only four years to meet the target. By 2009, all Beian's 238 administrative villages had at least one paved access road. Moreover, the county had paved a total of 750 kilometres of roads (39 km more than demanded); all the roads were paved at higher standards than the provincial ones (at a thickness of 20 cm instead of 18 cm as demanded by the province); and, in many of the villages, more than one access road had been paved. In some of the townships, roads were also wider than the provincial minimum demand of 3.5 metres. After a provincial inspection, the province included the county in their excellence list as one of the 10 best counties.[34] Unlike in Chenggu, the expectation in Beian was that all footpaths and alleys should be paved in redeveloped villages as well. Driving on bumpy dirt roads was slow and inconvenient and could become almost impossible after heavy rains or snow. Paving the roads made transportation between rural towns and villages, as well as between villages, quicker and significantly more comfortable than before.

Figure 3.5: A main paved village road, Beian County
Source: Author's photograph.

---

34 Interview with an official from the county's Transportation Bureau, Beian County, 22 March 2010.

Figure 3.6: An internal alley paved in a village, Beian County
Source: Author's photograph.

Changes inside Villagers' Homes

All the villagers I talked to who had moved to new houses or apartments expressed satisfaction with their move. All the apartments I visited in both counties were 'Western-style' modern apartments—a complete contrast to the houses they had left behind, many of which had old, (often) dirty cement floors and outdated facilities. The new apartments were equipped with granite or tile floors and modern facilities, such as running water, solar water heaters, modern kitchens with methane gas for cooking, hygienic toilets, internet facilities, air conditioners and, in some cases, central heating systems. Many of the apartments were painted in bright colours, with bright floor tiles, and had pastoral views of the countryside reflected through large windows (when they faced fields and not the neighbouring building).

In locales where villagers did not move to new residential districts, the changes inside the houses were more limited, mainly seen in the introduction of home biogas pits (*zhaoqi chi* 沼气池). These provided villagers with cheaper energy than methane gas or electricity for lighting and cooking, and hygienic toilets (since the biogas pits transform human manure into gas).[35] Beian officials also perceived the countywide installation of running water as an important goal. Consequently, the number of villages and villagers enjoying running water had increased consistently.

Changes in the Villages' Public Areas

Changes in public areas were prominent in all the villages under redevelopment, whether or not villagers were moving to new residences. In all villages, inhabitants tried to make the villages cleaner and greener than before. They planted trees, shrubs and flowers along the main roads and public areas and introduced or improved garbage disposal facilities. When needed, electricity networks were upgraded. Water drainage ditches were constructed, renovated or cleaned, as were the villages' reservoirs. Streetlights were installed along the villages' main roads. In Township D, Chenggu County, surveillance cameras were installed in the villages and residential communities 'to ensure the villagers' safety'.

After redevelopment, villages were also likely to offer better cultural facilities. Public squares and sports facilities such as croquet courts (in Chenggu County), basketball courts, ping pong tables and other outdoor sports facilities were introduced.

Reading rooms, which offered inhabitants reading material in their leisure time, were built in all the villages. (In a few villages these functioned as lending libraries.) In rich central villages in Chenggu, small-scale supermarkets that were significantly bigger than previous grocery stores were built, reducing the inconvenience of having to buy some daily products outside the village in the township seat or rural markets.[36] Village government offices, including meeting rooms to serve the village government and village assemblies, were also often rebuilt or renovated. In some villages, political and administrative activities were consolidated under the same roof alongside communal facilities and activities, such as a television room where villagers could gather at the end of the working day, a reading room and/or activities for older people. (In such

---

35 I only encountered home biogas pits in both counties; however, in other places in China, central biogas pits also exist, serving larger groups of households. Biogas pits have been encouraged by the central government as an environmentally friendly energy source and villagers enjoyed subsidies in 2009 that amounted to more than 50 per cent of the total cost. Villagers still needed to pay about RMB1,000, which, as I was told by several villagers, could be earned back after one year of use (by reducing the use, and therefore the cost, of other energy sources such as electricity or methane gas).

36 When residential communities were being built, supermarkets were considered an indispensable part of the services provided inside each of these compounds.

cases, the 'village office' could be quite a large building of two or even three floors.) Prosperous villages in Chenggu were also likely to build retirement homes, as mentioned earlier, to which villagers could move after the age of 60.

And yet, for local officials, successful redevelopment depended not only on the availability of better village facilities but also on the ability of the villagers (under the guidance of the local government) to change their 'backward' rural attitudes, habits and perceptions and, as officials occasionally said, improve their 'quality' (*suzhi* 素质).[37] Officials in Beian complained about the reluctance of villagers to pay for home biogas pits, since they were accustomed to using manure as fertiliser, despite the financial and hygienic benefits of biogas. Officials in Chenggu complained about the refusal of villagers to separate the living areas of humans and livestock and to house their husbandry animals in designated area—a condition for moving into the newly built communities.

Figure 3.7: Recreation facilities in a village, Chenggu County
Source: Author's photograph.

---

37   The concept of *suzhi* is controversial and difficult to translate. In this book, I only use it in the context of direct citations from interviews with local officials and government documents. For general discussion on the concept of *suzhi* see Murphy, 'Turning Peasants', 1–20; Kipnis, 'Suzhi: A Keyword Approach', 295–313; Kipnis, 'Neoliberalism Reified', 383–400; Anagnost, 'The Corporeal Politics of Quality', 189–208.

The cleanliness of villages was also a major issue. Despite the introduction of rubbish bins and disposal arrangements, it was ultimately up to individual villagers to decide whether to throw their rubbish in a bin or on the road. In many of the villages I visited (mostly in Beian, where the villagers stayed in their original villages), redevelopment had not finished and public areas were dirty again, with rubbish thrown in redeveloped water ditches, reservoirs and along the villages' roads and alleys. Many officials from both counties believed that changing people's 'backward' habits and consciousness was the most difficult task under the BNSC policy. In her PhD dissertation, Lili Lai inveighed against the urban narrative of villagers lacking hygiene. According to her, hygiene plays a significant part in villagers' lives. Pointing to what she calls a 'perceptible hierarchy of hygienic configuration', Lai argued for several dichotomies that guide villagers' perceptions of hygiene: interior (clean) *versus* exterior (dirty), up (clean) *versus* down (dirty), near (clean) *versus* far (dirty). According to her, these dichotomies are responsible for the environmental crisis in villages.[38] From the officials' point of view, it was exactly this kind of rural culture that needed to change if a 'new socialist countryside' was to be built.

Conclusion

This chapter has portrayed two distinct perceptions of the national Village Redevelopment Program. In industrialised Chenggu, local officials strongly supported the notion of rural reorganisation and moving villagers from traditional rural villages to large-scale, city-like communities. Yet, even under circumstances of being a national-level experimental site, and despite the overall support of province and local officials, townships did not implement the transition to rural communities blindly; nor did they impose it on all villages as a uniform policy. Local economic conditions played a decisive role in the development of the policy. Initially, the transition to rural communities involved mainly industrialised townships and villages that held the best prospects for success. In poorer areas, even when officials supported the idea of rural communities and merging villages, inhabitants were likely to stay in their original houses due to official recognition that villagers had to improve their household economies first.

---

38   Lai, 'Discerning the Cultural', ch. 1.

However, construction of new rural communities is a long-term project and what was true of the first four years of implementation may not necessarily prevail in the future. When asked about the reluctance of villagers to leave their old houses, officials tended to be disparaging. For them, the new residences represented a new dawn for the countryside. The new communities symbolised modernity and a pathway to improving villagers' wellbeing. Why would a rational person resist this opportunity? Officials, especially in the industrialised areas of the county, also tended to disparage economic constraints; indeed, in many villages and townships, I was told that these simply did not exist. For officials, any reluctance to move was first and foremost a manifestation of backwardness.

However, in practice, the construction of rural communities embodied a significant reorganisation of the 'old' countryside and there were numerous pitfalls, especially in relation to the weaker strata of society. An immediate problem was the potential discomfort villagers encountered in living further from their land. In cases in which several villages moved together, the common practice was to build the community around a central village, but this was not always convenient for further-out villages. This problem was most acute in rural townships where agriculture remained a significant part of households' daily labour. Officials tended to dismiss this by claiming that: a) even when villagers dwelt further from their land, it was not very far; and b) in any case, most households had transportation (mainly small motorcycles), making distance less of an issue. From the officials' point of view, the discomfort of dwelling further from agricultural land was cancelled out by the many benefits and comforts embodied in living in a modern environment.

This view was contradicted by a study I conducted in 2016 on the concentration of villages in the remote, poor and mountainous township of Middle Hill (county level) on the outskirts of the metropolis of Chongqing. With a very limited industrial sector and undeveloped labour market, many of Middle Hill's rural households relied on agriculture and work migration (mostly young villagers who migrated to China's south-east provinces for jobs) as sources of household income, which stood at only 60 per cent of the average rural per capita income in Chenggu (but 75–80 per cent of the average income in Chenggu's *rural* townships). After the announcement of the BNSC, the township government attempted to concentrate villagers into newly constructed villages or local urban centres, but with very limited success. Within a decade of implementation, only 20–30 per cent of the villagers had agreed to move; most villagers chose to stay in their non-developed villages. Apart from financial reasons (apartment prices in Middle Hill were similar to those in Chenggu, despite the households' lower income), villagers and local officials pointed to the villagers' high dependence on agriculture as the main impediment to relocation. My interviews with about two dozen villagers and local government and village leaders revealed that those who had moved were mainly villagers whose land was relatively close to the new resettlement locations, those who did not engage in agriculture anymore or those who could afford to forgo agriculture after the transition. For many others, the new settlement's location and the required changes in lifestyle were simply too inconvenient and did not fit their agricultural lifestyle.

In both Beian and Chenggu, in all the villages where people were moving away from their old houses, I was told that older people were among the most reluctant to relocate and that many refused to leave their long-term residences. Some were accustomed to their houses and lacked the energy to move. Others lacked the finances to move. For some, buying an apartment for their children was a higher priority than buying one for themselves. Without adequate finances and no employment, many were likely to end up in the cheapest apartments, on the fourth or fifth floors, which could be very inconvenient for older people.

Two points made this problem even more worrisome. First, in 2011, I was told that residential prices in several villages had already increased by 10–20 per cent or more. If this trend continued, the longer a person waited to buy an apartment, the more expensive it would become. This disadvantaged those who lacked the required finances to buy a new residence immediately. The second point refers to the involvement of large business groups and investors. In some cases, local business groups had taken a leading role in financing the construction of new communities. According to several officials, these groups were not interested in making a profit but had invested for the sake of their communities' wellbeing.[39] Nevertheless, one thing is clear. After the transition, villages would have more land available and new deals could be signed with investors, involving large amounts of money. To what extent these economic players, as well as the political leaders of villages and townships, would tolerate recalcitrance due to economic distress remained unclear. Many township officials did

---

39   Nevertheless, in Village C7, inhabitants claimed that contracts had already been signed with a local business group promising it rights on the clear land after transition. According to them, the details of the contract were not transparent and village officials had never consulted them.

not seem to be worried by this. In the worst case, they said, every township had a nursing home for older people. They spoke lightly about tearing such people away from their old homes and traditional communities. Village officials, for whom this problem could be more complicated (due to personal relations and personal acquaintance), suggested various solutions—ranging from establishing nursing homes (in the case of wealthy villages), to waiting for people to die, to offering special subsidies, to providing people with free accommodation.

Like the situation in Chenggu, there was a correlation between local interpretations of redevelopment and local economic conditions in Beian. The importance of adjusting policies to local economic conditions was obvious. And yet, considering the economic and political complexity of a township and even more so of a county, questions remain about the ability of Chenggu and Beian to adjust the policy's implementation to sub-county realities. Obviously, this would have a decisive impact on the ability of the Village Redevelopment Program to meet its goals. An answer to this question is presented in the following chapters.

4

Targets, Standards and Grassroots Investment: Power Distributions during the Village Redevelopment Program

In the previous chapter we saw that, in the absence of a clear direction from above, local officials' perceptions of both economic conditions and villagers' financial capacities played a decisive role in deciding how to interpret the Village Redevelopment Program. This chapter focuses on the main players in the redevelopment process and how power was distributed among them. Far from a uniform hierarchical system, it reveals a significant degree of divergence in governance strategies and practices applied by different economic-political systems (*xitong* 系统) in China when implementing the same policies from above. Here, a word of caution. As we will see in the following chapters, in both counties not all villages were included in the redevelopment project. In fact, at the time of my research, local officials had *not selected* a majority of the villages in Chenggu and an even higher percentage in Beian had not been selected to join the program. Therefore, it is important to bear in mind that this chapter applies only to a minority of villages that were under redevelopment. In the next two chapters I will zoom out again to a 'bird's-eye view' of Chenggu and Beian when discussing the tendency of officials to prioritise a distinct group of villages over others.

The Main Players from the Centre's View

During interviews, officials from both counties referred to the first national directive (*zhongfa yi hao* 中发一号) of the Chinese Communist Party (CCP) in 2006 as the vindication of the counties' actions. This directive introduced the Building a New Socialist Countryside (BNSC) policy and provided detailed lists of targets and guiding principles for implementation. The document demanded, as a key principle, that BNSC should be government led and specified what leading meant. Every level of the government was expected to lead its jurisdiction *politically* and *financially* by allocating financial support in accordance with its financial abilities. A second principle demanded that local governments implement the BNSC in accordance with local conditions (*yindi zhiyi* 因地制宜) and instructed them to avoid uniform implementation. Finally, the document stated that officials should encourage (*guli* 鼓励) the society (*shehui* 社会) to take part in the process and should avoid economic impositions on villagers. Interestingly, while local officials were to encourage society and villagers to participate in the creation of their own new villages, nowhere in the long document was the BNSC subject to villagers' willingness to participate. In the central government's view, building a 'new socialist countryside' was, first and foremost, a government venture.

While these three principles might be seen as complementing each other, it is easy to see how they also contradict each other. After all, the first principle emphasises the hierarchical nature of the Chinese rural political system and the role played by higher levels of the government; contrarily, the second empowers grassroots governing levels, which naturally possess the best information about the villages' capacities and needs; and the third encourages empowerment of society. How the counties reconciled these principles is the subject of this chapter.

Creating an Institutional Environment to Facilitate Implementation

Both counties took two initiatives immediately after BNSC was introduced to facilitate its implementation. The first was the establishment of a leading group (*lingdao xiaozu* 领导小组) headed by the county's party secretary in Chenggu and by the county head in Beian,[1] and comprising the leaders of all the county's party and government units relevant to BNSC (a total of 20 units in Beian and 32 units in Chenggu). The second initiative was to establish a 'BNSC office' (*xin nongcun jianshe bangongshi* 新农村建设办公室). In Chenggu, officials extended this institutional framework to the townships, with every township having its own leading group and BNSC office. As in the county government, in the townships, party secretary–headed leading groups hosted all relevant township bureaus. In Beian, unlike in Chenggu, townships did not have any special leading groups or offices, and village redevelopment was under the responsibility of the townships' deputy head who was normally responsible for agriculture. According to county and township officials, a special office in the townships was not needed, as they played only a marginal role in village redevelopment. Indeed, townships in Chenggu played a far more significant role in the redevelopment than in Beian. This was even more so after the Chenggu County government stepped back from intensive involvement in the first two years of implementation (2006–7) and dismantled the county government's BNSC office in 2008.

The leading groups had two main aims. First, as groups in which almost every bureau of the party and government had representation, they provided an opportunity for coordination between the different bureaus and offices. Second, since the top leaders in each county headed the leading groups, they symbolised both the importance of BNSC and that its implementation was a goal shared not just by one bureau or another but by the whole government and the party.

The county BNSC office's role was to engage in day-to-day implementation.[2] In contrast to the leading group, which was focused on BNSC from a macro perspective and met irregularly (normally a few times a year), the office was the government's main arm engaged in the Village Redevelopment Program on a day-to-day basis. Symbolically, it represented the government's push for desired change. But the importance of the office was much more than mere symbolism. Unlike in the past, now there were officials in both counties being paid solely to promote village redevelopment. Although these were not high-ranking officials (some were not even included in the government

---

1   Officials in Beian explained that the leading group was headed by the county head and not by the party secretary because implementing BNSC was a governmental undertaking—not a party one.

2   In a visit to Chenggu in 2011, I was told in several townships that special BNSC offices had ceased to exist and that the program had been incorporated into the regular work of various departments. For Chenggu, therefore, the following discussion refers to the first four years of implementation.

register of officials [*bianzhi wai* 编制外]), their superiors evaluated them according to their ability to successfully implement the redevelopment program.

Regional and county governments commonly establish offices and leading groups in China when superiors impose new targets from above. Graeme Smith has criticised the practice of establishing offices as a potential manifestation of political and economic corruption. In a trenchant article on political machinations in a rural county, he wrote: 'at one stage in my research it appeared that there was a new office opening each week … each new office and committee is an opportunity for friends and relatives to join the county payroll'.[3] However, and without negating the possibility of using offices for corrupt purposes, one should bear in mind that offices also have functional aspects.

Village redevelopment by itself was not a specific target, but a concept or a meta-target involving many local bureaus and offices that were expected to change priorities and to ensure the provision of public goods that previously were not provided to rural areas. The aim of the BNSC office was not to challenge these professional local units by taking over their duties and responsibilities but to coordinate them and to ensure that rural areas were a focus of their attention. Apart from being in touch with all the relevant units, the BNSC office was also responsible for ensuring that village redevelopment did not violate local or national policies and regulations. When taking into account the complexity of the rural fiscal system in China,[4] the narrow expertise of each bureau/office and the vertical flow of information,[5] the existence of designated budgets for village redevelopment (as will be elaborated further in this chapter) and the existence of a 'scientific' plan to guide villages' redevelopment, it is easy to understand why coordination was crucial to ensure better implementation of village redevelopment.

Thus, although belonging to different provincial systems, both Chenggu and Beian counties created similar institutional environments as the first step of implementation. Yet this is also where the similarity ends, as both counties pursued different types of implementation.

---

3   Smith, 'Political Machinations', 39–40.
4   See, for example, Tsai, *Accountability without Democracy*, especially ch. 2.
5   Lampton, 'The Implementation', 14.

Hierarchical Chenggu: Duplication, Targets and Standardisation

After the CCP announced the BNSC publicly in March 2006, local officials in Chenggu County held a conference to inaugurate the policy and circulated papers to participants presenting the county's plan (*fang'an* 方案)—its logic, guiding principles for implementation and targets. In the same month, all township party committees (*zhonggong X zhen weiyuanhui* 中共X镇委员会), together with their equivalent local governments (X *zhen renmin zhengfu* X镇人民政府), circulated documents presenting each township's own plan for building a 'new socialist countryside'. I could only obtain copies of the plans of the county and two of the townships.[6] Still, comparing the three plans reveals some striking notions about rural governance in the county. The book's appendix presents the county's and the two townships' targets. It also indicates for each target whether it appears in the other plans or not.

Reading the plans reveals that the central government and party rhetoric regarding the holistic nature of BNSC had reached the grassroots levels. On paper at least, the local plans were to introduce changes to almost every aspect of villagers' lives—the physical layout of villages, the environment, culture, employment, income, public goods, services and even improvement of villagers' personal *suzhi* ('quality'), which local officials typically conflated with 'old-fashioned' values and attitudes and a lack of knowledge.

However, comparing the county's plan to those of the townships reveals three interesting points. First, with a few minor exceptions, all the county targets were also township targets. Second, the same titles, content and, indeed, words appeared in both township and county plans. Last, it was impossible to find even one target in both township plans that did not also appear in the county's plan. In short, the township plans, presented as *their own* for BNSC, were—almost word for word—the same as the county's plan. Neither township added even one target of its own to better adjust the county's overall plan to suit their local circumstances.

---

6   A few officials claimed that they could not find a copy of the plan due to the long time that had passed since its announcement three years earlier. Others simply politely refused my request to obtain a copy of their plan.

To further exemplify this point, consider the desired ratios between agriculture, industrialisation, and commerce and services (known as primary, secondary and tertiary industries) as stated by the county and by each of the townships. The county stipulated a ratio of 3:72:25 as an immediate target (by 2010) and a ratio of 3:59:38 as a target for the longer run (the year 2015). Township A stipulated a ratio of 3:72:25, the exact ratio stated by the county as its goal. Township E stipulated a ratio of 5:70:25 as its goal, only slightly different from the county's target.[7] Had these two townships been similar to each other in terms of economic development, and/or had they been considered 'average' in the county, stating targets similar to that of the entire county might have made sense. But Township A was the most industrialised township in the county and Township E was an agricultural township with limited industrialisation that was considered *poor* by local standards. Township A's total GDP was eight times higher than Township E's and the ratio between the three economic sectors in terms of contribution to local GDP differed significantly between them. In industrialised Township A, agriculture and commerce and services (primary and tertiary industries) barely contributed to local GDP (4 per cent and 5 per cent, respectively). The bulk of local GDP (91 per cent) was derived from the developed industrial sector of this township. In rural Township E, the industrial sector contributed only 35 per cent of the local GDP, services and commerce were responsible for 21 per cent, while agriculture comprised the largest contributor to the township's GDP (44 per cent).[8] In 2009, Township E was in the midst of paving two new major roads (supported financially by the county) that, local officials hoped, would facilitate access to extra rural manpower for two of the county's largest industrial zones, both located outside the township. Attracting investments and developing local entrepreneurs was important to Township E's leaders, but they seemed pessimistic about the possibility of attracting significant investments and developing a large-scale industrialised sector. Their pessimism was due not only to the less favourable location of the township and the county's overall plan about land use but also to the township's agricultural history and lack of entrepreneurship among its inhabitants, as they perceived it.[9] Moreover, Township E was considered a leading agriculture township in the county (*nongye da zhen* 农业大镇) and the prefectural city recognised it as a leading livestock-rearing township (*xumu qiang zhen* 畜牧强镇). The township's

---

7   In contrast to the county's plan, townships' plans did not distinguish between short- and long-term targets.

8   *Chenggu County Statistical Yearbook*, 2008.

9   Interview with township officials, Township E, Chenggu County, 23 June 2009.

leaders were very proud of the area's agricultural achievements and presented themselves as the best agricultural area in the county. In both townships, therefore, meeting the stated ratios (3:72:25/5:70:25) would require such fundamental changes to their economic structure that it is difficult to envision how they could be met.

Although both townships' plans were almost word for word replicas of the county's plan, it is important to note that they were not exact copies. This may imply that the county's plan was not simply blindly circulated, and that local officials in both townships invested some thought before circulating them. Why would such different townships embrace the same developmental targets?

An academic with whom I discussed this issue told me that in the county he was studying in the province of Yunnan, it was common practice to write plans for the townships. Kevin O'Brien documented a similar phenomenon at the village level. Discussing the implementation of the Organic Law in what he called 'authoritarian villages', O'Brien wrote: 'Codes of conduct and charters are frequently prepared by townships (or counties) and blindly copied from village to village'.[10] I could not verify whether this practice prevailed in Chenggu and no-one mentioned anything about the county's plan being imposed on the townships. But, even if that was the case, why would the county, fully acknowledging the large differences in terms of economic development between the townships, expect every locality to promise similar economic results instead of embracing a macro-management view in which the county allocated every township a different ratio according to its strengths and abilities that, combined, would meet the county's macro-target of 3:72:25?

A possible answer is that the macro-management approach demanded a level of sophistication in planning that the county government did not have. But the county leadership was sophisticated enough to oversee rapid economic development in the county, and it managed economic projects costing huge amounts of money compared to what most other counties in China could attempt. Surely the county leadership understood that allocating the same economic development goals for all townships made no sense. Similarly, township officials were sophisticated enough to realise whether specific targets were applicable to them or not.

---

10   O'Brien, 'Implementing Political Reform', 54.

To answer this question, I wish to present a new concept to describe local governance in Chenggu County—the notion of *politics of duplication*. Politics of duplication refers to the tendency of lower levels to emphasise the hierarchical nature of the political system by embracing, almost blindly, higher interpretations and targets when superiors demand (and then evaluate) that policies from above are carried out. From this point of view, politics of duplication can be seen as a continuity of the legacy, though in lesser magnitude, of the Mao era when meeting targets from above constituted a main pillar of 'revolutionary' governance. This reinforces the general claim among governments worldwide for compliance in the operation of street-level bureaucracies to superiors' impositions of performance standards and evaluations.[11]

An official from the industrialised Township A dismissed my question regarding the inadequacy of the 3:72:25 ratio in meeting the township's economic conditions by claiming that 'this is only a plan'. But even if the politics of duplication was manifested as a pro forma only, with little probability of spurring real change in the townships' local economies, it nevertheless had a significant impact on the overall implementation of the Village Redevelopment Program in the county. When township officials in Chenggu were asked why they had not added targets of their own, they explained that they were only the implementers. To be sure, under the current political structure, meeting the demands of superiors is still a key to gaining personal benefits and securing promotions.[12] But this does not mean that townships can only strive for targets imposed from above or that they lack the ability to bargain with the county to pursue policies better attuned to their local conditions.[13] Yet, rather than seeking an opportunity to serve as government entrepreneurs, grassroots officials experienced the redevelopment program as another case of obeying targets that were listed by the levels above. This was also manifested in the notion of the 'list'.

When township officials were asked to explain how they decided what items to include in their redevelopment plans, their normal answer was to refer to the first national directive of the CCP in 2006, or to a document circulated by the prefectural city (and, in most cases, to both) titled 'The Prefecture's Main Index for BNSC Demonstration Villages' (*X shi shehuizhuyi xin*

---

11 Lipsky, *Street-Level Bureaucracy*, 48–53, 165–70; Edin, 'State Capacity', 35–52; Whiting, *Power and Wealth*, 12 and ch. 3. The debate of strategic agency versus compliance is discussed in Chapter 1.
12 O'Brien and Li, 'Selective Policy Implementation', 167–86; Smith, 'Political Machinations', especially 49–52; Whiting, *Power and Wealth*, ch. 3; Edin, 'State Capacity', 35–52.
13 Ahlers, *Rural Policy Implementation*.

nongcun shifan cun kaohe xize X 市社会主义新农村示范村考核细则).
Table 4.1 presents the list of targets circulated by the prefectural city. As can
be seen, the list covered more areas than just village redevelopment, but
village redevelopment certainly occupied a significant part of it.

Table 4.1: The prefecture's list of targets for inspection

Item	Main content and aims for inspection
Villagers' income (*nongmin shouru* 农民收入)	Average per capita annual income — more than RMB7,000
	More than 60 per cent of villagers engaged in secondary and tertiary industry
Annual collective income (*nian jiti shouru* 年集体收入)	For villages with fewer than 500 people — more than RMB100,000 For villages with 500–1,000 people — more than RMB150,000 For villages with more than 1,000 people — more than RMB200,000
Village construction (*cunzhuang jianshe* 村庄建设)	A plan drawn up by an authorised unit and more than 70 per cent of the plan already completed. The plan should include four maps: 1) current situation in the village; 2) general plan; 3) roads and traffic plan; 4) vertical plan of pipes, as well as the selected model(s) of residential units and an explanatory pamphlet
	Pave main roads, make village beautiful: 1) make village greener according to standards of well-off villages (*lüse xiaokang cun* 绿色小康村, namely, plant trees along the village's main roads, ensure suitable plants have been planted in more than 80 per cent of the houses' courtyards, around buildings and in the village's central public areas; 2) small alleys and households are clean and tidy; 3) the streets cleaned from piles of burning wood, garbage and dunghills
Basic facilities (*jichu sheshi* 基础设施)	A paved road leading to the village; more than 95 per cent of households have running water; 100 per cent of households use electricity; more than 80 per cent of households possess a telephone; more than 85 per cent of households have cable TV
Education and health (*jiaoyu weisheng* 教育卫生)	100 per cent of the children enter kindergarten; 100 per cent of healthy children of suitable age enter and remain in primary school
	100 per cent cover for medical insurance; an available clinic in the village or shared with neighbouring village(s)
Culture (*wenming jianshe* 文明建设)	Building a culture compound including a public courtyard; access to internet (remote education); a reading room; equipment (*qicai* 器材) etc.
	Building a sports courtyard (*tiyu changsuo* 体育场所) with more than two of the following components: 1) a standard concrete basketball court, 2) a standard croquet court, 3) an indoor activity room of no less than 40 square metres, 4) public sports facilities — not less than eight exercise machines
	Village should have a standardised propaganda wall for popularising science (1.8 x 0.6 metres in size, and information should be replaced six to seven times annually)
	No defiance of family planning; 100 per cent implementation of birth control

Item	Main content and aims for inspection
Environmental protection (*huanbao jieneng* 环保节能)	Fine environment; polluting emissions according to standards; industrial energy consumption according to national standards; expand clean energy (usage of electricity, gas, biogas and so on) to more than 90 per cent (of rural households)
Social security (*shehui baozhang* 社会保障)	Providing minimal level of life subsidy to all those in need — more than RMB900 (per person annually)
	Concentrating more than 70 per cent of *wubao hu* (五保户)* in the villages' or townships' nursing homes. In villages where special 'decentralised' contracts signed, a special person allocated to support them
Security and stability (*anquan wending* 安全稳定)	Comprehensive management measures in place; no significant criminal cases or interruption to public order; no major accident(s); no collective appeals to higher authorities or collective protests; conflicts resolved promptly
Organisations (*zuzhi jianshe* 组织建设)	All village organisations fully established (CCP branch, village committee, mediation and so on); more than 90 per cent of the people are satisfied with their performance**

Translated by the author.

* *Wubao hu* (households-receiving-five-kinds-of-support: food, clothing, medical care, housing and burial) refers to rural welfare recipients — mainly old people in poor economic conditions and with no financial support from younger relations. The term's origins lie in the Maoist period.

** Note that the prefectural list did not include types of housing. As noted in the previous chapter, whether redevelopment included restructuring of the villages and moving the villagers into new rural communities or only redeveloping the old villages' public areas was mainly decided according to the townships' and villages' local economic conditions.

It is not surprising that township officials referred to the prefecture's list of targets and not to their 'own' targets or the county's plan. The plans were crowded with details, and in many parts phrased very vaguely. The list, on the other hand, contained clear targets and served as a useful tool for officials to translate the broad 2006 document into operational tasks.[14] The embedded hidden risk, however, was that imposing targets and performance standards from above would diminish commonsense discretion by the grassroots levels, resulting in top-down style implementation with minor considerations of local conditions and needs.

Although many of the interviewed township officials claimed that the targets in the list were only to ensure a minimum standard of living in the villages, and certainly did not represent the final goals of village

---

14 Operationalisation of national policies by higher levels to concretise policies for both officials and the public is a common practice under the PRC. See, for example, Greenhalgh and Winckler, *Governing China's Population*, 53. See also Li, 'Jianshe xin nongcun qieji "yi dao qie"' [Avoiding uniform implementation during the construction of a new countryside].

redevelopment, which was a continuing process (since it is always possible to further upgrade people's lives and living environment), in the day-to-day implementation, the villages', townships' and county's efforts were to meet the prefectural list's demands. After all, these were the criteria on which the villages were inspected by the prefecture. Yet the prefecture was remote and detached from the villages. It lacked grassroots knowledge of the villages and their needs, and its policy was supposed to apply to all six of its counties and thousands of administrative villages, regardless of their differences. It certainly could not meet the central government's directive to implement according to local conditions. And yet, the county, in its plan, had added only one target that had not been raised by the prefecture—the construction of accessible supermarkets in the villages. In reality, the existence of a list of targets from above had castrated local creativity.

When BNSC was announced in Chenggu, the county government took it upon itself to lead the implementation during its first stage (2006–7), coordinating the redevelopment of 30 villages countywide. County officials from various bureaus and offices were attached to these 30 villages as supportive cadres (*bao cun ganbu* 包村干部) to lead and assist them during the process of redevelopment. They were not necessarily specialists in construction. The Office for Outside Relations (*waishiban* 外事办), for example, allocated two officials to guide two different villages.[15]

In 2008, the program entered a new stage and was expanded significantly to include about a quarter of the county's villages (for a detailed account see Chapter 5). The county stepped back from its day-to-day involvement and handed this to the townships and their designated BNSC offices. The county's office was dismantled and the responsibility for guiding the redevelopment was transferred to the county's recently established Office of Rural Works (*nonggongban* 农工办). From then on, the townships' offices took over the role of daily involvement with the villages and monitoring their redevelopment, while the county merely inspected the redeveloped villages. Township officials explained that villages were inspected gradually: first by the township, then by the county and finally by the prefectural city. This process was institutionalised and the county circulated its own list for inspection, titled 'key indicators for a demonstration village at the county level' (*Chenggu xian shehuizhuyi xin nongcun jianshe shifan cun zhuyao zhibiao*, Chenggu 县社会主义新农村建设示范村主要指标). As in the

---

15   A tacit rule was that supportive cadres were to be men and not women.

case of the prefecture's list, the county's list included targets and criteria to guide redevelopment, against which county officials inspected the villages. Township officials I asked insisted that, while targets were the same in the county's and the prefecture's lists, the criteria upon which villages were inspected were not. Yet, despite claiming in its title to represent the *county's* key indicators for a successful inspection, I could not find any difference between the two. Officials with whom I discussed this issue were unable to point to even one difference between the lists. As in the case of the county's and townships' plans, the county's list of targets was an exact copy of the prefectural city's list.[16] Again, the duplicative mechanism was evident.

The prefecture's list can be seen as a central institution that guided village redevelopment in the county, being incorporated into the work of the supporting cadres of township personnel that most of the townships allocated to the villages.[17] Passing the prefecture's inspection meant that supportive cadres had successfully met their task and the Village Redevelopment Program was officially no longer part of their role. In this way, the list was transformed into a threshold device to decide when governmental guidance was needed and, conversely, when it was not.

Standardisation

It is common for upper-level authorities to provide a checklist of responsibilities for lower-level cadres to fulfil.[18] Yet, the use of standardisation in Chenggu was almost obsessive. When a village in Chenggu started its redevelopment, its discretion was already minimal. Not only did the prefecture's list decide for the village the main changes required, but it also attached clear performance standards for every item, and these (as seen in Table 4.1) were often exact and specific. For example, a village was not only required to plant trees and suitable plants to meet the target of becoming greener but also had to plant them in at least 80 per cent of the village houses' courtyards and around the public buildings and public areas.

---

16   Warranting attention is the absence of the goal of construction of accessible supermarkets in the villages, the only goal the county added by itself to its BNSC plan.

17   It was a regular practice in Chenggu that townships dispatch their own personnel to the villages as supportive cadres to lead, assist and supervise the villages. The Village Redevelopment Program was yet another role these township personnel had to fulfil in addition to their regular work at the township bureaus and offices. In several townships, I was told that even some of the townships' leaders served as supportive cadres. Dispatching local government officials to villages as supporting cadres is a common practice in the operation of the Chinese political system and is not unique to Chenggu.

18   Kung, Cai and Sun, 'Rural Cadres', 62.

Similarly, the village enjoyed credit for having running water *only* if was available to more than 95 per cent of the households, for electricity *only* if 100 per cent of households had access, for cable TV *only* if more than 85 per cent of households had access and for telephones *only* if more than 80 per cent of households possessed one.

The above standards are understandable. Villagers should be able to enjoy the basic infrastructure and public goods that have long been taken for granted in the cities.[19] But the prefecture did not stop there. Every village was required to have at least three out of the following four sports facilities: a standard concrete basketball court, a standard croquet court, an indoor activity room and outdoor sports facilities. If a village chose to build an indoor activity room, it could not be smaller than 40 square metres. If it chose to have outdoor sports facilities, it could not have less than eight different exercise machines. More stringent yet was the prefecture's demand that each village install a bulletin board with a minimum size of 1.8 x 0.6 square metres, and that 'scientific' news pinned to the board be changed six to seven times a year.

What happened when a village chose, for example, to build a basketball court? Here again it had to adhere to minimum specific standards that were provided by the township government to guide construction—measurements for the size of the court, the materials the village should use, and even a list of vetted companies from which to buy basketball hoops and other equipment. To be sure, establishing standards for construction is not unique to China; nor it is necessarily negative. After all, standards seek to ensure minimum quality (for a few of the items, I was told that the standards were national). My purpose is not to evaluate or criticise these standards or even to ponder whether they are appropriate. The standards did not prevent villages from engaging in ostentatious construction, as villages were welcome to surpass them. My point is to emphasise the importance of meeting the standards, which local officials expressed as a main pillar of the redevelopment project. This was also notable in the allocation of subsidies.

---

19   In fact, the province demanded, and the prefecture conveyed, many of these items and standards to its subordinates. See Shandong Sheng Fazhan he Gaige Weiyuanhui, 'Shandong sheng jianshe shehuizhuyi xin nongcun jianshe zongti guihua, 2006-2020'. According to Françoise Robin, provision of public goods such as electricity and access to cable TV are necessary means for nation building, which also may facilitate state control by 'allow[ing] state media to be present in every village'. See Robin, 'The "Socialist New Villages"', 61.

Standardising Subsidies

What happened if a village did not meet the standard for a specific item it had constructed? The immediate implication would be a potential loss of money and effort. It was likely to fail the inspection and might find itself having to reconstruct the item before receiving the subsidy attached to that specific item.

As noted at the beginning of this chapter, every level of the government was expected to lead the BNSC project, politically and financially. Financial leadership in Chenggu has been translated into subsidies provided by the different levels of local government. In the first two years of implementation, villages passing the prefecture's inspection received a one-time grant shared by the county and the townships. But, after 2008, the method of allocating subsidies changed, and subsidies were allocated per item if the village met the required standards. The province (together with the central government) provided subsidies for paving roads between the villages as well as the main roads inside the villages (RMB70,000–80,000 per km). The prefecture was much more modest in its financial contribution and provided only RMB3,000 for villages that constructed outdoor sports facilities. The county provided subsidies for constructing basketball courts, croquet courts and an activities yard (*wenhua da yuan* 文化大院). Each of these entitled the village to RMB5,000.[20] Townships provided subsidies in line with their economic abilities. Industrialised townships provided significant subsidies while several rural ones did not provide subsidies at all, as can be seen in Table 4.2.

---

20 The county also bore part of the subsidies for home biogas pits that were shared together with the province and the central government. Further, the county provided subsidies for the drawing up of scientific plans for the villages based on village size. Also excluded from this calculation was the significant investment of the county and townships in public amenities and services, such as road and electricity networks, public transport and education systems, nursing homes and many other investments that supported rural inhabitants.

Table 4.2: Subsidies provided by various townships in Chenggu County for village redevelopment, mid-2009

Township	Content of subsidy	Sum in RMB
C	Croquet court	5,000
E	No subsidies given, but the township exempted the villages from construction taxes (3.27 per cent) for croquet court and public square	----
H	No subsidies given	----
F	No subsidies given. Money invested by the township in a few villages for special projects	----
D	**For the village***	
	Improving infrastructure (running water, paving roads etc.)	10,000
	Croquet court	4,000
	Reading room	2,000
	Security facilities (such as cameras, guarding station etc.)	5,000
	Village park	2,000
	For the residential community (shequ 社区)	
	Building a service centre	100,000
	Administrative office	Min 20,000
	Facilities required for providing services	5,000–10,000
	Improving infrastructure (running water, paving roads etc.)	Min 10,000
	High-standard reading room	10,000
	Computer room	20,000
	Installation of pipes	Paid by the township
	Security facilities (such as cameras, guarding station etc.)	5,000
A	Greenification Electricity Medical insurance Village office Sports facilities Installing running water Installing flushing toilets	Total of RMB100,000 per village on average. Detailed information was not provided
B	NA	NA
G	NA	NA

Source: Author's interviews.

*As noted in the previous chapter, Township D government's goal was that all rural households would move to communities by 2014. However, to improve the villagers' wellbeing in villages that were expected to move last into new communities, the township allocated special subsidies to support limited redevelopment in these villages. As can be seen in Table 4.2, the subsidies allocated to individual villages were significantly smaller than the subsidies allocated to support the construction of new rural communities.

A tacit rule was that every level that provided subsidies also provided standards for construction. Industrial townships therefore provided detailed standards for the items they subsidised. The emphasis on standardisation in the county was manifested in the somewhat ironic story of Village A2, a prosperous village in the most industrialised township in the county. After the township inspected the village's new sophisticated underground pipe system, it decided not to provide the village with a subsidy for this item— not because it did not meet the standards, but because the standards they used were too high and had exceeded those recognised by the township.[21]

To sum up, Chenggu presented a relatively transparent governance approach in which subsidies were allocated in accordance with publicly known criteria. Every village under redevelopment was, more or less, entitled to the same share of the local government subsidies pie. This was a government-oriented model in which targets set at higher levels occupied most of the local officials' attention. Through circulating a list of targets, the prefecture effectively smothered (even if not intentionally) local initiative and entrepreneurship. This resulted in a hierarchical structure of implementation in which the closer the government was to the villages (and thus naturally more familiar with the on-site realities), the less discretion it exercised in deciding the shape of redevelopment. Townships became (mainly) the non-decision-making overseers and villages became (mainly) the implementers. From an opportunity to upgrade villagers' lives in accordance with local conditions and needs, village redevelopment in Chenggu turned into a mechanical process of implementation whereby the lower levels implemented demands from above. Under this model, grassroots accountability was to be achieved through allocating detailed targets and performance standards. The notion of redevelopment in accordance with local conditions was manifested mainly by prosperous villages exceeding the demanded standards, if they did not mind spending more on their redevelopment. The case of Village A2 (mentioned above) was extreme; normally villages received the subsidy if they exceeded the required criteria. However, they were given the same subsidy as others who had built a facility according to the required standards.

---

21   Interview with village and township officials, Village A2, Chenggu County, 2 March 2009.

'Evaluating the Spirit' — the Case of Beian County

Similar to Shandong, in Beian the province of Anhui (with the central government) provided subsidies for paving roads. For every kilometre of paved road, the province allocated RMB125,000. But unlike Shandong, which allocated subsidies for villages' main roads and those between administrative villages, Anhui conformed with central government policies and provided subsidies only to roads between the administrative villages. Also unlike Shandong, Anhui Province allocated RMB3.3 million annually to support the redevelopment of 25 villages to serve as demonstration sites to lead implementation in the county. As a central financer of redevelopment, the Anhui provincial government was also much more involved with the grassroots levels than the government of Shandong and played an active role in monitoring redevelopment. At the end of each year, representatives of the provincial BNSC office would meet representatives of the county office for updates. At each meeting the county submitted a booklet describing the achievements and expenses of the villages' redevelopment during the past year as well as plans for the coming year. Data in the booklet referred separately to every village under redevelopment, and the reports were all signed and approved by the villages' governing committees, the township government and its financial department, and the county BNSC office as well as the county Financial Bureau. This, however, is not to say that the province supervised its Village Redevelopment Program efficiently or sufficiently. The number of employees in the provincial office was too small to supervise its 56 counties thoroughly, let alone every township or village under redevelopment. In fact, the provincial employees did not regularly visit the county, and, in several cases, they instructed county officials to meet them in another county where they happened to be conducting an inspection that year. In reality, therefore, provincial monitoring was largely symbolic, amounting to a reminder to the localities to take village redevelopment seriously.

Unlike Chenggu, the prefecture in Beian was a marginal player. It selected one outstanding village as an 'advanced village at the prefecture level' (*shi ji xianjin cun* 市级先进村) to which it provided financial awards every year (RMB200,000 in total as of 2010). It also provided modest support (a few dozens of thousands of RMB) to three to four villages that decided to redevelop even though they were not included on the provincial list of 25 demonstration villages. But generally, the county's officials tended to disregard the prefecture's financial and political role in village redevelopment. In fact, the prefecture, unlike in Chenggu, was not mentioned in most of my interviews and conversations with local officials. The county office's representatives met with the prefecture's representatives once a year to report and the prefecture conducted irregular inspection tours in the county. However, the prefecture did not enjoy its status as a link between the province and the county, since the county reported directly to the province as well.

Surprisingly, the province did not demand the county do anything, referring to the use of its annual RMB3.3 million, except to request it be used only to redevelop 25 demonstration villages, at least one in each township. It committed support to these villages for the first three years of redevelopment, starting in 2007. Officially, every year the province would decide on the exact amount of support according to the county's achievements. Yet, in reality, the province allocated the same amount (RMB3.3 million) every year over the first three years.[22] The county matched the village redevelopment funding with an additional RMB5 million annually from its own coffers, designated only to support village redevelopment and agricultural industrialisation (*nongye chanyehua* 农业产业化).

With the marginal role of the prefecture and the inability of the province to ensure thorough monitoring, with the economic weakness of the townships and their inability to support redevelopment significantly and with total control over more than RMB8 million annually (the aggregation of the province's and the county's designated allocations), the county was the main government organ involved in the processes of redevelopment.

Deciding the Targets

Unlike Chenggu in which the prefecture circulated a detailed list of targets, there were no lists imposed from above in Beian. Who then decided the main features of redevelopment? To be sure, policymakers' targets (as appeared in the 2006 first national directive of the CCP or in other related central/provincial documents)—such as those for cleaner and greener villages, the use of cleaner energy, introducing 'cultural' facilities, building an office to serve governing organisations in the village etc., as well as paving all village

---

22   Unlike Chenggu, where village redevelopment started in 2006, in Beian it started in 2007. Provincial support in the 25 chosen villages was supposed to end in 2010. However, in mid-2010, the province announced an extension for a fourth year.

roads—were compulsory. But, in contrast to Chenggu, grassroots officials experienced redevelopment less as a process of meeting targets from above and were more likely to adjust redevelopment to the villages' local conditions and wishes. To note a few examples: in one of the hamlets of Village I1, the hamlet decided to build a bridge with a pavilion over the main water reservoir at the centre of the hamlet for recreation purposes. Another hamlet on the other side of the county decided to rebuild the village's ponds, install a public address system in the village and shift the original road leading into the village to another location where a beautiful gate could be installed to mark the entrance to the 'new' village. In another hamlet, fences along the main roads were built by the villagers and flowering bushes were planted along them.

Apart from the absence of any list of targets imposed on the county from above, two additional differences contributed to Beian's more villager-oriented model of implementation: the redevelopment financers and the method of allocating subsidies.

The Redevelopment Financers

When asked about the main implementation players, Chenggu officials tended to emphasise the government's role while Beian officials indicated the villagers. As in Chenggu, redevelopment in Beian involved significant village-funded financial investment. However, since most of the villages in Beian did not have sufficient collective income to support redevelopment, the contribution of 'society' was crucial. This came from various sources such as donations from local industries (if there were any in the village) or donations from rich villagers. However, the bulk of 'society's' investment in most of the villages that I studied came from ordinary households. The amounts were quite significant, from a few thousand RMB per household to RMB20,000 per household in one village.[23] This was the main reason, according to the county office's officials, why they did not impose stiff targets or standards on the villages. 'How can we tell the villagers what to do with *their* money?' they repeatedly asked. It was their money and their villages, and the government was only there to support them. As in the case of the decision not to ask the villagers to move to new houses, the county officials were trying to walk a fine line—implementing policies from

---

23   Generally, investment was shared equally between the village's households. But, in some of villages, the size of the household was also taken into consideration and large households paid more than small ones.

above and involving the villagers without stepping over the line to mass discontent. One of their main strategies to meet these demands was to be attuned to local needs and wishes as much as possible. As long as the villages had met the compulsory items, they could freely add their own preferences for redevelopment. This, of course, was also true of Chenggu. What was different, though, was the method by which subsidies were allocated.

Allocating Subsidies — Evaluating the Villagers' Spirit

When officials in Beian were asked how the county allocated subsidies, they tended to cite a slogan of the central government and CCP—'[those who] do much, will get much; [those who] do less will get less; [those who] do not do, will not get' (*duo gan duo bu; shao gan shao bu; bu gan bu bu* 多干多补；少干少补；不干不补). This principle was valid also in Chenggu: those who constructed more items were entitled to more subsidies from the government(s). But there were clear differences between the two counties. Only for two items could Beian officials point to a rough figure for determining government subsidies: installing running water (RMB800–1,000 per household, depending on the location of the village and how close or far it was to a water reservoir) and paving roads between the administrative villages (RMB40,000 per km paid by the county excluding the RMB125,000 paid jointly by the central and provincial governments). For all other items, officials claimed that there were no clear rules and the county leading group decided on subsidies and their allocations to reward the 'spirit' (*jingshen* 精神) of the villagers. Every year annual working contracts (*zeren shu* 责任书) were signed between villages under redevelopment and the township and county governments.[24] The contracts included the villages' main tasks and the amount of the subsidies they could struggle for. 'Spirit' referred to the ability and willingness of the inhabitants to invest in their village redevelopment. It had two facets: the objective and the subjective. The objective facet referred to the total annual investment by a village in its redevelopment, its ability to meet the annual contract and the quality of the redevelopment. For a village to obtain subsidies, it first had to meet its annual contract. The office's officials claimed that, while they were not very strict with the villages, they expected them to take this task seriously and to

---

24 According to several officials in Chenggu, no performance contracts were signed in the context of the Village Redevelopment Program. However, compulsory quotas were imposed for the number of villages slated for redevelopment, as elaborated in the following chapters.

meet at least most of it. The quality of the redevelopment was also important, but officials were less concerned about meeting specific standards than in Chenggu. As long as villages did not violate construction rules or build ridiculous items, they were free to decide the standards themselves (in one of the villages I even witnessed a triangular basketball court). If villages met these two conditions, then the county was likely to provide subsidies relative to the total size of the investment (although, according to local officials, other criteria such as the average income of the villagers and the existence of government financial resources could also influence the decision).

The subsidies' allocation in Beian differed from Chenggu in two notable ways. First, subsidies were not attached to specific items and villages gained financial credit for everything they redeveloped (as an expression of having a 'positive spirit'). Second, unlike in Chenggu where villages were entitled to the same amount of subsidy for redevelopment, in Beian, subsidies were calculated mainly based on the *total* investment of the villagers. The subsidy pie, therefore, was not divided equally between the villages. Take, for example, three villages that I had the opportunity to study. In the administrative village of M2, a small hamlet with only 20 households was chosen to lead the village redevelopment; in the N1 administrative village, a hamlet with 58 households was chosen; and in the administrative village of J1, the most industrialised and prosperous village in the county, all of the 3,350 villagers were designated to move to new housing in the next few years. All three villages (located in three different townships) were considered successful in their redevelopment and the first two had, more or less, finished their redevelopment when I visited. All reported getting a similar percentage of assistance from the government: 20–30 per cent of their total investment. But, in real terms, the government assistance significantly differed between the villages. In the first village, the total investment was RMB450,000, of which the government paid RMB150,000 as subsidies; in the second village, the total investment was RMB1 million, of which the government paid RMB300,000 as subsidies; in the third village, where 82 households had already moved to new houses, the total investment had already reached RMB8 million (excluding housing that had already cost RMB12 million), of which 1.5 million was paid by the government as subsidies. Thus, richer and larger villages gained a larger part of the pie. The consequence was even more egregious when remembering that provincial support was guaranteed for a limited time only. No-one could guarantee that the subsidies would still be there by the time weaker villages secured the needed funds.

Table 4.3: List of criteria to be inspected by the county, Beian, 2007

Content of inspection		Value (points)	Criteria for inspection
Village plan (cunzhuang guihua 村庄规划) (15 points)	Drawing up a village plan	5	Prepare plan on time
	Publicity	5	Publicise plan in a prominent place in the village
	Implementation	5	Prepare intensively for implementation of village plan; report and approve according to law any land use for living and infrastructure
Production development (shengchan fazhan 生产发展) (30 points)	Development plan	10	Implement the policy of 'one village one product' (yi cun yi pin 一村一品) and having plan to raise villagers' income
	Characteristic agriculture	15	Establish leading industry and characteristic agriculture product(s) in villages; value of leading agriculture product is (at least) 10 per cent of entire agriculture output
	Villagers' income	5	Annual increase of more than 7 per cent in villagers' income
Basic infrastructure (jichu jianshe 基础建设) (60 points)*	Safe drinking water	10	100 per cent of villagers with access to running water or introducing other water provision means beyond non-centralised water tanks or every household digging its own well
	Paved roads (between administrative villages, inside hamlets and between households)	20	All main roads leading to administrative village and all roads inside the hamlets under redevelopment are paved
	Households with phone	5	(At least) 90 per cent of households have phone
	Households having TV	5	(At least) 80 per cent of villagers have cable TV
	Street lighting	10	Enough lighting along villages' main roads and public areas
	Greenery	15	Trees, bushes and flowers planted along both sides of main roads, between houses, along rivers and in villages public activities' areas

Content of inspection		Value (points)	Criteria for inspection
Clean villages (*cunrong zhengjie* 村容整洁) (50 points)	Cleaning up garbage	10	No weeds or sludge around the buildings in the villages; villagers houses' courtyards are clean; at least one designated waste dump site in each village
	Cleaning up sludge	5	Elimination of open cesspits and dirty drainage ditches; drainage ditches along both sides of main roads or underground drainage; clean and level old water reservoirs and sludge pits; no sludge around villages' buildings and public areas
	Cleaning up roadblocks	10	No chaotic construction; no violation of construction rules; no dilapidated walls and old houses that prevent improving villages' appearance; no agricultural crops blocking roads; no 'three piles' along main roads (refers to piles of land, manure and firewood)
	Clean courtyards	10	Villagers' courtyards are clean and tidy; firewood, miscellaneous objects and agriculture tools are orderly; appropriate storage and disposal of everyday waste; separation between human residences and animal areas; create animal pens; beautiful courtyards with vegetation
	Sanitation management and system	5	Having a cleaning group or (at least) one designated cleaner to clean the garbage
	One pit and three changes	10	(At least) 80 per cent of households use biogas pits; (at least) 80 per cent of households implement the 'four changes' (refers to water, kitchens, toilets and animal pens)

121

Content of inspection		Value (points)	Criteria for inspection
Civilised villages (*xiangfeng wenming* 乡风文明) (10 points)	Rate of villagers with medical insurance	5	More than 90 per cent of villagers have purchased new cooperative medical insurance; compliance with policy of family planning; constructing a standardised village health clinic
	Sports activities site**	5	Having a communal activities centre and sports activities site; initiating 'healthy culture'; extensively rating 'civilised households'; implementing a family planning policy; prenatal and postnatal care; no pornography, gambling or drugs; no superstitions and illegal religious activities; law and order is kept, no criminal cases have occurred
Managing democracy (*guanli minzhu* 管理民主) (10 points)	Democratic management and transparency in village affairs	5	Villages' organisations are completely built-up; good coordination between organisations and smooth operations; transparency in villages' and the local party's affairs and democratic management; reporting (to the villagers) on village affairs at least four times a year
	Party work	5	Actively implementing pioneering process of 'two training two leading' (*shuang pei shuang dai* 双培双带), which refers to training village party members and officials to become development experts, and training village development experts to become officials and party members; leading (oneself) towards getting rich; leading masses towards getting rich; allocating tasks to party members with no official roles and making them agents to serve people; developing party activities among political and economic leaders, former soldiers, young villagers who come back to villages, central industries and villagers who work outside villages; recruiting at least one new party member per village per year

Content of inspection		Value (points)	Criteria for inspection
Organising publicity (zuzhi xuanchuan 组织宣传) (10 points)	Establishing a council (lishihui 理事会)	5	Electing a designated leading group; having a detailed implementation plan; establishing a 'new socialist countryside council' in hamlets under redevelopment and standardising its work; posting a bulletin; more than 98 per cent of villagers are familiar with the redevelopment program
	Submitted materials	5	Submitting materials on demand; participating in 'unified organisation' activity (tongyi zuzhi de huodong 统一组织的活动, refers to ensuring all inhabitants are taking part in the redevelopment program)
Organisation and implementation of township government (xiangzhen zhengfu zuzhi shishi 乡镇政府组织实施) (5 points)	Organisation; plan implementation; work initiatives; submitting materials	5	Drawing a plan of township's new countryside; a detailed implementation plan, layout work plans, clear annual targets and missions; submit materials reflecting the township's situation by request from county government units
	Budget and social finances	10	A minimum investment by township and the village of RMB100,000, an investment by various elements of the society of (at least) RMB200,000
Total		200 points	

Translated by the author.

*Note: There is an inconsistency between the overall score of the category (60 points) and the aggregate score of its sub-categories (65 points). This inconsistency originated in the county's documents.

**Note: There is an inconsistency between the original table and its appendix of criteria for inspection, as the criteria do not refer only to having a designated sports site in the village. This inconsistency originated in the county's documents.

The subjective aspect of 'spirit' aimed also to ensure that villagers contributed funding to the investments, which officials were so dependent on. Deliberately fostered by the county, this was manifested in an internal competition between the 25 chosen villages.[25] At the end of each year, the leading group evaluated every village. An outstanding performance would entitle the village to public financial rewards and a poor performance would subject it to sanctions. As in Chenggu, the county used a list of targets to inspect the villages. An inspection was conducted and assessed in the following way: each criterion amounted to a certain number of points that the village gained if it passed inspection. In total, these points could amount to the maximum score of 200. Table 4.3 presents the list of items and the criteria attached to them. It also presents the number of points each item was worth if met completely.

This list is not to be confused with the one in Chenggu, as their uses were completely different. Unlike in Chenggu, where the prefecture circulated the list, in Beian the county composed it for its internal use. Beian's list was less detailed than the one in Chenggu and the county specified measurable standards only for those targets that referred to basic infrastructure items; the centre had attached high importance to these and they were subject to provincial scrutiny. But the main difference between the lists was in their uses. In Chenggu, the list measured the redevelopment's outcomes and decided the stage at which the prefecture recognised the village as redeveloped. In Beian, on the other hand, the aim of the list was to encourage local investment by measuring the villages' performance against each other. To put this another way: villages in Chenggu needed to perform well enough to meet a list of objective criteria, while villages in Beian needed to ensure that their performance was better than that of their counterparts.

No village wanted to be ranked at the bottom of the list. In the eyes of the county government, there was only one reason for a village to be ranked last: lack of motivation ('spirit'). The bottom-ranked village could be deprived of government subsidies that year. Similarly, villages could receive only part of the promised subsidies if their performance failed to meet the county's expectations. In addition, each year the county announced a list of excellent villages. To heighten the importance of this list, the county head announced the excellent villages at the BNSC annual conference,

---

25 This mechanism was also observed by Gunter Schubert and Anna L. Ahlers in their research in three counties in the provinces of Shaanxi, Zhejiang and Jiangxi. See Schubert and Ahlers, 'County and Township Cadres', 83.

in which relevant leaders from the county, townships and villages under redevelopment participated. The county awarded the villages that had performed extremely well with trophies and money for their positive spirit. The county divided villages into three levels of excellence. Level C entitled the village to an annual subsidy of RMB40,000; Level B was worth RMB50,000; and Level A was worth RMB80,000 in 2008 and RMB60,000 in 2009. The criteria for the evaluation were not clear and the decision was made in collaboration with the leading group. In total, in 2009, about a third of the 25 villages were included in the excellence list; however, only one was included at Level A. One of the richest villages in the county, it was one of the demonstration sites to which officials were eager to take guests (including this author) due to its good economic conditions and the friendly political connections the village officials had with the township and county governments.

Conclusion

This chapter commenced with a question: how did officials in Chenggu and Beian reconcile the seeming contradiction between three principles— government leadership, locally defined implementation and the involvement of society—in their efforts to redevelop villages? As this chapter has shown, the two counties walked very different paths and presented distinct approaches towards implementation. Table 4.4 encapsulates the differences in these approaches.

Table 4.4: Main characteristics of village redevelopment implementation in Chenggu and Beian

Chenggu	Beian
Formal	Less formal
Hierarchical	Less hierarchical
Transparent	Less transparent
More government oriented and less inviting of local initiatives	Less government oriented and more inviting of local initiatives

Source: Author's research.

Chenggu took a government-oriented approach that focused on formalism, hierarchical relations between supervisors and subordinates, and transparency. Beian, on the other hand, took a more village-oriented approach and was more welcoming to local initiatives. It placed less emphasis on the hierarchical nature of the local political system and its approach was less formal and standardised than in Chenggu. It was also less transparent than Chenggu, with the county making financial decisions according to the vague notion of villagers' 'spirit'. Clearly, since the county was fully in charge of the provincial financial allocations, and since there was a lack of any significant monitoring from above, one could suspect that this model was also more open to malpractices such as embezzlement and corruption, though I saw no evidence of this.

What were the roots of such different approaches? Why would two counties walk such different paths when implementing the same policy from above? Without a doubt, understanding these differences must begin with higher-level decisions on whether to intervene during implementation or not. The case of Chenggu strongly demonstrates the potency of higher levels to shape subordinates' conduct in the political system. Even in an industrialised county such as Chenggu, the existence of a list of detailed targets and intensive involvement of the prefecture in monitoring implementation and measuring performance eliminated local discretion, and the whole system synchronised itself around meeting the prefectural list. The allocation of subsidies in Chenggu dampened local discretion as well, as villages could enjoy subsidies only for a distinct list of items. Even if unintentionally, the existence of a list of targets from above pushed the county towards standardisation. Andrew Kipnis, in an article on school consolidation in the county of Zouping, Shandong, claimed that prosperity may provide leverage against standardisation.[26] In the case of the Village Redevelopment Program, this was manifest in those (mainly prosperous) villages that exceeded the government's minimum standards, constructing beautiful political-social-cultural facilities in the villages. It was less evident, though, in rethinking or bargaining vis-a-vis redevelopment and the requirements from above.

A second point to note touches upon officials' perceptions and attitudes towards the villages. Many of the township officials I met in Chenggu expressed doubts about the ability of the villages to carry out redevelopment by themselves, and some even expressed doubts about the integrity of the

---

26   Kipnis, 'School Consolidation in Rural China', 123.

villagers and their grassroots leadership. Such officials felt that, without tight supervision, redevelopment was likely to fail. A Chenggu township official explained to me why subsidies were always given after construction and not before, saying:

> Will the village carry out construction according to the standards? We cannot know that in advance. They may use this money for other things and the village will not be able to finish the construction on time. When building a croquet court, for example, they must build it in accordance to our demands; we will check what they constructed and approve it and only then will be able to give them the subsidy.[27]

The last point refers to the lack of government motivation to involve villagers in the process of their village's redevelopment. As noted, the central policymakers urged the local governments to involve 'society' in the process of BNSC. In the eyes of local officials, involvement meant, first and foremost, economic investment. However, as industrialised villages, redevelopment was mostly paid for out of the collective income of the villages (excluding housing, which, as noted in Chapter 3, villagers were expected to pay for themselves). On the positive side, paying for redevelopment out of the villages' collective income benefited the villagers, since they enjoyed a redeveloped environment for free. On the negative side, redevelopment turned into an inter-government(s) matter, and there were no real incentives for officials to involve ordinary villagers in the process.

Despite officials' claims—and in line with the Law on Urban and Rural Planning, which states that before redevelopment can start, villagers must approve 'scientific' plans in an assembly of the whole village (or villagers' representatives in the case of larger villages)—the *real* extent of villagers' involvement in Chenggu was questionable. Real involvement from below was even more dubious in cases in which redevelopment involved construction of new rural communities.

As noted in the previous chapter, in 2009, Chenggu County drew up a new residential plan and villages were expected to be merged into 173 residential communities. According to officials from the county's Civil Affairs Bureau, the decision about which villages would be merged together was made primarily on grounds of geographical proximity, the size of the village population and villages' economic conditions. Much less important was villagers' consent, as is evident in the following anecdotes.

---

27 Interview with a township official, Township D, Chenggu County, 16 June 2009.

Several villagers I talked with in the industrialised C7 village claimed that no-one asked their opinion about the village plan and transition to apartment buildings, which the township dictated (township officials supported this claim). In village H1, which, at the time of my visit in 2009, had started its redevelopment with 40 households having moved to new residences, the village plan was still officially a draft since it had not yet been approved by the villagers' representative assembly (one may wonder about the worth of this approval and how seriously officials took it if redevelopment had already commenced). In Township G, five nearby villages were to be merged into one large community. One of them, which enjoyed better economic conditions than the others, convinced the township that it could construct its own community. As a result, the original location of the residential compound was changed to the other side of that village. According to local villagers in one of the four remaining villages, including a member of the local CCP branch, no-one had asked their opinion about this change. They had never seen a plan and the township, according to them, was building the same model of housing everywhere.[28] In another village in Township H, where redevelopment had not started yet and there were no villagers' representatives (due to the small size of the village), a villager I conversed with dismissed my question about villagers' involvement in village affairs, stating: 'Even when the village officials convene a meeting people don't come. Who has the time to go to these things?'[29]

In Beian, the lack of significant involvement from above combined with the expectation of higher measures of success obliged the county government to take the leading role in initiating and monitoring redevelopment. Given the townships' financial weakness and the lack of villages' collective income, officials were in desperate need of villagers' investment, without which they would not be able to meet their superiors' expectations. This reflects an important regional variation in bureaucratic capacity compared to Chenggu. The need to spur local investment without invoking social unrest is the key to understanding implementation in Beian. To ensure villagers' investment, local officials embraced two main mechanisms. The first was attentiveness to local needs and willingness to set local initiatives according to villagers' own wishes and financial abilities. Provided targets set by higher levels were met, the county was more open to offsetting some

28   This township was not included in my research permit and my access to this village was through a local friend who lived there. Therefore, I was not able to interview officials in this township to verify this claim.

29   Interview with a villager, Township H, Chenggu County, 25 June 2009.

of the costs of additional local initiatives and investments.[30] The second mechanism was fostering competition between villages over subsidies, making additional incentives available to the excellent and subjecting poor performers to financial sanctions. In officials' minds, the discourse between the government and the villages was less about meeting targets from above and more about partnership. This, of course, is not to say that local officials trusted the villagers and their local leaders more than in Chenggu; rather, that under local circumstances, distrusting villagers and disregarding their self-perceived needs and wishes was less an option to officials in Beian.

But what were the implications of embracing such different approaches to implementation against the prospects of the Village Redevelopment Program meeting its goals? To answer this question, two prior questions must be considered: 1) which villages were redeveloped and 2) how were they selected? These questions are answered in the next chapter.

---

30   This is not to claim that the decision-making processes in villages in Beian were more democratic in nature than in Chenggu or that ordinary villagers in Beian had a larger impact on village-level decision-making. Studying decision-making processes at the village level and evaluating the *genuine* extent of ordinary villagers' involvement in these processes would have required systematic research that exceeded the scope and permits of this research.

5

The Main Beneficiaries: 'Demonstration Villages' in Chenggu and Beian

In its attempt to redevelop villages, the Chinese Communist Party (CCP) and State Council drew upon the South Korean village redevelopment movement (known as the Saemaul Movement), initiated in 1970, as a model experience, hoping to emulate its success. In May 2005, a high-level delegation was dispatched to South Korea to investigate the Korean experience. Zheng Xinli (郑新立), the deputy director of the Central Committee's Policy Research Office (*Zhonggong zhongyang zhengce yanjiu shi* 中共中央政策研究室), headed the delegation, which included representatives of the Central Office of Rural Works (*zhongnongban* 中农办), the Ministry of Finance, the Ministry of Construction, the People's Bank and others. Thereafter, the two countries signed contracts institutionalising a training framework for Chinese officials. Since then, thousands of officials have travelled to Korea on official study tours.[1]

In several of my interviews in Chenggu, officials referred to the Korean case as an aspirational goal. In Beian, this positive attitude to the Korean example was taken even further. In 2006, the county, townships and central villages' leaders went on a study tour to Korea, organised by Anhui Province and

---

1   Hunan Provincial People's Government, 'Xin nongcun jianshe yinfa chuguo kaocha chao: san wan guanyuan jiang fu Hanguo' [A tide of initiating study tours abroad as part of the new socialist countryside: Thirty thousand officials will go to South Korea), hunan.gov.cn/hnyw/zwdt/201212/t20121210_4708820.html, accessed 21 October 2021.

headed by the provincial secretary of the CCP.[2] Yet, neither Chenggu nor Beian meticulously followed the 'Korean model'. A main deviation referred to the question of which villages should enjoy redevelopment.

In Korea, all villages in the country participated in redevelopment from the beginning. The government provided each of Korea's 32,267 villages with 335 free bags of cement to be used for communal projects. Based on the villages' achievements in 'the spirit of self-help, participation, cooperation, unity and the determination to work for themselves',[3] the government classified them into three main groups: basic villages, self-helping villages and self-sufficient villages. The government gave more—an extra 500 cement sacks and another ton of steel rods—to the last two groups, to show appreciation for their efforts and achievements and to further boost their redevelopment.[4] In Beian and Chenggu, on the other hand, villages were redeveloped cluster by cluster, with some villages left out. As of the period of my fieldwork, redevelopment had occurred mainly in what local officials called 'demonstration villages' (*shifan cun* / *shifan dian* 示范村 / 示范点).

Three main questions guide this chapter:

1. What characterised a 'demonstration village'?
2. How did local officials decide their priorities (i.e. which villages to redevelop first and which later)?
3. How did local officials conceive of 'demonstration villages'?

The chapter claims that, although the central government announced the Building a New Socialist Countryside (BNSC) and the Village Redevelopment Program as a national policy for all villages, in reality, local officials prioritised a very distinct group of villages while overlooking others. The importance of this prioritisation was not only symbolic (i.e. designation of certain villages as demonstration units); it also had real financial consequences, as designation as a demonstration village resulted in government subsidies that were not available to other villages (these were discussed in the previous chapter).

---

2   An internal document published by the prefectural city to which Chenggu belongs accounted for a delegation of 40 people, including party secretaries from 18 selected villages, who visited South Korea as well. Yet during my fieldwork I did not hear about this activity from my interviewees.

3   Kim, *Korea's Development*, 134.

4   Ibid., 134, 137. For more details about the Saemaul Movement, see Han, 'The New Community Movement', 69–93; Moore, 'Mobilization and Disillusion', 577–98.

The chapter comprises two main parts. The first provides a general discussion of the exemplary society in contemporary rural China, providing a theoretical background to evaluate 'demonstration villages' and their performance. The second part presents fieldwork findings from Chenggu and Beian.

The Exemplary Society in Rural China

Public anointment of exemplary models is a prominent governing principle in China and an important channel for the state to mark its moral and political power.[5] In rural areas it regularly involves rewarding individuals, households, intra-village groups and whole villages, praising them for their achievements and marking them publicly as subjects for emulation. The wideranging spectrum of criteria includes, for example, relations inside households and between families, economic achievements, 'civilised' behaviour, special contribution to the state and successful implementation of government policies. Despite a considerable divergence in terms of genre of performance and types of exemplary behaviour, all exemplars share a common feature: they are anointed by the authorities in the hope that they will influence others to follow their path and hopefully emulate their success. A basic typology can be used to distinguish between three popular types of exemplars: models, non-models and demonstration units.

Models (*mofan* 模范)

The premise that people learn primarily through the imitation of virtuous models, and that a person's legitimate goal is to seek to be a model for others, is one of Confucianism's most fundamental premises. Models have existed for thousands of years as an indispensable part of Chinese culture and governance.[6] Traditionally, models refer to individuals 'held up to others as an example of a quality or behavior that others should emulate'.[7] The practice of guiding the people ('masses') through virtuous models is strongly supported by the CCP. Under the communist regime, China 'has gone farther than other societies in institutionalising the selection and publicising of models as vehicles of socialisation and as a means of discipline and social

---

5 Bakken, *The Exemplary Society*, ch. 5; Thøgersen, 'Cultural Life', 139.

6 Munro, *The Concept of Man*, 136.

7 Burch, 'Models as Agents of Change in China', 123.

control'.[8] Out of its revolutionary ideology, the CCP has extended the understanding of models beyond the individual level to include collective 'revolutionary' groups as well. To note one famous example, in 1964 Mao elevated the village ('production brigade') of Dazhai as a collective model for national guidance due to its inhabitants' alleged superior ability to implement, despite tremendous difficulties and under terrible conditions, what were perceived as the core values of socialism/Maoism: 'the principle of putting politics in command and placing ideology in the lead; the spirit of self-reliance and hard struggle; and the communist style of loving the country and the collective'.[9] However, in contrast with the Mao era—when national models were commonly introduced and campaigns for learning from national models were quite aggressive—most of the models that people encounter in their everyday lives today are more locally oriented, and are confined in their potential influence mainly to their immediate community.

Whether individual or collective in character, and whether nationally or locally applicable, all models depend on three main conditions to successfully influence their audience. First, they must convey a message to the people. Models are expected to serve as living examples. Second, the extent of the distance between the model's messages and its audience's real lives should not be too large, otherwise the audience will experience its messages as unrealistic. If a model is successful due to special gifts that others do not have, to an optimal geographic location that others do not enjoy, to excellent financial conditions that others do not share or to state support that others do not receive, it is more likely to discourage its audience than to mobilise it. A model needs to convey the message that success is possible if the people are willing to invest the required effort.[10] Finally, rewards for the models (or punishment in cases of negative models) should be conducted in public for maximum effect.[11]

---

8   Ibid.
9   Zhao and Woudstra, '"In Agriculture Learn from Dazhai"', 182.
10   Diamond, 'Model Villages', 163–81; Bakken, *The Exemplary Society*, 176–79; Burch, 'Models as Agents of Change', 124, 132.
11   Bakken, *The Exemplary Society*, 174.

Since being a model entitles one to public acknowledgment, honour and respect,[12] models are expected to foster competition between individuals or groups, and to exceed standards and set new ones. Consequently, models have the potential to serve as a mechanism to foster social progress and excellence, providing channels for social mobility that, at least theoretically, are open to all members of the society (as long as they are not officially excluded from the possibility of becoming a model, e.g. bad-class people during the Mao era).

In both Chenggu and Beian, local officials (and often their superiors) have invested considerable effort in anointing models as a means to influence local inhabitants. To note a few examples: county officials in both counties commended women as models for exercising good relations with their mothers-in-law (*hao xifu* 好媳妇) or with their daughters-in-law (*hao popo* 好婆婆). It was hoped that the potential to gain public recognition would invoke better behaviour and would assist in maintaining public order and harmony inside the villages. Similarly, households were designated models for achieving excellent economic results and rising into prosperity ('wealth champions' [*zhifu zhuangyuan* 致富状元]). Officials were selected as models for demonstrating leadership aptitude and/or excellent implementation of policies and fulfilling demands from above. For example, in 2009, the prefectural city to which Beian belongs chose and publicised two village officials from Beian to serve as models for the rest of the villages due to their efficient implementation of the Village Redevelopment Program. It was common for local authorities to provide such models with a certificate, acknowledging publicly their achievements and small symbolic gifts or money.

Non-Models

The rural exemplary society includes other types of exemplars apart from models. At the time of my visits to Chenggu, the county still implemented the well-documented movement of 'the ten stars of civilisation' (*shi xing ji wenming hu* 十星级文明户), and successful households still hung the 10-star sign (*wenming xing ji pai* 文明星级牌) at the main entrance of their

---

12 Unlike models in the USSR, becoming a model in Communist China was not supposed to entitle the anointed person to gain material benefits. See, for example, Munro, 'The Chinese View', 347. In reality, however, this principle was often violated. See, for example, Zhang, 'Laodong mofan: zai daode yu quanli zhijian—cong shehuixue de shijiao kan yi zhong daode jiaoyu zhidu' [Model workers: Between morality and power—a sociological perspective on moral education system].

homes.[13] Similarly, households with party members or soldiers were likely to proudly announce this by hanging signs on their main door, exalting them as a 'party-member household' (*dangyuan jiating* 党员家庭) or a 'household of glorious people' (*guangrong renjia* 光荣人家). Township G in Chenggu County anointed village officials as 'excellent village cadres' (*youxiu cun ganbu* 优秀村干部) if they adhered to the family planning policy in their villages.

Like models, such exemplars were expected to influence others to follow their path. Yet I call them 'non-model' exemplars because they diverge significantly from some of the most basic attributes of the model. Stig Thøgersen, in a paper on cultural life and cultural control in rural China, wrote:

> At the same time, it [the ten stars of civilisation] acquires a detailed knowledge of the present state of mind among all villagers, because *every* household is involved, as opposed to earlier campaigns such as the nomination of 'five-good-households' where local political activists *competed* for the honour.[14]

Thøgersen has rightly pointed to one of the main differences between models and other elements of the exemplary society. While some elements may apply to the entire social group (e.g. it is hoped that all households will reach the standard of the '10 stars' or will meticulously adhere to the family planning policy), models involve competition over scarce resources, as they only apply to the most excellent exemplars of the society. Both forms of exemplars involve adherence to standards decided from above; however, anointment of non-model exemplars tends to establish common practices (and thus may be referred to as templates [*yangban* 样板]), while the anointment of models is expected to produce a refinement of standards and behaviour as its corollary, paving a moral path for others to walk on.

Demonstration (*shifan* 示范) Sites

The title 'demonstration' can be granted to social, cultural, political or economic units (e.g. households, cooperatives, factories, government units, schools etc.) that authorities wish to present as examples to others. In this chapter I focus on the case of 'demonstration villages' (*shifan cun* 示范村) whose construction facilitated the Building a New Socialist Countryside

---

13   On the 10-star movement, see, for example, Thøgersen, 'Cultural Life', 138–40; Bakken, *The Exemplary Society*, 175–79.

14   Thøgersen, 'Cultural Life', 139–40 (emphasis added). The 'ten stars of civilisation' and the 'five-good-households' were re-accentuated as national policies in China's 13th Five-Year Plan (2016–20).

and Village Redevelopment Program. Unlike cases of non-local exemplary models through which the state and its moral education and propaganda organs convey and mediate lessons, demonstration villages are mainly expected to influence their audience through direct and unmediated interaction. Trips to learn from exemplary locations were promoted by the CCP as a governing tool even before 1949 and remain a common practice in today's China.[15] The earlier mentioned tours to Korea to study its village redevelopment can also be viewed as part of this practice.

While villages can be selected as demonstration sites due to outstanding achievements *before* their designation, it is also common for authorities to select villages due to their *potential* to successfully implement a certain policy or government activity or to reach a certain standard of development. In these cases, it is hoped that *after* successful implementation, these villages will influence others to learn from their experience.

Construction of 'demonstration villages' manifests a very different type of state–society relationship compared to the anointment of models (and, in many respects, of non-model exemplars as well). In the latter case, the need to have models constitutes a relationship in which the state is dependent on society. While the state may decide what constitutes a model,[16] its ability to present models is dependent on the availability of social players who meet the criteria through their behaviour. The system is not supposed to force individuals or groups to become models nor is it about designating in advance who is to become a model. Originally, the state's role was to detect excellent exemplars in society, nurture them and finally present them publicly.[17] In the case of demonstration villages, however, and amid the absence of excellent exemplars, the state takes on the role of creator: it decides not *who* is excellent but who has the *potential* to become excellent— and also takes on the task of conversion. Often, this entails the government allocating resources that are not available to others. This is partly because construction of demonstration villages often has another goal: to serve as sites for piloting and experimentation.

Decentralised experimentation is an essential part of the Chinese policy process. At the policymaking level, central authorities expect local governments to 'try out new ways of problem-solving and then feed

---

15 Heilmann, 'From Local Experiments', 1–30.
16 Some scholars have also emphasised the power of social players to influence the state's priorities and national agenda. See, for example, Weigelin-Schwiedrzik, 'The Distance', 216–25.
17 Munro, 'The Chinese View', 344–45.

the local experiences back into national policy formulation'.[18] A main principle in the experimentation methodology is 'proceeding from point to surface' (*youdian daomian* 由点到面); policies are tested in selected sites and then, upon gaining enough experience and successes, are expanded to other localities/communities. In the central policymakers' viewpoint, therefore, policymaking and its implementation must be gradual, careful and interrelated. Indeed, decentralised experimentation is perceived as endowing the Chinese regime with 'extraordinary learning and adaptive capacity', enabling it 'calmly to respond to all sorts of challenges under a radically changing environment'.[19]

At the implementation level, experimentation is expected to guide the implementers. Since central authorities typically 'develop policies or administrative fiats that are intended to be applicable and implemented in all regions and localities or in the entire policy arena',[20] national policies often convey general targets and guidelines. Realising that conditions may vary significantly between localities, experiments are perceived as an important mechanism to provide local officials with relevant ground-based information to develop policy instruments in accordance with their own conditions (*yindi zhiyi* 因地制宜).[21] Good candidates, therefore, are villages with the capacity to enable successful implementation but that are not too different from ordinary villages.[22]

Construction of Demonstration Villages During the Village Redevelopment Program

In 2006, the Ministry of Agriculture issued documents supporting the construction of demonstration villages as an indispensable part of the Village Redevelopment Program's implementation.[23] Subsequently, this ideal proliferated nationwide.[24]

---

18 Heilmann, 'From Local Experiments', 1.
19 Wang, 'Learning through Practice', 128.
20 Zhou, 'The Institutional Logic of Collusion', 56.
21 Heilmann, 'From Local Experiments', 1–3.
22 Diamond, 'Model Villages', 179; Han and Wang, 'Woguo gonggong zhengce zhixing de shifan fangshi shixiao fenxi: jiyu shifan cun jianshe ge'an de yanjiu' [Analysis of failures in the demonstration mode in China's public policy implementation: the case of constructing demonstration villages], 41.
23 See *Nongye bu guanyu shishi 'jiu da xingdong' de yijian* [The Ministry of Agriculture's opinion on the implementation of 'the nine big actions'] and its attachment *Shehuizhuyi xin nongcun jianshe shifan xingdong fang'an* [A program of demonstration actions in the (campaign of) Building a New Socialist Countryside].
24 Han and Wang, 'Woguo gonggong zhengce zhixing de shifan fangshi shixiao fenxi', 38.

The Beian County government invested in the construction of 25 demonstration villages to lead (*daitou* 带头) the process of redevelopment. According to officials in the county, these villages were to achieve two main goals. After their redevelopment, officials expected the demonstration villages to share their experience with other local communities and, by providing a visual demonstration of the many benefits of redevelopment for the villages and their dwellers, to attract other villages to take the initiative to improve themselves. The second goal was to serve as experimental sites (*shiyan qu* 实验区). County officials hoped to gather knowledge and experience as to the most efficient methods to facilitate further local implementation of the redevelopment program and BNSC as a whole.[25] Thus, during and after their redevelopment, these villages were to serve as local arenas for officials and others to learn from their experience.

Anhui Province allocated to the county a quota of 25 demonstration villages. According to local officials, the provincial government set quotas to each of its counties in accordance with the size of the rural population and number of villages (larger counties were allocated larger quotas). The number of province-supported demonstration villages in each county was transparent and was published on the province's website. According to local officials, provincial allocations were fair. While the province allocated the number of demonstration villages to be redeveloped, it did not interfere with the selection of specific villages. It was up to townships to decide which of the county's 243 administrative villages would be chosen and which hamlets would be redeveloped, subject to approval by the villages and the county. As mentioned in the previous chapter, the province committed itself to financially support the redevelopment of the chosen 25 demonstration villages for the first three years of BNSC, and the county matched the funding with RMB5 million annually spent from its own coffers. Thus, the townships and the county held the power to decide who would enjoy financial support and who would be deprived of it.

The province decided that every township should have at least one demonstration village. This was to ensure the existence of an accessible demonstration site for the rest of the villages. Although the county was allowed to add more villages to its redevelopment list (on the condition that

---

25   In my interviews, it became clear that for many of my interviewees—villagers, officials and even academics—BNSC remained a vague concept, even though it had been three years since its inception. In one of my conversations with the head of Beian County's BNSC office, I shared my own perceptions of BNSC and its importance. He laughed, saying that only now, after talking to a foreigner, did he understand what BNSC was.

these would not enjoy provincial financial support), in reality the county synchronised its effort with the provincial quota, and, during the first three years of implementation, invested mainly in the redevelopment of the 25 chosen villages.[26]

A primary condition for demonstration village status was political obedience. Although not a written rule, officials agreed that they would not choose villages where social unrest had occurred or where the policy of family planning had been violated because such villages could not serve as exemplars in a wider sense. All local officials in Beian concurred: as the government was leading the program, this meant, first and foremost, adherence to its most important policies. Although local officials never admitted as much, it was easy to sense the desire not to benefit villages that had endangered local leaders' political careers because of villagers' unwillingness to adhere to county policies.[27]

Having met this condition, county-circulated documents had the following criteria for villages to be chosen for redevelopment:

> Convenient transportation, a concentrated population, villagers with a positive spirit, good organisation and strong groups at the village level, relatively clear commercial features, appropriate basic conditions [to implement the redevelopment program], which will enable [these villages] to attain relatively quick results after a short period of redevelopment.[28]

Townships applied these demands when they selected their candidate villages. Township M, for example, selected the village of M3 because it enjoyed 'good natural conditions, convenient transportation and high activism among the villagers toward redeveloping their hamlet'.[29] Put in other words, the most important criteria for choosing the candidates to enjoy government generosity were: 1) willingness to participate in the redevelopment program; 2) political obedience and social harmony; and 3) favourable pre-2006 economic, physical and geographic conditions. Hence, villages that were already prosperous had a better chance of being chosen than less prosperous ones.

---

26 Two exceptions were the provision of safe drinkable water to the villages and paving roads between administrative villages, which were implemented throughout the whole county.
27 Family planning and social stability are considered as 'veto targets' in the contracts signed under the cadre evaluation system (see Chapter 1, footnote 39). See also Edin, 'State Capacity', 35–52; Whiting, *Power and Wealth*, ch. 3; O'Brien and Li, 'Selective Policy Implementation', 168–76.
28 Beian County, internal document, 2009, copy in author's possession.
29 Township M, internal document, 2009, copy in author's possession.

In a few cases, local officials chose villages because of their 'positive spirit'. To explain this, let us elaborate on the quota of 25 villages. In 2007, the province ordered the county to present a list of 20 villages the province should support. However, out of the 20 candidates, the province approved only 15. According to local officials, this was due to provincial financial constraints (not to a refusal to accept the choice of candidates). A year later, the province ordered the county to submit another list of 10 villages, all of which the province approved. A few of the villages included in the second list had already decided to redevelop by themselves, even though they were not included in the first list and were not entitled to provincial subsidies. Since these villages were 'a safe bet', and out of true appreciation for their efforts, they were included in the second list. This explains why the county approved two administrative villages for redevelopment in Township N, a remote township, while most townships had only one administrative village under redevelopment. Yet these cases were few and by no means represented the majority of the chosen villages, which tended to be among the most prosperous villages in the county. Moreover, 'positive spirit' was not enough in those few self-initiating villages, where villagers needed to be prosperous enough as a group to afford investing in self-redevelopment.

Typically, after choosing an appropriate administrative village, the preference was to begin by redeveloping the central village (*zhongxin cun* 中心村) inside the administrative village. This makes sense because, in most cases, these are the largest hamlets in the administrative village and constitute the centre of the villages' administrative, political and commercial life. This is where the village committee office, the clinic, the primary school and small-scale commercial undertakings are likely to be located. According to local officials, most of the hamlets under redevelopment were central villages.

Yet this was only a preference and not a compulsory condition and there were exceptions, which pointed to different scenarios. First, some of the richer central hamlets had already invested in their own redevelopment. Local officials could decide to expand the program quickly to other hamlets within the same administrative village. In Village K1, for example, the central village redevelopment was almost complete and four hamlets were already under redevelopment when I visited the county. According to the village party secretary, they planned to spread redevelopment in 2010 to another five hamlets.[30] A second, already discussed scenario, were the

---

30 Typically, the redevelopment of 'regular' hamlets was less comprehensive due to their smaller size and more marginal position within the administrative village system.

villages that were included in the list of 25 due to their own initiative. In N1 administrative village, to note one example, a small and remote hamlet of 58 households was chosen for redevelopment. According to county officials, had the villagers not started to redevelop their village by themselves, the village would not have been chosen. Another scenario was a situation in which some hamlets enjoyed significantly better economic conditions than the central village. A notable example was the case of a very small hamlet (20 households) within the administrative village of M2, where villagers enjoyed higher incomes and could spend a high amount of money for redevelopment (RMB20,000 per household). However, regardless of the scenario under which a village was chosen to take part in the redevelopment program, having good economic conditions was paramount.

Personal relations also seemed to play a role in the choice of villages. Among the villages I studied, two were exceptional due to their small population of about 20 households. Besides good economic conditions, both villages shared another common denominator—they enjoyed extremely good contacts with the township government. In one, the supportive cadre was none other than the township deputy head responsible for implementing BNSC; in the other, the village's party secretary was simultaneously one of the township's deputy-heads. The county office's officials never admitted that personal relations played a significant role in the politics behind the redevelopment, but they did not deny it either ('like everywhere, it can happen', I was told). To what extent personal relations influenced the selection of villages in the county is difficult to calculate, but it is safe to say that among those villages that had already reached economic prosperity, having good relations with the local government sometimes played a role in prioritising their selection over others.

At the time of my fieldwork, one to two demonstration administrative villages were being redeveloped in each of the county's townships. Officials estimated the total number of hamlets under redevelopment to be 30–35, less than 1 per cent of the hamlets in the county. In fact, local officials did not use the term 'demonstration villages' (*shifan cun* 示范村) when referring to villages under redevelopment. According to them, a village would become a 'demonstration village' only when (and if) the whole administrative village had been redeveloped. Meanwhile, they used the term 'advanced village' (*xianjin cun* 先进村) when referring to the whole administrative village and 'demonstration area' (*shifan dian* 示范点) or 'experimental area' (*shiyan qu* 实验区) when referring to hamlets under redevelopment.

Demonstration villages, as they were perceived and applied in Beian, deviated from both the modelling and demonstration functions discussed at the beginning of this chapter. As noted, the success of exemplary villages or experimental sites to convey applicable lessons depends upon a selection of typical cases. But, in Beian, those chosen had the best economic conditions. Officials did not even try to disguise this. It was publicly stated in official documents and was openly discussed in my interviews. What made this a problem was that the county expected villages to bear most of the redevelopment costs by themselves, and expenses were significant (this is discussed in detail in Chapter 6). Under these circumstances, one may rightly wonder what kind of example already prosperous villages could possibly offer to others? What lessons, for example, could a village with a collective annual income of RMB1 million, such as Village J1, or villages where households enjoyed exceptionally high incomes and had sufficient finances to invest in their village's redevelopment, teach those that did not share this capacity and could not secure the required funds to redevelop their village? And what was the worthiness of the experience gained by officials from the redevelopment of these prosperous villages when many of them faced very few difficulties during the redevelopment? It is not surprising that by 2010, as officials admitted, only a few hamlets felt encouraged to start redevelopment by themselves. It was not only a question of being mobilised; many of them simply did not have the financial means to embark on redevelopment. When I asked officials from the county's BNSC office how a poor village could participate in the redevelopment program, since the villagers could not secure the required funds due to financial constraints, their response contradicted entirely the concepts of modelling and demonstration: 'if they cannot secure the money, there is nothing we can do about it' (*mei banfa* 没办法). Thus, the already better off demonstration villages could present a vision that most of the villages in the county would not be able to realise. In this sense, creating demonstration villages in Beian resembled the creation of focal points (*zhongdian* 重点), a popular institution under the CCP regime. The main difference between exemplars and focal points is that exemplars are expected to present achievable goals, while focal points are constructed through allocations of generous resources to ensure they will enjoy the best conditions, which will enable them to produce the best results. A focal point school in a city is allocated the best teachers and the most funding and recruits the best students—all to present major universities with the best educated candidates. A focal point institution hence presents a vision that others would find very hard to emulate. An article printed in the *People's Daily* in 1983 about the construction of 'key schools' depicted this point well:

> The key schools are too key, the ordinary schools are too weak. The ordinary schools cannot learn from the experience of the key schools, so the key schools are isolated from the ordinary.[31]

Demonstration Villages in Chenggu County

In March 2006, during the conference held in Chenggu County to inaugurate BNSC, the county's party secretary stated the following as the first step of implementation: 'the county would select 20–30 villages to become "BNSC's demonstration villages" (*xin nongcun jianshe shifan cun* 新农村建设示范村), to lead the implementation of BNSC in the county'.[32] This was the county's part in the larger project titled 'Mobilise one-ten-hundred demonstration projects' (*yi shi bai shifan daidong gongcheng* 一十百示范带动工程), which referred to selecting one county (Chenggu), 10 townships and 100 villages to serve as demonstration units for others, announced by the prefectural city as the first stage of implementation. Accordingly, the county chose 30 villages to be redeveloped and become demonstration villages. To ensure access to these villages and to symbolise that BNSC and villages' redevelopment was to apply to all rural areas, it was important to Chenggu County that at least one demonstration village would be constructed in every township. As in Beian, however, the county prioritised villages that were 'well located and with a good economic infrastructure, high potential for development, a good starting point, and with high standards and efficient management'.[33] Thus, as in Beian, the county chose villages with the best chances of being successful quickly. Interviews with township officials confirmed that all the townships in Chenggu applied these criteria after the county stepped back in 2008 and handed responsibility for redevelopment construction to the townships. Thus, in both counties, authorities put villages with poor economic conditions, remote villages and villages that were politically problematic (which mainly referred to violations of family planning policy and social unrest) near the bottom of the list. In Beian, local officials, from their own understanding, established a link between exemplariness (becoming

---

31 Cited in Rosen, 'Restoring Key Secondary Schools', 349.
32 Chenggu County, internal document, 2006, copy in author's possession.
33 Ibid.

a demonstration village) and political moral standing (a village's adherence to the family planning policy and maintaining social stability). By contrast, in Chenggu, the prefectural city articulated these notions and incorporated them into the prefectural list that itemised the compulsory conditions a village needed to meet to be deemed a demonstration village (see Chapter 4, Table 4.1).

As in Beian, quotas played a decisive role in managing the process. Officials from most of the townships in Chenggu admitted to receiving county quotas of the numbers of villages to be redeveloped, and, as in Beian, it was township officials who decided which villages were to be redeveloped and when. But this was where the similarities ended. In brief, while the conceptualisation of demonstration villages in Beian diverged significantly from methodologies of modelling and decentralised experimentation, the conceptualisation in Chenggu diverged even further. This was noticeable in three main points: 1) local officials' declared expectations about the role of the demonstration villages in the implementation process, 2) the criteria for awarding village-demonstration status and 3) local officials' hopes for the future regarding the construction of demonstration villages.

1) Declared Expectations

As we have seen, dissonance characterised local officials in Beian: the villages they chose for redevelopment did not coincide with their stated expectations for redevelopment. By contrast, when village and township officials in Chenggu explained the rationale behind the redevelopment of demonstration villages, they tended to significantly reduce the villages' instructional role. In accordance with the demonstration methodology, study tours to demonstration villages were organised by the townships to bring villagers from nearby villages to witness and study these exemplars. At the same time (and similar to Beian), many of the township officials I interviewed admitted that the capacity of these wealthy demonstrators to mobilise worse-off villages was limited without first improving the villagers' financial capacity. They perceived the 'demonstration villages' as passive entities that symbolised (*daibiaoxing* 代表性) the many benefits that redevelopment could bring to villages and their residents but nothing more.

2) Criteria for Awarding Demonstration Village Status

When would a village be officially recognised as a 'demonstration village'? Local officials in Beian provided a vague statement along the lines that they recognised a village as a *shifan cun* when it was able to introduce significant changes in its physical environment. In Chenggu, on the other hand, the definition was very clear. After a village had met the prefectural city's list of targets and successfully passed prefectural inspection, it would be recognised as a 'demonstration village at the prefecture level' (*shi ji shifan cun* 市级示范村). Thus, in Chenggu, the concept of a 'demonstration village' was a bureaucratic title and an award for villages that met specific targets imposed from above. Over time, an increasing number of villages were able to meet these goals.

In 2007, most of the 30 villages local authorities had selected for redevelopment had already been redeveloped enough to pass the prefecture's inspection. In 2008, the prefectural city expanded the scope of the redevelopment program by launching a new project—building 1,000 demonstration villages by 2010. The prefecture allocated Chenggu a quota of 240 villages, more than any other county under its jurisdiction. The county met this demand successfully and more than a quarter of the county's villages became 'demonstration villages'. Table 5.1 summarises the distribution of these redeveloped villages in each of the townships I studied. The information was provided by the county's Agriculture Office, the unit in charge of managing and leading the BNSC program following the dismantling of the county's BNSC office (discussed in Chapter 4). It also presents the percentage of these villages out of the total number of villages in each of the townships and the townships' basic economic characteristics.

Table 5.1 reveals a clear tendency to concentrate demonstration villages in the county's industrialised areas. While the prefecture recognised a quarter to half of the villages in the industrialised townships (15–29 villages in each), it recognised only slightly more than 10 per cent of villages in the rural areas (9–10 villages each). Out of the county's 13 townships, almost 60 per cent of the demonstration villages were located in the county's five most industrialised townships. Thus, in Chenggu, the title 'demonstration village' was, in effect, a popular title granted to villages that already enjoyed excellent economic circumstances.

Table 5.1: Demonstration villages per township, Chenggu County, end of 2010

Township name	A	B	C	D	E	F	G	H
Number of demonstration villages	22	29	16	15	10	9	10	9
Percentage of total villages	48	26	44	38	24	12	21	13
Total GDP (in RMB10,000)	389,579	190,420	95,746	68,459	50,058	47,799	41,940	38,465
Total rural population	37,088	72,421	33,308	29,278	34,163	47,784	36,817	35,590
Per capita rural annual income (2007)	6,812*	6,079	6,368	6,515	5,359	4,978	5,334	5,182

Source: Author's interviews. Townships' statistical data is gathered from *Chenggu County Statistical Yearbook*, 2008.

* The figure of 6,812 refers to the average of all villagers in the township. Yet, there was one village where people enjoyed exceptionally high incomes (RMB16,000 on average per year), the highest in the county (see also Chapter 2).

3) Hopes for the Future

Officials in Beian hoped to reach a stage in which each administrative village would have its own demonstration hamlet to mobilise the rest of its hamlets. Conversely, officials in Chenggu hoped that all villages would ultimately become demonstration villages. The peculiarity of this statement is plain for all to see. As noted earlier, the aim of demonstration villages was to facilitate local implementation by providing ground-based information and mobilising other villages to emulate their success—not to turn the entire society into demonstration units. Chenggu's vision begs the question: what is the meaning of being a demonstration village? The only scenario whereby all villages could become '*shifan cun*' was if the meaning of the term was altered. In Chenggu, becoming a 'demonstration village' took on a new definition: it meant to reach a bureaucratic goalpost and pass official inspection.

Conclusion

Since the announcement of BNSC and the inception of the Village Redevelopment Program, officials in Chenggu and Beian have channelled their efforts into what they called 'demonstration villages'. Evaluating these villages from the view of modelling and decentralised experimentation raises some real concerns about official selections. Obviously, selecting the most prosperous villages to take part in the redevelopment project significantly decreased their capacity to serve as successful exemplars, as the residents of other less well-off villages knew that the chosen villages had innate economic advantages as well as government subsidies that they did not have. Similarly, it is difficult to see what generalisable lessons local officials could draw by implementing programs only in the most prosperous villages. From the perspective of the Chinese conception of modelling, these privileged villages represented the form (i.e. the common practice of rewarding exemplars) but not the content, which, in practice, consisted of a bureaucratic configuration.

Local officials in Chenggu and Beian acknowledged the futility of presenting wealthy exemplars to non-wealthy communities. When I asked the head of the BNSC office in Beian when the redevelopment program would be finished, he laughed—suggesting that by then we would both be long retired. If anything, redeveloping the better off villages mainly enabled local officials to moderate their investment in the project.

Notwithstanding this shared fault, officials in Beian and Chenggu differed significantly in their rhetoric and understanding of 'demonstration villages'. Local officials in Beian adhered to the 'instructional' discourse and therefore showed a dissonance between rhetoric and reality. In Chenggu, on the other hand, officials did not expect any genuine modelling from their exemplars. They hoped that eventually all villages would become demonstration villages, which, in their view, symbolised that a village was able—economically and politically—to meet a series of prefectural bureaucratic criteria to fulfil the BNSC's Village Redevelopment Program.

What explains these differences in officials' discourses? Why did officials in Beian retain the traditional elements of demonstration sites despite their poor selection of village candidates? And why did officials in Chenggu almost entirely ignore these qualities? The answer to these questions,

I suggest, lies again in the intersection between the two shapers of policy implementation that are the foci of this book: local economic conditions and the hierarchical nature of politics.

The starting point is that, in both counties, higher levels of government imposed the demonstration villages strategy and local authorities followed it by designating quotas to meet the higher-level government's regulations for implementation. However, the pace of redevelopment differed significantly between the localities. After four years of implementation, Chenggu had redeveloped about a third of its villages, while in Beian, redevelopment had been implemented in less than 1 per cent of the county's hamlets. Moreover, Anhui Province originally secured its subsidies for three years only and these were about to end when I visited the county. The fate of future provincial financial support was indistinct. As we saw in the previous chapter, provincial subsidies played an important role in instigating villagers' participation, since most villages in Beian did not have significant collective income and could not support redevelopment. Termination (or significant reduction) of provincial subsidies would significantly diminish any possibility of the government encouraging and mobilising villagers. Under these circumstances, officials needed exemplars in the most traditional sense not only to demonstrate the benefits of redeveloped villages but also to encourage other villagers to walk this path by themselves (at least those who could afford it).

Chenggu presented a very different situation. As we saw in the previous chapter, the existence of a clear list of targets and the fact that many villages enjoyed significant collective income made implementation a matter of discussion within and between government(s), which were less attentive to the opinions of villagers. The county perceived meeting the prefecture's quota of 240 demonstration villages as easy. There were still many candidates for redevelopment and officials estimated that most villages in industrialised townships would soon meet the criteria of a 'demonstration village'. In fact, they claimed that many villages had already met the prefecture's list of targets and would have been recognised as 'demonstration villages' had the townships been allocated larger quotas. The financial conditions of these townships permitted them to provide subsidies to a larger number of villages than demanded by the set quotas, even though only certain villages could enjoy the county's and prefecture's subsidies. Under these circumstances, officials did not think of the poorer villages. An official from one of the non-industrialised townships in Chenggu estimated that about 60 per cent of his township's villages would be able to meet the prefecture's demands by the end of the process (a period of at least 15 years, according to him). 'What about the other 40 per cent?' I asked. 'We still have not really thought about that', he replied.

The fast pace of redevelopment (due to better economic capacities), the belief that all villages would be included in future quotas, and the prefectural city's decision to ensure success and accountability by imposing a list of items to construct resulted in routinisation. Routinisation replaced the idea of modelling. With enough candidates to meet the prefecture's quotas and a list of very specific targets, demonstration villages in Chenggu became an assembly line product. The title 'demonstration village' was turned into bureaucratic label that anointed and rewarded any village that was financially able to meet the prefectural city's list of targets.

In both counties, the holistic nature of the Village Redevelopment Program faded, the project being converted into a reward almost solely for the already prosperous. Bearing in mind that the original goal of the BNSC and Village Redevelopment Program was to decrease social disparities and inequality, why did local officials deliberately increase inequality in their rural areas by channelling more resources to villages that already enjoyed better conditions and whose residents were already wealthier than others? It is true that officials in Chenggu were optimistic about the possibility that all villages would eventually become 'demonstration villages' but they estimated that this would take 15 and perhaps even 20 years to achieve, acknowledging the many difficulties embodied in the program. Who knows what policies will prevail in 15 years time? Will government subsidies still be available? Meanwhile, government financial allocations have been channelled to those who are least in need of them. Why did officials in Beian deliberately choose villages that were likely to fail in their demonstration task? Why not wait for ordinary villages to redevelop themselves, learn from their experience and then present them as exemplars? Answering these questions constitutes the core of the next chapter.

6

Trapped in the System

So far we have seen that the Chinese bureaucracy in different regions can demonstrate significant degrees of divergence and flexibility when implementing the same policy issued from above. In previous chapters it was observed that Chenggu and Beian differed significantly in almost every possible aspect: they interpreted the Village Redevelopment Program differently; they implemented it differently; and, even what may initially have been seen as a common governance practice—the creation of demonstration villages—turned out, after investigation, to be another significant difference. And yet, ultimately, the beneficiaries of the program were the same. In both counties, officials deliberately prioritised and benefited the already better off villages, providing them access to government financial support that was denied from the rest. Why they did this is the main question of this chapter.

The first part of the chapter expands on the claim that local officials prioritised the already developed and better off villages. It shows that, since the inception of the Village Redevelopment Program, even in industrialised Chenggu County where significantly more villages enjoyed the benefits of the program, the prospects of local officials selecting poor or even average villages to participate and consequently enjoy the program's benefits were much lower than those of the better off. The second part of the chapter discusses the reasons for this.

Prioritising the Better Off

As noted in the previous chapter, by 2010 redevelopment had influenced less than 1 per cent of hamlets in Beian, while in Chenggu prefecture officials had already designated about a quarter of the county's villages as demonstration villages and many more, according to local officials, were ready for inspection. Clearly, the definition of 'better off' takes on a different meaning when describing a quarter of the county's villages. Yet even in industrialised townships, the tendency to select the better off first and entitle them to government subsidies was notable—though, in their case it was the better off of the better off. As was discussed in the previous chapter, almost 60 per cent of the demonstration villages were located in the five most industrialised townships.

The tendency to choose the better off was also noticeable when comparing the average income of inhabitants in the demonstration villages to the total average income of rural inhabitants in the townships, as can be seen in Table 6.1. It presents the average annual per capita income in selected demonstration villages in Chenggu as a proportion of the average income of the total rural population in each of the townships to which these villages belonged. As can be seen, in most demonstration villages, the average income exceeded 100 per cent. This suggests that rural inhabitants in these villages enjoyed higher incomes than those in other villages.

Table 6.1: Average income in selected demonstration villages as a percentage of townships' average rural income, Chenggu County, 2007

Demonstration village	Proportion of average income (%)	Second demonstration village	Proportion of average income (%)	Third demonstration village	Proportion of average income (%)
A4	235	A2	105.7	A1	99.8
B1	147.9				
C7	125.6	C1	103.6		
D1	107.4				
E1	99.6				
F1	103.1				
H2	135.3	H1	126.6		

Source: Author's calculations, *Chenggu County's Statistical Yearbook*, 2008.

In fact, the tendency to concentrate efforts in the more industrialised townships was notable even from the early stages of implementation. In all four industrialised Chenggu townships that I researched (A–D), all villages had their 'scientific plans' drawn up by as early as 2006–7. In the rural townships, however, only a few of the villages had their plans drawn up by mid-2009. As noted in Chapter 3, having a scientific plan was a necessary condition to start village redevelopment. This formed an official threshold, deciding which villages could enjoy subsidised redevelopment and which could not.

It should be stressed that 'better off' is a relative term and what was considered as 'better off' in industrialised townships may be very different from the 'better off' in other rural townships of the county. To demonstrate this point, note, for example, two extreme cases: the village of B1 in the well-off Township B and the village of F1 in the relatively poor rural Township F. Both villages were included in the first group of 30 demonstration villages in 2006. Yet their realities could not have been more different. In Village B1, one of the most prosperous villages in the county with an annual collective income of RMB8 million, the village party secretary could not even provide me a rough estimation of the subsidies the village had received from the government. So large was their own investment that these subsidies were considered insignificant. In Village F1, on the other hand, the collective income amounted to only RMB50,000 annually. The main roads in this village had been paved in 2004, but with many financial constraints. The village received a small subsidy from the county (14 per cent of the cost) and the township (5 per cent) but the village was expected to bear most of the cost by itself (the total cost of paving the village's main roads was RMB570,000). The village bore 34 per cent of the total investment out of its own collective income, but the bulk of the paving cost (47 per cent) was borne by the villagers themselves (RMB200 per person). The demand in 2006 to improve other aspects of the physical environment to become a demonstration village imposed another serious financial burden on the village. Under such financial circumstances, constructing a new residential area was out of the question. Although officials in this township supported the idea of a transition to multistorey apartment buildings, the decision was that villagers would stay in their original rural houses until economic conditions improved.

With collective income limited, money and labour contributed by residents offset the village government's expenses—though the total extra investment to meet the prefectural city's list of criteria was still quite significant, amounting to RMB395,000. The party secretary of the village donated the money to buy trees and plants to meet the demand for greener villages, and the villagers themselves carried out most of the redevelopment. They used their own cars; they built the village committee's office and the culture yard with their own hands; and, whereas Village B1 bought a 150-year-old tree to beautify the village, the villagers in F1 planted tiny saplings themselves. To cut expenses even more, they used materials from old houses (the doors and doorposts of the new village committee's office were all recycled from an old, abandoned house in the village). It was important to the party secretary to emphasise that, unlike richer villages in other townships, his village had not been able to use construction companies to redevelop the village. They built everything with their own hands. In his view, they deserved to be awarded the title 'demonstration village' much more than their rich counterparts.

However, the village of F1 was not representative; in most cases, officials chose significantly more prosperous villages to participate in the redevelopment program. In any case, Village F1 was considered one of the most prosperous villages in rural Township F and a proper candidate for demonstration village redevelopment. Why would local officials, by giving more to those who already had more, increase disparities between rural communities when implementing a policy that aimed to achieve the exact opposite?

Institutional Obstacles during Implementation

All the county and township officials I interviewed stressed that choosing the candidate villages for redevelopment was their responsibility and their own choice, subject to the chosen villages' consent. If we concentrate on a narrow understanding of the word 'selection', then these officials are correct; in none of the counties did higher levels specify which villages were to be chosen first. Nevertheless, when a broader conceptualisation of the notion of 'selection' is applied—namely, not only the act itself but also the motivations behind it—our understanding of grassroots officials' role in the selection of villages for redevelopment changes dramatically.

It has long been recognised that the Chinese political system involves the coexistence of decentralisation and centralisation patterns, which are often translated as horizontal local powers (*kuaikuai* 块块) versus a top-down chain of command (*tiaotiao* 条条).[1] However, scholars differ in the way they place local officials' decision-making and conduct on the continuum of decentralisation versus centralisation. Those who focus on decentralisation tend to attribute higher levels of autonomy and discretion to local officials than those who focus on centralisation. They perceive high-level authorities as mainly 'direct[ing] the attention of [the] local officials to issues and areas intended by the policy makers'[2] and 'set[ting] the main parameters of policy targets'[3] (e.g. through imposing quotas and incentive mechanisms), while providing local authorities (i.e. the implementers) with considerable discretion in deciding on specific methods and strategies of implementation.[4] According to Zhou Xueguang, this presumed local discretion increases the prospects of successful implementation in three ways. First, it provides the opportunity for adjusting national policies, which often convey general targets and guidelines, to fit local conditions. Second, it gives authority to local governments, which best know the local conditions. Finally, it saves resources by delegating supervision to immediate superiors, who are in the best position to supervise effectively.[5]

However, experience shows that, in reality, not every national policy is implemented, and that implementation does not always coincide with the central authorities' expectations. Scholars tend to explain such undesirable outcomes by pointing to structural deficiencies in the Chinese political system, especially to the need of local officials to present successes to their superiors through a system that lacks monitoring capacity and accountability.[6] When 'facing unrealistic policy targets and strong incentive pressures',[7] local officials might be enticed into developing coping strategies for 'meeting' policy targets and manipulatively promoting their self-interest.[8] Often they are criticised for concentrating on 'image-construction projects' (*xingxiang gongcheng* 形象工程), chasing after quick successes, and 'betting on the strong' as a means of enhancing their image in the eyes of

---

1 Unger, 'The Struggle to Dictate', 15–45.

2 Zhou, 'The Institutional Logic of Collusion', 63.

3 Ibid., 58. See also O'Brien and Li, 'Selective Policy Implementation', 167–86; Edin, 'State Capacity', 35–52.

4 Lieberthal, *Governing China*, 167. See also Göbel, *The Politics of Rural Reform*, 52–53; Ahlers and Schubert, 'Strategic Modelling', 840; Schubert and Ahlers, 'County and Township Cadres', 67–86.

5 Zhou, 'The Institutional Logic of Collusion', 56–57.

6 Cai, 'Irresponsible State', 23; Zhou, 'The Institutional Logic of Collusion', 65; Zhao, 'The Power System', 16.

7 Zhou, 'The Institutional Logic of Collusion', 65.

8 Ibid., 65–68; Göbel, *The Politics of Rural Reform*, 52–53; Cai, 'Irresponsible State', 23; O'Brien and Li, 'Selective Policy Implementation', 167–86.

their superiors. It is sometimes argued that they pursue individual political interests while distorting policies and disregarding economic costs at the expense of the public interest. Cai Yongshun concluded that the prevalence of such behaviour makes China an 'irresponsible state'.[9]

Several scholars have taken this approach to explain the implementation and outcomes of the BNSC policy. Elizabeth J. Perry wrote:

> Even well-meaning cadres are sometimes carried away by the campaign spirit. Overly exuberant local officials have been accused of harbouring 'Great Leap Forward expectations'. Their selection of test-points and models, for example, is said to overlook backward villages in favour of wealthier villages that can more easily be presented as success stories.[10]

Anna L. Ahlers and Gunter Schubert provided the following observation regarding two case studies in the provinces of Shaanxi and Zhejiang: 'It was quite obvious that model [demonstration] villages served as showcases for successful policy implementation to boost the cadres' legitimacy'.[11] Walking the same path, Graeme Smith described a case study in the province of Anhui:

> Cadres made one thing clear—another large central government campaign [i.e. the BNSC program] meant business as usual. Communist traditions of showcasing, output obsession, betting on the strong, and campaign-style governance were back in vogue, and influencing patterns of selective policy implementation.[12]

Indeed, many scholars, both outside and within the PRC, had referred to opportunism and unrestrained striving after self-interest as guides to grassroots officials' behaviour long before the inauguration of the BNSC program.[13]

Others, however, have attributed higher importance to aspects of centralisation and commandism as the keys to local officials' decision-making and deeds. While still following the same conceptual framework that perceives local officials' conduct as driven by calculations of potential rewards and sanctions, they tend to focus more on institutional impediments

---

9   Cai, 'Irresponsible State', 20–41.
10   Perry, 'From Mass Campaigns', 42.
11   Ahlers and Schubert, '"Building a New Socialist Countryside"', 55.
12   Smith, 'Political Machinations', 56–57.
13   O'Brien and Li, 'Selective Policy Implementation', 175; Cai, 'Irresponsible State', 20–41.

and commandism as narrowing grassroots officials' genuine autonomy to shape policy implementation. A leading figure in this school is Zhao Shukai, a Chinese government official in charge of a central government research unit, who is one of the most prominent Chinese authors on rural governance. In his words:

> Surveys of the operational mechanisms of grass-roots governments showed that the townships revolve entirely around directives from higher levels. All tasks and quotas are formulated and passed down by the higher authorities; inspections and assessments are determined by the higher-ups, as are all incentives and sanctions. The assessments are closely linked with promotions and material remunerations of the township leaders. Failure to meet quotas not only precludes the possibility of commendations and promotions, but also entails 'yellow card warnings' and even summary 'dismissals from office'.[14]

In another paper, Zhao summarises the bitter reality of grassroots officials:

> Under heavy pressure, township leaders must do their utmost to carry out these missions … What can be carried out is carried out, and what can be faked is faked. What can neither be carried out nor faked is done by illegal means.[15]

While still agreeing that grassroots officials may manipulate or corrupt the process, Zhao points the blame for this at the system much more than at the grassroots officials.[16]

My findings in the case of the Village Redevelopment Program fit with Zhao's view of officials as located in a system characterised by a top-down chain of command, which *pushes* them to engage in certain behaviours rather than allowing them genuine autonomy and discretion. Unlike Zhao, whose analysis covers township officials only, I extend my claim to the county level as well.[17]

---

14   Zhao, 'The Debt Chaos', 44.
15   Zhao, 'The Power System', 16. A similar approach was taken by Zhao Shukai to explain the unfortunate phenomenon of townships' debt. According to him, much more than reflecting poor management and slack administration, this was an expression of a structural problem. See Zhao, 'The Debt Chaos', 43–44.
16   For a similar account in the context of peasant burden, see Göbel, *The Politics of Rural Reform*, ch. 3. In the context of cadres' corruption, see Lü, *Cadres and Corruption*.
17   As noted in the Chapter 1, a new approach of 'strategic agency' has recently emerged, claiming for larger leeway of local officials to bargain and manoeuvre mechanisms of commandism. See, for example, Ahlers, *Rural Policy Implementation*; Heberer and Senz, 'Streamlining Local Behaviour', 77–112; Heberer and Trappel, 'Evaluation Process', 1048–66. This book, however, does not support this approach.

To be sure, grassroots officials in Chenggu and Beian were definitely concerned to boost their own standing in the eyes of higher levels. Yet, unlike scholars who would portray the tendency of local officials to redevelop wealthy villages as a conscious strategy to gain promotion and commendations, and despite grassroots officials' claims of significant discretion, my research reveals that, as the lowest ranks of a very hierarchical political system, their *genuine* discretion and autonomy to decide the candidates for redevelopment was, in fact, extremely limited. Much more than genuine agency, choosing the better off villages first reflected grassroots officials' weakness and compliance to a series of governance principles and premises imposed from above. These constituted a powerful, tacit thrust that pushed them towards the only possible 'choice' available for them as rational players—selecting the better off first. This system constitutes the underlying unity of the very different implementation strategies seen in Chenggu and Beian and attaches them to a larger unified bureaucracy. It also explains the dissonance between the grassroots officials' claims for discretion and their statement that there was nothing they could do (*mei banfa*) about the poorer villages missing out on redevelopment benefits.

At the heart of the discussion is a hypothetical question. Could grassroots officials have behaved differently had they wanted to? If a township's party secretary, or even a county's party secretary, wanted to redevelop non-industrialised villages first, out of a true understanding of the genuine aim of BNSC to decrease social disparities and tackle rural problems, would they have been able to do so? My answer is that, under the circumstances that prevailed, it would have been very difficult and politically risky to do so. This chapter claims that although BNSC and the Village Redevelopment Program were meant to diminish inequality and solve rural development problems, superiors at high levels of the local state shaped the program such that it could only benefit the better off villages.

This chapter highlights the existence of 'institutional obstacles' in the Village Redevelopment Program. I call them 'institutional obstacles' because they reflect a well-established core of Chinese institutional thinking. The fact that such obstacles prevailed in two different counties in two different provinces suggests that they may represent a wider phenomenon and may not be unique to Beian and Chenggu. Therefore, revealing these obstacles enables a better understanding not only of the redevelopment program but also of rural governance in China today.

Obstacle 1: Habituation to the Need to Introduce Exemplars

As noted, mobilisation through exemplars is deeply rooted in Chinese culture and governance. In the case of the Village Redevelopment Program, as we saw in the previous chapter, demonstration villages played a crucial role in local implementation, as most officials' efforts were channelled towards redeveloping these particular villages. Grassroots officials and officials at the highest levels of the local state—the prefectural city in Shandong and the province of Anhui—supported the idea of invoking social mobilisation via presenting visual successes. Of course, presenting exemplars is not the only possible strategy available for state officials to mobilise society. In the previous chapter, I recounted the case of village redevelopment in South Korea. In this case, the Korean state undertook a different approach. All villages started redevelopment simultaneously and further government support was offered based on their performance. In Beian and Chenggu, however, the Chinese bureaucracy walked a different path, selecting some villages to participate before others, and deeming exemplars to be necessary. Yet, without successful exemplars to present, local authorities took over the entire process of creating exemplars. This by itself does not necessarily mean the corruption of modelling capacity, as local officials could have waited for ordinary villages to redevelop themselves and then present them as examples. Yet, this process would have taken a while and was not a real option for local officials. In fact, higher levels of command made almost every possible effort to impede such villages from gaining 'demonstration' status, as I describe below. Under these circumstances, compromises in the selection of exemplars were inevitable. Ironically, the Korean way better serves the Chinese idea of modelling since, at least theoretically, it provided all villages with the opportunity of performing well and becoming exemplars on a competitive basis.

Obstacle 2: Quantification of Success

The province of Anhui and the prefecture to which Chenggu belongs did not pose any direct demands regarding the selection of villages for redevelopment (apart from the provincial demand for at least one demonstration village in every township in Beian). Yet, by their quantitative interpretation of success, they significantly decreased the ability of the townships and even the county to exercise discretion when choosing villages. Quantification of campaign goals has been a well-documented obsession that has infected the entire chain of command under the Chinese hierarchical political system for the past seven decades. In a paper on the accountability of township governments, Zhao Shukai claimed that 'the reason given for quantifying the audits was that assessment should be conducted in a scientific manner'.[18] In several other papers, however, Zhao warned against the significant undesired impact that such quantification had on grassroots officials' decision-making behaviour.[19] Similarly, Andrew B. Kipnis, in a criticism of the audit culture in China, wrote:

> Performance audits, whatever form their ideological justifications take, often lead to such non- and anti-neoliberal outcomes as the production of new social ties and the related nonindividuated forms of personhood among the people audited and the development of new, efficiency-hindering practices, such as deception, formalism, and the shifting of employee attention away from organizational goals to the politics of selecting, measuring, and fulfilling audit criteria.[20]

The prefectural city chose Chenggu County in 2006 as the foremost demonstration arena in which to implement BNSC and expected Chenggu to report on its successes. The city's leadership measured success by the number of villages that passed inspection (i.e. demonstration villages). As noted in the previous chapter, this expectation did not remain at the abstract level. The prefectural city operationalised it into specific quotas of villages to pass its inspection at each stage of the implementation process (30 villages in 2006–7 and 240 villages in 2008–10). The prefecture expected redevelopment to occur in about two to three years. To ensure success, the county allocated annual quotas to its townships, specifying the number of villages that it and the prefecture would inspect. Officials, therefore, had to look for quick successes.

In a somewhat similar vein, in Beian, meeting the expectations of political superiors meant redeveloping 25 chosen villages. The county leaders' choice was driven by a prize of up to RMB3.3 million annually dangled in front of them by the province, but this was not awarded unconditionally. Each year, representatives of the county had to meet with provincial personnel to report on their achievements during the past year and to draw up plans for the next year. Based on these reports, and on the county's ability to present achievements, the province approved a specified amount of subsidy

---

18   Zhao, 'The Accountability System', 64–73.
19   Ibid.; Zhao, 'The Power System', 15–16; Zhao, 'Obligatory Interactions', 17–25.
20   Kipnis, 'Audit Cultures', 285.

each year.[21] Moreover, the fact that Anhui Province allocated subsidies for only three years meant that, as in Shandong, officials in Anhui expected quick successes. It is difficult to imagine township or even county officials gambling by selecting unpromising cases for redevelopment first, risking their chances of presenting achievements and receiving the provincial subsidies. The opposite, striving after quick successes to win provincial satisfaction and subsidies had prevailed.

Obstacle 3: The Method to Allocate Subsidies

The previous obstacle referred to the need for officials to move quickly and to introduce rapid changes in redeveloped villages. However, since the redevelopment of villages was subsidised, what prevented local officials from presenting quick successes in less well-off villages?

Table 6.2: Villages' redevelopment expenses in various villages in Chenggu and Beian

Village name	Expenditure paid by the village (in RMB)	Percentage of total investment paid by the village (%)
Chenggu		
H2	800,000–900,000	92
A2	600,000+	90
D1	1,000,000	90
F1	965,000*	86
E1	1,200,000	75
Beian		
J1	8,000,000	80
N1	1,000,000	70
M2	450,000	67
I1	1,500,000+	66+

Source: Author's interviews, based on officials' estimations.

* The case of Village F1 was recounted earlier in this chapter. The amount of RMB965,000 is an aggregation of RMB570,000, spent in 2004 for paving the village's main roads, and RMB395,000, which the village spent to meet the rest of the prefecture's demands to become a BNSC 'demonstration village'.

21　As noted, the county successfully met the province's expectations and was allocated RMB3.3 million annually.

The answer relates to the way in which higher-level governments allocated subsidies. Table 6.2 summarises the expenditure paid by various villages in Beian and Chenggu at the time of my visits, and the percentages that villages were expected to pay of the total redevelopment cost (excluding the construction of townhouses/apartments, which villagers paid for themselves).

As can be seen from the above table, in both counties the total government subsidies covered only a small part of the total expenditure (10–25 per cent in Chenggu and 20–33 per cent in Beian). In Chenggu, villages' collective income paid for most village redevelopment. In Beian, the village residents paid for most of the redevelopment. Not every village in Chenggu could afford the expenditure out of its collective income and only in the prosperous could villagers themselves afford the investment of several thousands of RMB, the average expense in Beian.

Moreover, in both counties the villages were entitled to receive subsidies only after finishing redevelopment projects. Providing government subsidies as reimbursement is a common practice in China, and, in the case of Beian, this was a direct order of Anhui Province. Sascha Klotzbücher et al. see this practice as ensuring that policy implementation is cost effective;[22] Chenggu officials also expressed this view. As discussed in Chapter 4, granting subsidies after redevelopment revealed local officials' distrust of village officials' ability to carry out the program and control the finances. Yet, reimbursing redevelopment costs after the project's completion significantly diminished the prospects that poorer villages could afford to participate. This was especially so since, in both counties, local officials insisted that redevelopment would start with improving basic infrastructure (such as paving roads and installing running water), which comprised a significant part of the villages' total redevelopment expense, and which many villages would find it hard to pay for up-front.

Even more encumbering than lack of trust between supervisors and subordinates was the adherence of officials to the principle that village redevelopment was not about the government building new villages for residents, but about villagers building their own new villages under government guidance and leadership. The national government promoted this arrangement in the wake of the BNSC's announcement. Its importance lay in its implications and consequences; according to officials in Beian and

---

22   Klotzbücher et al., 'What is New', 38–57.

Chenggu, it was the main reason why it was not possible to favour the weak and provide them with preferential assistance. The government subsidies were provided as awards (*jiangli* 奖励) for achievements and not as financial support. This rationale for allocating funds made subsidies accessible mainly to the better off.

Obstacle 4: Perceiving BNSC as a Long-Term Policy

Why were local officials not disturbed about channelling more resources to the better off? The BNSC, they said, was announced as a long-term policy and should be implemented in accordance with local conditions. Clearly, the original intention of these national principles was to ensure that officials would be attentive to local villages' needs and abilities. There is no doubt that, under the current governance system, had local officials implemented redevelopment rapidly in all villages, it would have been extremely difficult financially for many villagers. At the same time, a long timeframe provided an official excuse to push those in greater need to the bottom of the list. When asked whether the decision to choose the better off first was unethical (i.e. giving government finances to those least in need), officials said that *all* villages needed redevelopment, and that those who could redevelop themselves quickly would do it sooner and those without the funds would do it later (i.e. wait their turn). Since higher-level officials were only concerned with handing down quotas designating how many villages needed to be redeveloped, and cared less about whether poorer villages participated, why would grassroots officials, who were bound by instructions and the quotas from above, behave differently?

Obstacle 5: Subjecting Village Redevelopment to Local Economic Conditions

> The most important thing is to raise the villagers' income ... If you have raised the villagers' income you have succeeded in obtaining the most fundamental solution to rural problems.[23]

Wandering around and witnessing the many changes that redevelopment has brought to villages in Chenggu, it was easy to assume that village redevelopment held special importance in the local understanding of

---

23   Interview with a township official, Township C, Chenggu County, 1 July 2009.

BNSC. The establishment of leading groups and special offices in the county (dismantled in 2008) and in all townships to manage and regulate the Village Redevelopment Program strengthened this impression.

As noted in previous chapters, BNSC covered a wide range of aspects of life in the villages. Consequently, when villages in Chenggu were evaluated by the prefectural city, they were judged not only for their physical environment but also for their entire situation (see Table 4.1). Interestingly, officials in Chenggu provided different accounts on how the prefecture conducted the evaluation. According to a township official, each item in the prefectural list was worth a certain number of points that together totalled 100 points. A successful inspection meant that the village succeeded in scoring more than 90 points. Accordingly, what mainly counted for villages was not how much they scored on a specific item, but their total BNSC score.[24] As each item was worth a different number of points, the lists distributed from above were very useful to learn about higher levels' priorities (the more points attached to a target the more important it was and vice versa).

Unfortunately, the prefectural list that I was given did not show the distribution of points per target, and the township officials I talked to claimed that they were not familiar with the distribution of points and, indeed, had never seen such a list. According to them, if a village failed inspection, the prefectural city would provide them with a letter specifying the reasons for the failure and recommendations for further improvement. Yet, when asked which of the many items demanded by the prefectural city were most important, there was unanimity in the county. All claimed that the most important item was improving the villages' economic conditions and, particularly, raising the villagers' incomes. This statement coincided with provincial and prefectural inspections prior to the announcement of BNSC. In 2005, the province of Shandong conducted a survey among its counties to learn about their pre-BNSC situation as part of the provincial preparations to implement BNSC. The criteria in Table 6.3 were used to evaluate the counties. This shows the number of points a county could obtain for meeting each of the items.

---

24 Local governments commonly allocate points to evaluate and monitor performances. See, for example, Zhao, 'The Accountability System', 64–73; Zhao, 'Township–Village Relations', 74–93.

Table 6.3: Provincial criteria for pre-BNSC county assessments

Area	Item	Number of points
Production capacities (*shengchan fazhan* 生产发展) Total points = 46	Average local government income per capita	12
	Ratio of local manpower working in sec. and ter. industries	7
	Ratio of urbanisation	7
	Ratio of administrative villages with collective income higher than RMB50,000 at their disposal	6
	Average rural income per person	14
Wellbeing (*shenghuo kuanyu* 生活宽裕) Total points = 22	Rural Engel coefficient	5
	Ratio of expenditure for culture and recreation activities	5
	Ratio of villagers participating in pension insurance	4
	Ratio of villagers participating in the new rural cooperative medical insurance	4
	Square metre of living area per person in reinforced concrete or brick houses	4
Communal civility (*xiangfeng wenming* 乡风文明) Total points = 8	Average years of education among villagers	6
	Rate of criminal cases per 10,000 villagers	2
Village appearance (*cunrong zhengjie* 村容整洁) Total points = 14	Rate of administrative villages implementing a new scientific plan	3
	Rate of administrative villages with paved main roads and greenery	3
	Rate of administrative villages with running water	4
	Rate of administrative villages with garbage collection and disposal facilities	4
Democratic management (*guanli minzhu* 管理民主) Total points = 10	Rate of villages implementing transparency in government affairs (*zhengwu gongkai* 政务公开)	4
	Rate of 'five goods villages'*	6
		Total: 100 points

* 'Five goods village' refers to five demands: good leadership (*lingdao banzi hao* 领导班子好), good party members and good cadres (*dangyuan ganbu duiwu hao* 党员干部队伍好), good working mechanisms (*gongzuo jizhi hao* 工作机制好), good construction of a well-off society (*xiaokang jianshe yeji hao* 小康建设业绩好) and good feedback from the villagers on village officials' conduct (*nongmin qunzhong fanying hao* 农民群众反映好).

Source: Fu et al., 'Shandong sheng shehuizhuyi xin nongcun jianshe xian ji fenlei zhibiao tixi yanjiu', [Research on Building a New Socialist Countryside's indicators at the county level in the province of Shandong], 37–54.

As can be seen in Table 6.3, out of 18 assessable items, five related to the category of 'production capacities', five to 'wellbeing', two to 'communal civility', four to 'villages' appearance' and two to 'democratic management'. Yet, summarising the points for each category reveals a clear stress on economic factors. The category of 'production capacities' was worth 46 per cent of the total evaluation points. If the rural Engel coefficient, an item that related directly to the villages' economic conditions,[25] is added to 'production capacities', economic factors were worth more than 50 per cent of the total evaluation. Items that related to improving the villages' physical environment, on the other hand, entitled the village to 14 per cent of the total score. Clearly, from the provincial point of view, economic factors were the most important in the BNSC vision.

In the same year (2005), the prefectural city conducted its own survey among each of its villages. The method of inspection was similar to the province's, but the list of criteria was different. Table 6.4 presents the list of prefectural city targets and the value of each target in points.

Table 6.4: Prefectural city criteria for assessing pre-BNSC villages

Area	Item	Number of points
Production capacities (*shengchan fazhan* 生产发展) Total = 40 points	Annual village collective income	15
	Average annual per capita income	15
	Rate of income derived from sec. and ter. industries	5
	Ratio of labour in sec. or ter. industries	5
Wellbeing (*shenghuo kuanyu* 生活宽裕) Total = 25 points	Residential patterns	4
	Are there established roads and a bus route?	3
	Per cent with access to cable TV	3
	Per cent in possession of a telephone	3
	Per cent using electricity	3
	Per cent with running water in their houses	3
	Per cent with new cooperative medical insurance	3
	Per cent with pension insurance	3

---

25 An Engel coefficient measures the proportion of income spent on food. Its basic assumption is that as income rises, the proportion of income spent on food falls. The lower the coefficient (e.g. between 0 and 1), the better off the locality.

Area	Item	Number of points
Communal civility (*xiangfeng wenming* 乡风文明) Total = 15 points	No petitions submitted	3
	No major criminal cases	2
	No safety incidents	2
	Praised by higher-level officials for its level of civil behaviour	2
	Is there an area for cultural activities?	2
	Average years of education	2
	Per cent of children entering school	2
Village appearance (*cunrong zhengjie* 村容整洁) Total = 10 points	Is there a village redevelopment plan?	3
	No piles of firewood, manure and garbage along village roads	3
	Ratio of paved roads inside the villages	2
	Ratio of households using gas (*ranqi* 燃气)	2
Democratic management (*guanli minzhu* 管理民主) Total = 10 points	Fully established party branch and village committee	2
	All village-level organisations are fully established	2
	Supporting 'democratic administration day'* activities	2
	Transparency in village and budgetary affairs	2
	Is the policy of 'one issue, one opinion' (*yishi yiyi* 一是一议) implemented?	2
		Total: 100 points

* 'Democratic administration day' started in the county in the early 2000s to increase transparency in government conduct. On the 5th of every month, leaders of every village, township and the county meet with representatives of the inhabitants to update them and discuss the main current political affairs. Placards on village committee walls tout 'democratic administration day' as the local answer to the centre's demand for democratic and transparent governance in the villages. This encompasses the 'four democratics' (*si minzhu* 四民主) — democratic policies, democratic management, democratic elections and democratic supervision (*minzhu zhengce, minzhu guanli, minzhu xuanju, minzhu jiandu* 民主决策、民主管理、民主选举, 民主监督) — and 'two transparencies' (*liang gongkai* 两公开) — transparency in financial affairs and village affairs (*caiwu he cunwu gongkai* 财务和村务公开).

As in the case of the provincial survey, economic factors dominated the prefectural survey. The category of 'production capacities' was worth 40 per cent of the points, more than any other category in the list. Villages' appearance (redevelopment), on the other hand, was worth only 10 per cent.

County officials with whom I discussed the evaluation process claimed there were even more stringent criteria for a village to pass the prefectural city's inspection. They denied the existence of points' allocation and the requirement to earn 90 points to pass, claiming that, for a successful inspection, it was mandatory for every village to meet all targets and standards as specified in the prefecture's list—no exceptions. This may explain why the prefectural list of targets, unlike, for example, the earlier discussed 2005 prefectural survey, did not include points' distribution and why all the township officials I spoke to claimed never to have seen any points' allocation. Clearly, if the county officials' account was correct (i.e. that a village under inspection must meet all targets and standards), this would have further negated the possibility of selecting poorer villages, as there was no leeway for clemency at all.

The tendency to focus on economic conditions as the heart of the BNSC is understandable. After all, economic development is necessary for improving material lives in the villages. But, from the perspective of village redevelopment, the prioritisation of economic factors (i.e. villages' collective income, villagers' per capita income, and percentage of villagers engaged in secondary and tertiary economic activities) dealt a blow to the possibility that grassroots officials would even consider redeveloping the less well-off. Physical redevelopment was fairly easy *if* a village had the required means. Most of the villages I studied from the first group of 30 selected villages needed only one to one-and-a-half years to pass prefectural inspection. The total investment required was not considered very significant in these villages, equivalent to the collective income they normally generated in only one to two years. Improving economic conditions in less industrialised villages was a different story. It required attracting investors, improving infrastructure and so on, which could not be achieved quickly, if at all, in remote and poorly located villages. Even in the best-case scenario, if physical redevelopment was worth only 10–14 per cent of the points but economic indicators were worth 40–50 per cent, and if a village needed to score 90 per cent to pass inspection, the immediate implication was that without preferable economic conditions, no matter how well a village redeveloped, it would not be able to pass prefectural inspection. This, of course, reduced even further any motivation on the part of local officials to choose the less well-off.

Interestingly, Beian did not impose the local economic condition obstacle. As noted, there was no list of targets for demonstration villages, and the county used an internal list to mobilise villages by evaluating their performances compared to each other (see Table 4.3). The list was divided into categories that were worth a total of 200 points. Unlike in Chenggu, economic factors in this list entitled a village to only a maximum of 15 per cent of the total possible score. Improving physical aspects of villages, on the other hand, was worth 55 per cent. Different economic circumstances explain these differences. In industrialised Chenggu, economic development could be the focus, while in economically drowsy Beian, village infrastructure and physical layout was the emphasis, enabling inhabitants to achieve results in a shorter time. However, this is not to say that economic development was less important to Beian officials. On the contrary, local officials invested considerable effort in developing local industries and commerce and attracting investors. Not unlike deciding on redevelopment targets (discussed in Chapter 4), Beian's worse-off economic conditions were translated by local officials into greater attentiveness to villages' local circumstances. Thus, while the prefecture expected villages in Chenggu to meet a per capita standard of more than RMB7,000 to grant a village a full score, Beian officials instead expected villages to meet an annual increase of 7 per cent in villagers' incomes. A percentage increase is easier to meet because it is relative to each village's own financial conditions, rather than the ability to meet a fixed standard. However, this did not assist other villages in Beian, as the county was bound by quotas from above and thus kept supporting the same 25 villages.

Obstacle 6: Perceiving the County as the Unit of Reference

As with the previous obstacle, this one refers to Chenggu only. Although considered prosperous, the overall economic indexes of Shandong are misleading, as they conceal a very high level of economic disparity between the counties. For example, in 2005, on the eve of BNSC, the total GDP of the 30 economically strongest counties in the province constituted 37.4 per cent of the total provincial GDP, while the total GDP of the 30 weakest counties in the province constituted only 10 per cent of the total. Local government revenue of the strongest 30 counties constituted 24.2 per cent of the total provincial local government revenue, while revenue of the 30 weakest counties constituted only 4.7 per cent.[26] The total GDP and local government revenue in the 30 strongest county-level units (*xian* 县, *qu* 区, *shi* 市) were, respectively, 372 per cent and 517 per cent higher than the

---

26 Fu et al., 'Guanyu dui Shandong sheng shehuizhuyi xin nongcun jianshe jiaqiang fenlei zhidao de zonghe yanjiu baogao', 5.

30 weakest,[27] while the difference between the county-level units with the highest and lowest rural per capita incomes was as high as 223 per cent.[28] The earlier mentioned provincial survey conducted in 2005 also revealed extremely high levels of inequality between the counties. Among the province's 135 county-level units, six scored an excellent grade of more than 90 (90.4–96.6), of which three belong to prosperous Qingdao; 24 counties scored 80–89.9 (80–89.1); 28 scored 70–79.9 (70.5–79.6); 32 scored 60–69.9 (61–69.9); 32 scored 50–59.9 (51.6–59.7); 12 scored 40–49.9 (40.9–49.2) and one scored as low as 36.7.[29]

The province responded to these discrepancies by dividing its 135 county-level units into three main groups—the strongest 45 counties (one of which was Chenggu), 60 moderate counties and 30 least industrialised—and formulated different policies for each of these groups according to their economic conditions. Table 6.5 presents each group's policies required under BNSC, divided into 'the threes' and 'the fives'.

As can be seen, the province attached different targets and expectations to each group. In the most industrialised county-level group, the time had come to leave traditional rural residential patterns behind. Provincial authorities expected villagers to be concentrated in rural cities and in dense, city-like communal buildings in villages, and for industries to be concentrated in large industrial areas. Rural and urban systems were to be merged towards breaking the dual economic-social structure. These counties presented the ultimate provincial vision of a developed countryside and were to serve as the core of economic activities in the province, pulling others upward through the example of their economic success. Less was expected of non-industrialised counties. Such counties were expected to shift away from traditional agriculture into modern agriculture and to improve their economic capacities; to improve the physical environment inside villages, making them cleaner, modernised and prettier; to improve the skills of excess workers, enabling them to leave the villages and integrate successfully into external labour markets; and to improve basic infrastructure

27   The highest ratio in the province in average local government revenue per person was 5,066 per cent. See Yu et al., 'Shandong sheng caizheng zhichi xin nongcun jianshe fenlei fuchi zhengce yanjiu' [Research on Shandong Province's financial policies for supporting the new socialist countryside], 75–80.

28   Ibid.; Fu et al., 'Guanyu dui Shandong sheng shehuizhuyi xin nongcun jianshe jiaqiang fenlei zhidao de zonghe yanjiu baogao', 5.

29   Fu et al., 'Shandong sheng shehuizhuyi xin nongcun jianshe xian ji fenlei zhibiao tixi yanjiu', [Research on Building a New Socialist Countryside's indicators at the county level in the province of Shandong], 53–54.

and amenities inside the villages and village officials' leadership. Unlike industrialised counties where the provincial focus had been on integration between rural and urban communities, in less developed counties the focus was on improving local conditions inside the villages as rural units, in the hope that, with time, they would be able to meet 'the threes and the fives' of the moderately developed counties and, later, even those of the industrialised ones.

Table 6.5: The threes and the fives — provincial policies under BNSC

	Group 1 (45 strongest counties)	Group 2 (60 middle counties)	Group 3 (30 least industrialised counties)
Threes	Three concentrations (*san ge jizhong* 三个集中): 1. concentrating industries in industrial zones 2. concentrating population in the counties' and central townships' seats 3. concentrating villagers in rural communities (*nongcun xin shequ* 农村新社区).	Three 'isations' (*san hua* 三化), promoting: 1. agricultural industrialisation 2. new types of industrialisation 3. urbanisation.	Three changes (*san ge zhuanbian* 三个转变): 1. from traditional agriculture to efficient ecological agriculture 2. from traditional backward to beautiful villages (*xiumei cunzhuang* 秀美村庄) 3. from traditional villagers to new-style villagers.
Fives	Five [integration] systems (*wu da tixi* 五大体系) integrating urban–rural: 1. economy 2. infrastructure 3. employment and social welfare 4. environmental protection and development 5. social and administrative management.	Five articles (*wu pian wenzhang* 五篇文章) to carry out: 1. high-quality agriculture 2. industrialisation of the county seat and industrial zones 3. urbanisation and better integration between urban and rural communities 4. social undertakings in the villages, townships and county 5. democratic management at the village level.	Five processes (*wu xiang gongcheng* 五项工程): 1. establishing a leading agricultural industry 2. remediating living environment inside the villages 3. preparing, facilitating and professionally training the villagers towards successful integration in external labour markets 4. establishing basic infrastructure in the villages 5. building village-level organisations and increasing local leadership's quality.

Source: Fu et al., 'Guanyu dui Shandong sheng shehuizhuyi xin nongcun jianshe', 12–17.

Allocating different levels of development between industrialised and rural counties was important to meet the national government requirement of adjusting BNSC to local conditions. However, as discussed in detail in the introductory chapter of this book, a county is not a homogeneous unit and can encompass a significant level of inequality. As I noted, the level of inequality between townships inside Chenggu was higher than the overall inequality between Chenggu and Beian. It is unfortunate that the province ignored the issue of inequality inside the counties and did not formulate policies to tackle this under the agenda of BNSC. Luckily, as described in Chapter 3, the province did not impose its vision strictly on the villages and the county enjoyed enough discretion to differentiate in its residential policies between its industrialised and rural villages.

The bigger obstacle to choosing any but the better off villages came from the prefectural city's failure to adjust BNSC in other respects to local conditions. The prefectural city expected villages under its jurisdiction to meet the same targets and judged them by the same criteria as those for a demonstration village. The requirements were simply too high for the majority of the villages to obtain. Table 6.6 presents the economic standards villages had to meet to pass prefectural inspection and the provincial criteria to be achieved by 2010. As the lists are different and refer to different units (villages versus counties) there were only three mutual criteria available for comparison.

Table 6.6: Prefectural and provincial economic criteria compared

	Prefectural city's requirements for a demonstration village (2008)	Provincial targets for counties (by 2010)
Average per capita annual rural income	More than RMB7,000	RMB5,500
Villages' annual collective income	Villages with less than 500 villagers: more than RMB100,000	
	Villages with 500–1,000 villagers: more than RMB150,000	Minimum of 50 per cent of the villages should have more than RMB50,000 in annual collective income
	Villages with more than 1,000 villagers: more than RMB200,000	
Ratio of manpower working outside of agriculture	More than 60 per cent	60 per cent

Source: For Shandong Province's targets, see Fu et al., 'Guanyu dui Shandong sheng shehuizhuyi xin nongcun jianshe', 33. For prefectural targets, see Chapter 4, Table 4.1.

Both the prefecture and the province expected excess manpower to shift away from agriculture to non-agricultural work. This standard was fairly easy to meet as villagers' work migration, as mentioned in previous chapters, had already become a national phenomenon, a result of China's rapidly developing economy, the lack of land or work opportunities in most villages, and villagers' need to make a living. The only difference was that, in Chenggu, most villagers could leave agriculture and still stay close to their homes, while in less industrialised counties, most job-seekers had to migrate to more prosperous areas inside or outside the province.

The other two criteria warrant our attention. The first refers to the criterion of average annual individual income. The province announced the target of RMB5,500 by 2010. The prefectural city, on the other hand, only passed a village after inspection if the villagers' average annual per capita income was more than RMB7,000. The criterion of RMB7,000 was very high, even in industrialised Chenggu. According to official data, in 2007 the average per capita rural income in Chenggu was RMB6,038. Yet only 2.5 per cent of the townships' villages met the standard of RMB7,000, while 42 per cent of the villages had an average annual per capita income of less than the provincial standard of RMB5,500.[30]

The second criterion refers to the villages' collective incomes. The province set a minimum level for annual collective income of RMB50,000 and stated that at least 50 per cent of a county's villages should meet this criterion. My own interviews in Chenggu revealed that an annual collective income of RMB50,000 was fairly low in the county. Most of the villages I visited, both those that had started redevelopment and those that had not, met this level. Yet, the prefecture had raised the required standards to more than RMB100,000 in small villages with a population of fewer than 500 inhabitants, more than RMB150,000 for medium-sized villages with 500–1,000 inhabitants and more than RMB200,000 for large villages with more than 1,000 inhabitants. Industrialised villages in Chenggu were likely to enjoy high collective incomes, and RMB200,000 was fairly low for them. But, for many of the non-industrialised villages, where prospects for increasing collective income were limited, the prefectural standard was out of reach. With inspection standards heavily weighted on high prefectural-set economic measures, only the better off villages were in a position to pass inspection.

---

30   Author's calculation based on *Chenggu County Statistical Yearbook*, 2008.

Conclusion

Local officials are rational actors. As such, they are motivated to undertake rational actions that will ensure maximum personal gains and benefits and minimum sanctions. The unique structure of the Chinese political system and the coexistence of patterns of vertical administrative hierarchy (*tiaotiao*) and local regional controls (*kuaikuai*) as potential determinants for local officials' behaviour have been well discussed in the literature. In reality, however, it seems that too often scholars have tended to overlook the basic question of autonomy and (genuine) discretion. Indeed, as this chapter has shown, a blind attribution of high levels of discretion and autonomy to grassroots officials' conduct and decision-making risks over-simplifying a much more complex story. By presenting a series of institutional obstacles, my research shows that, although township and county officials have indeed selected the better off villages and invested in redeveloping them first, pushing rural, remote and poor villages to the bottom of the list, it would be unfair to judge them negatively for this. As the lowest ranked operatives in the political hierarchy, they were unable to resist the system that pushed them towards a single rational solution. That better off villages were the easiest to redevelop, giving them guaranteed access to their political superiors' commendation, was a bonus. They were under pressure to present quick, quantitative successes; villages were expected to bear most of the redevelopment's costs; and there were no preferential policies to assist villages with financial constraints. In Chenggu, villages that did not enjoy preferable economic conditions would not have been able to pass inspection, no matter how well they redeveloped their physical environment. Together with a need to present exemplars, and in circumstances where no-one in the hierarchy endured sleepless nights for leaving the poor behind, the die was cast: village redevelopment became a subsidised program for richer villages, and there was very little that grassroots officials could do about it. Indeed, selecting better off villages as demonstration units and creating 'showcases' was a manifestation of grassroots officials' weakness and their submission to their superiors in a system that sanctifies the politics of command as its backbone.

But why was the Village Redevelopment Program constructed this way? Why did authorities at the highest level not intervene when government subsidies were channelled mainly to prosperous villages? Why would the prefectural city in Shandong demand such high standards knowing (after surveying its villages in 2005) that they were too high for many of the villages to meet? And why, instead of confronting inequality and economic disparities (e.g. by privileging the weaker villages), did the redevelopment program do the contrary, exacerbating discrepancies between the best off and worst off in each county and region?

This chapter points to a fundamental failure in the implementation of the Village Redevelopment Program. Instead of confronting the generators of inequality and economic disparities, authorities incorporated the redevelopment program into 'old' policy lines. What I have called institutional obstacles are, in fact, long-practised governing principles that have guided policy implementation and superior–subordinate relations in rural China since the early days of the People's Republic. From all indications, the local leaders are accustomed to this approach and accept it without question. Most notable are mobilisation to present visual successes (even when circumstances are less than ideal), the practice of benefiting the strong and the already better off, and top-down auditing policies. Indeed, a study on the implementation of BNSC found that when provinces abandoned the practice of constructing demonstration villages, local governments applied more egalitarian methods of resource allocation.[31]

---

31 Ahlers and Schubert, 'Strategic Modelling', 831–49.

7

Conclusion

The emergence of a market economy in China in the 1980s was accompanied by an expansion of economic and social disparities and inequality between rural and urban populaces. The income gap increased steadily; rural services, public amenities and village infrastructure were typically significantly worse than those of the cities and even rural towns; and, in many areas, relations between villagers and grassroots officials deteriorated. In the early 2000s, rural China went through a governance crisis and a deterioration in social stability. This unfortunate reality was an outcome not only of market forces and liberalisation but also of the state's deliberate discrimination against rural areas and their inhabitants through the persistence of socialist-era discriminatory institutions and, since the mid-1980s, a state policy to develop cities and urban economies while deliberately neglecting rural areas.

Inequality was also followed by a significant change in the official narrative. During the Mao era, the state perceived villagers as spearheading the revolution and its goal of establishing a new society. Following this view, officials exalted rural austerity as fostering revolutionary consciousness. This view of rural settlements and society, however, changed dramatically during the reform era. Now authorities criticised villages as 'dirty (zang 脏), chaotic (luan 乱) and poor (cha 差)'. They saw inadequate rural infrastructure and public amenities, poor access to low-quality services, poor hygiene and a lack of planned development as detrimental to China's project of modernisation. Many criticised villages as habitats of 'low quality' (suzhi di 素质低)—people who suffered from backward thinking and old-fashioned customs and behaviour. Under such perceptions, the entire structure of the countryside was a problem. Traditional rural housing was too large and wasted too much land, and villages were too dispersed to allow improvements in infrastructure, public amenities and services due to the high cost of upgrading each and every village. The die was cast: if China was to succeed in its modernisation project, the government had to change its rural areas.

The Village Redevelopment Program was announced as a central component of China's vision of converting rural areas into a 'new socialist countryside'. Its importance lay in its ambitious attempt to reshape rural lives and introduce permanent changes into the living environment. This was most notable in areas that had started implementing the centre's policy of constructing rural communities (*nongcun shequ* 农村社区), such as in Chenggu. Under this program, local officials led a total reshaping of the countryside, merging villages together into city-like residential compounds, often dominated by multistorey apartment buildings. In these new residential areas, China's central planners expected villagers to enjoy a modern living environment with high-quality infrastructure and highly accessible basic services; modern apartments; commercial services; cultural and leisure-time activities; high-standard hygienic conditions; better transportation and accessibility; and communal services such as welfare support, civil mediation, social security and policing. Equally importantly, the construction of apartment buildings was expected to save land, an essential resource for development.

Officials in industrialised Chenggu welcomed this policy as an important step towards further boosting the local economy and better integrating the county's rural and urban populaces. In line with these aims, local officials placed many of the new rural communities adjacent to rural towns where they served as de facto suburbs, sharing the towns' services and infrastructure. The county also invested in development of its excellent road networks and public transportation services, with buses running regularly from all the villages and new-style rural communities to the towns and the county's economic zones.

While planners expected increasing numbers of villagers in Chenggu to eventually move to new residences, most notably to multistorey buildings in large residential communities, the officials in predominantly agricultural and economically drowsy Beian were more sceptical about how appropriate such restructuring was to their local economic circumstances. Consequently, villagers in Beian were likely to stay in their original villages and housing. Yet the Village Redevelopment Program introduced significant changes in Beian's rural areas. Paving roads was a major project: in just four years, the county was able to establish a comprehensive rural paved-road network, with all the administrative villages in the county having, for the first time, at least one paved access road. Installation of running water was another major project, and the number of villages and villagers enjoying running water increased steadily. Villages that were chosen to participate in the redevelopment program experienced significant upgrading of their physical living environments, which included paving the village's entire road system and alleys, introducing garbage disposal facilities, building cultural and sports facilities, greenification and more. The number of rural households in the county with home biogas pits also steadily increased, providing villagers with cheap energy for lighting and cooking as well as hygienic toilets.

While Chenggu and Beian counties implemented the Village Redevelopment Program very differently, important aspects of the outcomes were ultimately similar. In both counties, officials diverged significantly from the program's original goal of decreasing social disparities and inequality, instead channelling government resources to those who were not lacking, while leaving behind those with greater need. To reconcile the puzzle of different implementation resulting in similar outcomes, this book has shown how the implementers were embedded in a larger economic-political-social environment that shaped much of their decision-making and conduct.

Variance in Policy Implementation

It may not be surprising to detect variance in local governments' modus operandi in a country as large as China and under a political regime that has welcomed decentralisation as part of its rule, that values the importance of experiments and the need to adjust local undertakings to reality, and in which power fragmentation and lack of accountability are prevalent. Yet, without systemic research, the extent of divergence between localities in China remains indistinct. The case of the Village Redevelopment Program shows that, at least in some contexts, divergence is significant.

Apart from different interpretations of the policy (whether villagers should be pushed to move to new housing or not), we have also seen that, in the two counties, different levels of the local state played very different roles during implementation. In Beian, the provincial government played a significant role in providing subsidies to support redevelopment projects and was directly involved in supervising the implementation, while in Chenggu, grassroots officials perceived the province as being detached from implementation (apart from providing subsidies for road paving).

The prefectural city, however, played a very significant role in supervising and monitoring implementation in Chenggu, while local officials in Beian tended to disregard the prefecture as an insignificant player (partly because provincial involvement overshadowed the prefecture).

Chenggu and Beian also presented distinct approaches to local implementation. Chenggu took a government-oriented approach that emphasised formalism, hierarchical relations between supervisors and subordinates, and transparency. In this approach, local officials valued standardisation as a means of guiding and controlling villages' redevelopment and allocated subsidies in a way that increased the accountability of both the implementers and the recipients. They attached subsidies to specific items and allocated them in accordance to publicly known criteria. Inspection was highly institutionalised with several governmental levels conducting strict and standardised on-the-spot inspections in every village under redevelopment.

In Beian, on the other hand, implementation was less hierarchical and less formal. The county took a more village-oriented approach and was more welcoming to local initiatives. Officials did not attach subsidies to specific items and villages received financial credit for everything they constructed. Subsidies, however, were calculated mainly based on the total investment of the villagers, a clear advantage to better off villages to grab larger parts of the government subsidies' pie.

At the heart of these changes lay significant differences in officials' perception of villagers and of their role in implementation. The prominent attitude among township and county officials in Chenggu was that the Village Redevelopment Program was, first and foremost, a government project, and many pointed towards the government as the most important player in the operationalisation and implementation of the policy. They openly distrusted the villagers' integrity and tightly regulated their conduct. In their view, the villagers were mainly expected to approve and to implement a generic list of targets and performance standards, dictated by the prefectural city, which they inspected and subsidised. In cases where the construction of rural communities and multistorey buildings had begun, attentiveness to the villagers' vantage point declined even further. Local officials and even village leaders in Chenggu disparaged households who were reluctant to participate due to economic distress. They had little tolerance for villagers who desired not to spend so much of their own money on new residences, or for villagers who refused to leave their familiar living environment and change their familiar rural lifestyle. Officials considered these as nothing more than manifestations of rural 'backwardness', which needed to be rectified.

Conversely, in Beian, local officials tended to point towards the villagers as the most important players in implementation. Some township and county officials even referred to them as partners. They were less critical regarding the villagers' integrity (at least publicly). Provided redevelopment met the higher-level authorities' basic demands, they were willing to accommodate villagers' self-perceived needs and their preferred investments. And, as long as the villagers' reconstruction efforts were reasonable, they cared less for fixed standards.

Divergence was also noticeable in the way the two counties handled the same governing principles and institutions. Although both counties supported the strategy of developing 'demonstration villages', and although both diverged significantly from genuine modelling and decentralised experimentation, Chenggu and Beian differed significantly from each other in their articulation of 'demonstration villages'. Officials in Beian walked a more traditional path by assigning an active modelling role to such villages. Their hope was to present exemplars to influence the rest of their communities, and there was an absence of clear and stiff criteria to recognise a village as a 'demonstration village'.

By contrast, in Chenggu, the prefectural city routinised the creation of demonstration villages by imposing quotas from above and articulating clear and measurable targets for a village to become a demonstration unit. As part of this perception, officials viewed the title 'demonstration village' as a bureaucratic title and did not really expect any modelling qualities to emanate from their shining examples, while hoping that eventually all villages would become 'demonstration villages'.

Similar Outcomes

Prioritising the better off in the selection of villages for redevelopment was not undertaken in a clandestine manner. It was transparent and explicit in local official documents and was openly discussed during my interviews. Thus, officials in both counties totally ignored the Village Redevelopment Program's original goal of decreasing economic disparities and inequality. This was most noticeable in Chenggu, where a significantly larger number of villages participated in the program. Even when redevelopment was expanded to include more than a quarter of the county's villages, local officials continued to redevelop villages mainly in the county's most industrialised areas.

Redeveloping the Villages: The Main Shapers

What influenced local officials in each of the counties to operate in the ways they did? Why did each of the counties take a different implementation approach and why were outcomes in each of the counties ultimately similar? The claim of this book is that officials' conduct in both counties, as well as their overall attitude towards rural society, was primarily an outcome of two main shapers that influenced their decision-making and conduct: local economic conditions and the politics of command.

Economic conditions played a significant role in local officials' support of the idea of creating new 'rural communities' and merging villages in Chenggu. In such an industrialised county, officials perceived that villagers could afford to buy new apartments or townhouses. Moreover, Chenggu had already reached a level of development where officials could see benefits in urbanising rural areas by constructing rural communities to save land; in better integrating rural and urban areas; and in providing a modern, city-like living environment for the villagers. Yet, although officials supported the idea of moving villagers into multistorey buildings, they did not impose residential models in most townships in the early years of implementing the redevelopment program (2006–8). The result was a large variety of different housing between villages. In the most prosperous villages, inhabitants moved to multistorey buildings (in a few cases, as noted in Chapter 3, this was also a result of direct instructions by the township government), while other villages built multistorey housing side by side with new townhouses. In a few villages, residents deemed multistorey buildings not desirable (due to perceptions of inconvenience or due to the high costs involved in the construction of these buildings) and housing construction consisted of new townhouses only. Yet, in 2009—two years after the county was included in the Ministry of Civil Affairs' national list of counties chosen to experiment with the construction of rural communities— attentiveness to local desires was pushed aside in favour of the politics of command when the county government drew up its plan to concentrate all villages in 173 residential communities. Very soon thereafter, several townships changed their housing regulations to support the county's master plan of constructing rural communities, forbidding any form of construction other than apartment buildings. Construction of rural communities gained high momentum, especially in the industrialised townships.

Local officials in Beian, on the other hand, could not see many advantages in moving villagers. In their view, relocating residents would impose significant expenses on them and on the county government, which would find it hard to pay compensation. They also perceived that being forced to purchase new housing was contrary to the interests of many of the local people who migrate away from the villages for most of the year. For county officials, the most urgent need was to strengthen the rural towns' economies. Only then would they consider reshaping the rural areas.

The interaction between higher-level officials' intervention (or lack thereof) on the one hand, and local economic conditions on the other, also played an important role in shaping local approaches towards implementation. In Chenggu, the decision of the prefectural city to circulate a list of quantitative targets and detailed performance standards, and its tight supervision of redevelopment, resulted in a paucity of local discretion. The whole system was shaped around meeting the prefectural city's list. Even if not intentionally, the existence of a list of targets from above pushed the county towards standardisation. I used the term 'politics of duplication' to describe the tendency of lower levels to emphasise the hierarchical nature of the political system by almost blindly embracing and institutionalising higher-level policy interpretations and targets. The monetary strength of villages in Chenggu and their ability to finance redevelopment expenses out of collective income, as well as inherent distrust in the villagers' integrity and their grassroots leadership, also contributed to redevelopment in Chenggu becoming a highly supervised inter-government project.

In Beian, high-level officials did not involve themselves in the redevelopment, and the county government took the leading monitoring role. Yet the province expected success and only gave subsidies on condition of proven successful redevelopment. Under these circumstances, and when townships lacked finance and villages lacked collective income, county officials needed provincial subsidies and villagers' investments in their homes and infrastructure to meet provincial expectations. As I demonstrated in Chapter 4, the need to spur local investment without provoking social unrest and discontent served as an important shaper of the program's implementation in Beian. To encourage villagers' investments, the county officials introduced two mechanisms: 1) attentiveness to local needs and self-investments and 2) fostering competition between villages over resources. Under these circumstances, ignoring the villagers' desires and alienating them from decision-making processes regarding the redevelopment of their own villages was less of an option in Beian than in wealthy Chenggu.

State intervention and local economic conditions also played a role in regulating the creation of 'demonstration villages'. In industrialised Chenggu, the prefecture set higher quotas of villages for redevelopment than the province of Anhui, and the creation of demonstration villages fell into a routine. By 2010, the prefectural city had already recognised about a quarter of the villages as 'demonstration villages', and officials expected this number to continue rising in the coming years.

Walking different paths of implementation, however, was arguably less important than the fact that both counties prioritised the better off villages over others. Ironically, both counties shaped a national policy that initially proclaimed its intention to decrease inequalities into a program that left the poor behind. Explaining this irony, I concluded that higher levels of the regional and local states, by their instructions and expectations, crafted a governing environment in which grassroots officials, as rational players, had no option but to choose the better off first.

Policy Implementation in Contemporary Rural China: Studying Discretion

The question of discretion can assist in understanding policy implementation by enabling us to view implementation through the eyes of the implementers. It helps explain the special position of the implementers and offers a paradigmatic view of the entire process of policy implementation. By doing so, it becomes evident that while many scholars have, in fact, touched the elephant, as in the story of the blind men and the elephant,[1] it is only at the aggregate level that the elephant itself can be revealed.

---

1   The story of the 'Blind Men and the Elephant' is about several blind men who encountered an elephant for the first time. Since they could not see it, they touched it to understand its shape. However, each one of them touched a different part of the elephant and therefore concluded a different shape. When they discussed what the elephant looked like they fell into quarrel, not being able to realise the complex shape of the elephant. When applied to social science, this story implies that social phenomena are often complex and scholars in their debates may touch various aspects of a complicated reality but often fail to see the aggregated whole.

To conceptualise discretion, let us briefly observe the structure of the Chinese political system and the position of the implementers in linking state and society. In contrast to other regimes (most notably a federal regime) in which the central/national level and local/municipal levels are distinct in their responsibilities—formulating policies and executing them (as long as the municipal/local level does not violate national principles, rules and regulations)—this distinction is very blurred in China. While every level in the political hierarchy is responsible for managing its own jurisdiction according to local needs and circumstances, it is also responsible simultaneously for executing higher-level policies and regulations. For the higher levels, this dual position of enactor and executor is not a real day-to-day matter, as they are detached from rural reality, and the higher level's responsibility as executor may be summed up as formulating policy documents and circulating them to the level beneath. But, this becomes a real dilemma for grassroots officials, especially when policies from above stand in contrast to local needs and interests. It is this triangle—the need to execute policies and demands from above; the need to manage and regulate their own area of jurisdiction, and to sustain the local bureaucratic machine; and the need to serve the people and local communities—that forms the most basic framework for understanding and evaluating grassroots officials' decision-making and conduct.[2]

The presumption when studying discretion is that each of these factors make separate demands on grassroots officials that they must reconcile during implementation. Only after reconciling these pressures can grassroots officials exercise *genuine* discretion—if there is any space left for them—to shape implementation (and therefore its outcomes). From this view, policy implementation is a delicate contexture of subjection to pressures on the one hand and genuine discretion on the other.

A thorough understanding of policy implementation must refer to three major questions: 1) why are policies implemented, 2) how are they implemented and 3) what outcomes and impacts have they achieved? Discretion relates directly to the first two questions and indirectly to the third question. In the following I will elaborate on each of the first two questions. When added together, this can be viewed as a two-step model for analysing policy implementation. After

---

2   Thomas Bernstein and Xiaobo Lü have depicted this well. In their words:

> A good many village cadres felt trapped by their situation: 'We are all peasants, our families contract for land, we understand the peasants, but who understands us? ... We get blamed by both sides. The higher levels demand money from us ... each year we have to ask several times, causing the elders and our relatives to feel offended.' It is quite plausible that some of these cross-pressured cadres might have led collective protest.

See Bernstein and Lü, 'Taxation without Representation', 758.

discussing discretion, I will show that applying this perspective to analyse the case of the Village Redevelopment Program teaches us some new lessons about China and the operation of its state bureaucracy.

Step 1: Why Do Grassroots Officials Implement Policies?

The question of why grassroots officials implement or refrain from implementing policies has attracted much attention from scholars. Based on the literature and the case of the Village Redevelopment Program, Chart 7.1 offers a general mapping of the main influences on the decisions of grassroots officials about whether to implement a policy or not.

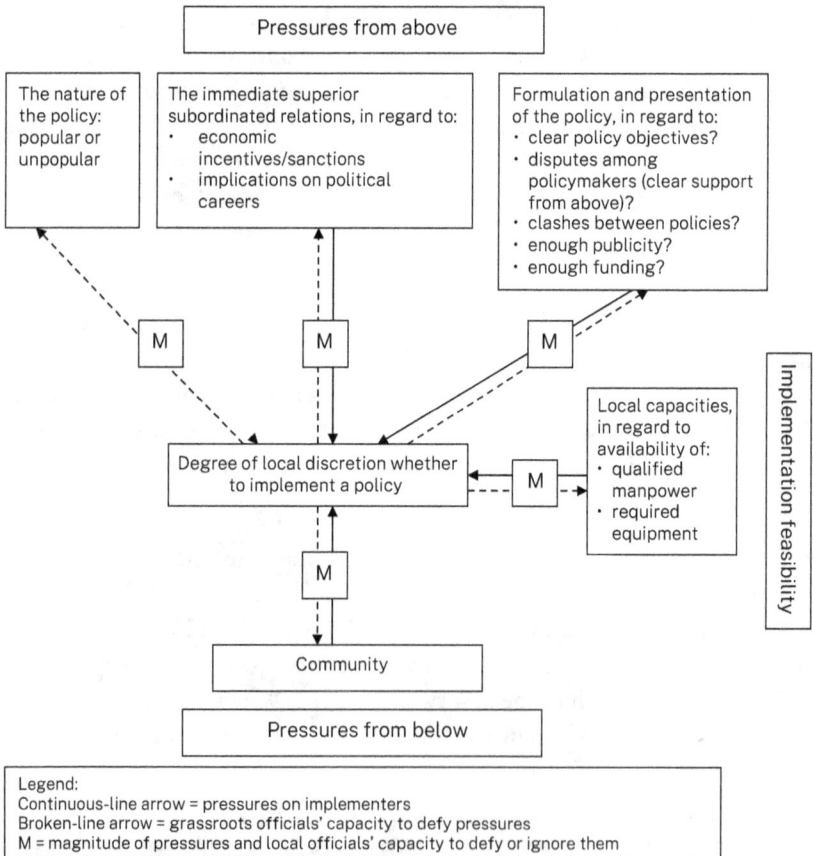

Chart 7.1: Why are policies implemented?
Source: Compiled by author.

It is common for scholars to point to power relations and means of coercion to explain why some policies are implemented while others are not. This is not entirely surprising, as most studies of policy implementation focus on cases of selective implementation of unpopular policies. A general typology of the body of knowledge would entail what we can call 'pressures from above', 'pressures from below' and 'implementation feasibility'. Scholars who have studied pressures from above have tended to focus on the hierarchical nature of the Chinese political system and the politics of command as the main explanatory factors. Some have focused on several policy questions, for example: To what extent has the national party-state succeeded in conveying a message that a policy is high priority and must be obeyed? Are messages regarding the policy and its targets clear? Does the message conveyed by the centre suggest unanimous support at the top for the policy? Do the policy goals clash with other policies and does this decrease (or increase) the prospects that it will ultimately be implemented by grassroots officials?[3] The question of funding is also seen as an important factor that may have an impact on local officials' decisions. This is especially important when remembering that most localities in China are in heavy debt.[4] Others have suggested focusing on the immediate relations between superiors and subordinates, giving special attention to mechanisms such as the 'one-level-down management' and the 'Cadres' Responsibility System', which the central government introduced in the 1980s in its attempt to control local agents and secure their loyalty.[5]

Local communities may also pressure grassroots officials to influence the implementers to carry out popular policies and refrain from taking on unpopular ones. Formal mechanisms, such as grassroots elections, and less formal mechanisms, such as rightful resistance, writing letters of complaint and petitions, protests and appeals to social affinity, are examples of what rural communities can undertake in their attempt to influence the implementers.[6] Local capacities also play a role in deciding local officials'

---

3   Rosen, 'Restoring Key Secondary Schools', 351; O'Brien and Li, 'Accommodating "Democracy"', 478–81; Lieberthal, 'China's Governing System', 6–7; Zweig, 'Context and Content', 255–83; White, 'Implementing the "One-Child-Per-Couple"', 284–317; Edin, 'State Capacity', 36; Wright, 'State Capacity in Contemporary China', 185–86; Kennedy, 'State Capacity and Support', 383–410; Harding, *Organizing China*, 350–51.

4   Zhao, 'The Debt Chaos', 36–44; Zhao, 'Hard-Pressed Township Finances', 45–54; Göbel, *The Politics of Rural Reform*, especially ch. 2.

5   Ho, *Rural China in Transition*, 221–25; Edin, 'State Capacity', 35–52; Whiting, *Power and Wealth*, ch. 3; O'Brien and Li, 'Selective Policy Implementation', 171–74.

6   See, for example, O'Brien and Li, 'Selective Policy Implementation', 176–80; O'Brien and Li, *Rightful Resistance*; Bernstein and Lü, *Taxation without Representation*; Tsai, *Accountability without Democracy*.

approach towards a policy. For example, whether or not a local government has the professional ability and equipment may be crucial to its ability to meet required goals.[7]

Of course, we should not assume that every time officials are required to implement a policy or meet a certain goal they are likely to confront all of these pressures. Depending on the context, various pressures may or may not be present. But, even when pressures are applied, local officials may still have a wide range of options to defy them according to their own interests. The question of the magnitude of existing pressures and of grassroots officials' ability to defy them, therefore, is essential to understanding local officials' priorities. The most notable examples are the goals of social stability and adherence to family planning, for which any violations may endanger local officials' professional careers. In such cases, the magnitude of superior–subordinate relations are so strong that it obscures all other considerations. After the officials have reconciled all of the pressures, they are then likely to decide a policy's destiny.

The Village Redevelopment Program fits poorly into this body of policies that has so far dominated the literature. This is because it represents a group of policies that scholars have paid insufficient attention to while researching policy implementation in China. These are policies that officials do not implement because of coerciveness but (mainly) because they welcome them as coinciding with local needs and interests.

To be sure, commandism and subjection to superiors are indispensable parts of the implementation of any policy in China. In the case of the Village Redevelopment Program, almost none of the villages in Beian and Chenggu had redeveloped themselves before the announcement of BNSC. Officials from both counties made it perfectly clear that superiors expected them to implement this program, which was among the foci of the Chinese Communist Party's and State Council's national agenda. The involvement of higher levels and the act of institutionalising the program by establishing designated offices and leading groups, headed by the most senior political figures in the county party/government, and the incorporation of villages' redevelopment into performance evaluations of the townships' work, all conveyed a clear message to grassroots officials that rejecting or ignoring the redevelopment program was not an option.

---

7   See, for example, Swanson, Kuhn and Xu, 'Environmental Policy Implementation', 486–87.

However, county and township officials in both counties did not refer to commandism or coercion to explain the reasons for implementation in their localities. From their viewpoint, the state was not implementing this policy against their will and they did not perceive their superiors as coercive figures. On the contrary, officials often expressed great support for redeveloping their villages, and praised the centre for announcing the BNSC policy. They perceived higher government levels as partners for achieving a common goal despite their role as inspectors and monitors.

Local support was an aggregated outcome. First, grassroots officials in both counties agreed that solving social disparities and decreasing inequality between rural and urban populaces, two main goals of BNSC, were needed not only for the sake of China's social stability and a prosperous national economy but also, more concretely, to boost the counties' local economy and their residents' wellbeing. Second, local officials did not experience implementation as burdensome. Most important was the fact that many villagers, similar to local officials, supported the policy and its goals. As those who were located on the inferior side of the urban–rural disparities equation, they shared the desire and were willing to contribute to introducing significant changes into their rural reality. The allocation of government subsidies to support the redevelopment project facilitated further local support. Although covering only a small part of the total expense, even in wealthy villages where redevelopment costs did not impose any economic burden on local coffers, villagers expressed their gratitude to the central and local government(s) for their material support. From the villagers' viewpoint, this was another facet of the larger picture of a new stage of state–society relations that had emerged following the announcement of the BNSC program. Significant government investments in rural areas in education and healthcare insurance, as well as direct subsidies[8] to agriculture, strengthened this view.

Another important factor that influenced local views was the expectation that local communities would bear most of the redevelopment cost and not the government. Although there was an implicit expectation that governments at all levels would support redevelopment projects financially, in both counties, superiors paid attention to townships' and village governments' economic conditions, and poor townships were largely exempted from bearing this financial cost. Moreover, since in both counties redevelopment

---

8   On the central government allocating direct subsidies to rural areas in the 2000s, see Lin and Wong, 'Are Beijing's Equalization Policies', 23–45. See also Chapter 1 (this book).

did not involve all villages, local officials had not (yet) had to confront cases of reluctance. Last, by delineating only the general lines of the policy, the centre left enough room for the local state's bureaucracies to interpret and operationalise the policy according to their perception of local conditions.

Step 2: How Are Policies Implemented?

After a decision to carry out a policy has been made, officials organise implementation. As noted, local government modus operandi has not been subject to systematic research, and this book meets this gap in the literature. By integrating the questions of *why* and *how* policies are implemented into a unified model for analysing the entire process of policy implementation, I am suggesting that the modus operandi of the local state should also be analysed from the same theoretical perspective as the question of why policies are implemented—that is, as a culmination of reconciling pressures on the one hand and genuine discretion on the other hand. Locating the modus operandi in between discretion and coercion applies to popular and unpopular policies alike, leading to the question of how to ensure successful implementation.

Since policy implementation normally occurs at the lowest ranks of the political system, we can expect the main possible shapers to involve the immediate superiors (as the link between grassroots levels and higher levels of the political hierarchy) and/or local communities as recipients of the policy (although factors such as whether a local government has the professional ability and equipment may influence modes of implementation as well). Chart 7.2 presents a general mapping of the main shapers of the modus operandi of grassroots officials.

While studies of implementation have observed the significant role supervisors play in setting targets and pushing their subordinates to meet them, they have not taken the further step to question the role supervisors play in deciding how these targets are to be met. The case of the Village Redevelopment Program shows that supervisors can play a very significant role in how policies are eventually carried out on the ground. Practices of setting quotas and quantitative targets, operationalising the policy, delineating clear criteria for inspection and supervising have all reinforced loyalty to superiors' instructions and significantly decreased implementers' discretion regarding the implementation strategies and modus operandi.

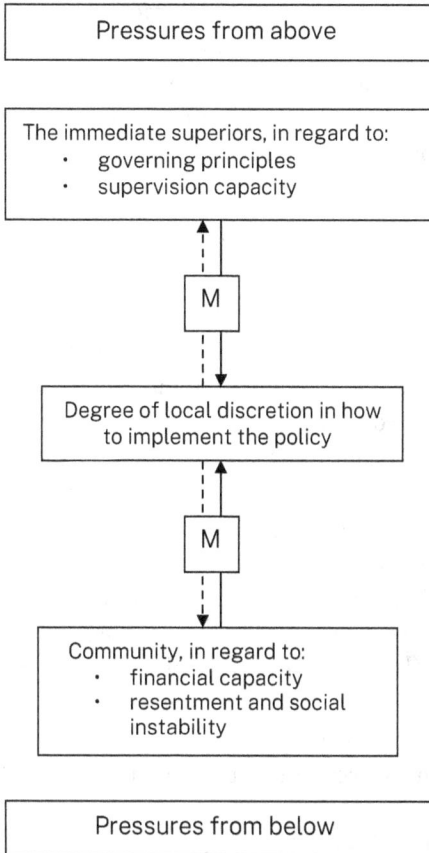

Chart 7.2: Possible shapers of the modus operandi of grassroots officials
Source: Compiled by author.

Regarding local communities, scholars have blurred the questions of how and why local officials implement policies as against general questions about these communities' ability to curb local officials' discretion and predatory behaviour. Researchers have discussed mechanisms such as electing grassroots officials, writing letters and lodging complaints to the media or the 'letters and visits offices' (*xinfang bangongshi* 信访办公室), learning relevant laws and suing officials for malpractice, 'resisting rightfully', protesting and using violence, and appealing to social affinity as possibly influencing implementers' decisions and their modus operandi. In addition, in the village redevelopment case, as we saw in previous chapters, avoiding social instability and taking account of the financial capacities of the different communities played a significant role in shaping conduct and implementation approaches.

Looking at 'discretion' in the modus operandi, the case of the Village Redevelopment Program teaches us significant lessons about contemporary China. First, it testifies to the vitality and importance of a politics of command, in shaping implementers' decision to go (or not to go) ahead and how to do so. One of the differences in modes of implementation between Chenggu and Beian was the manifestation and magnitude of a politics of command in each of the counties. As we saw, officials in Chenggu expressed high levels of loyalty and conformity to their superiors. This was also true of officials in Beian in cases where higher levels intervened with clear instructions (such as the provincial demand to redevelop 25 'demonstration villages'; although the county could have chosen to redevelop more, it chose to follow the exact original quota as imposed from above). Conformity to local commands and governing principles also pushed local officials in both counties to choose the better off first and bolstered their notion that there was nothing they could do to assist the poorer communities. When they had to decide between conformity with superiors' views or attentiveness to communal needs, the implementers' choice was clear: loyalty to superiors came first.

Shifting away from issues of unpopular policies and selective policy implementation, the Village Redevelopment Program presents a new kind of accountability that, to date, has attracted much less scholarly attention. In this kind of policy implementation, the 'traditional' top-to-bottom coercive structure to impose unwanted policy targets from above diminished, in favour of cooperation and attentiveness, creating symbiotic relations between residents, villages and local governments in which each player was dependent on the others for successes and benefits. This was a direct result of the delicate social-political-economic construction of the redevelopment program. Its desire to meet a *real* need was what facilitated its welcome by grassroots officials and villagers. Subordinating redevelopment to avoidance of resentment and social instability served as a buffer against 'crash-campaign implementation'.[9] The lack of unrealistic

---

9   The notion of a 'crash campaign' is taken from Greenhalgh and Winckler, *Governing China's Population*.

targets from above created a relaxed implementation atmosphere in both counties, and the existence of government financial support to distribute to villages encouraged grassroots participation. Unlike cases of unpopular and/or extractive policies, or even previous developmental policies that were often used to justify ill-conceived investments and wasteful construction,[10] successful implementation was not perceived as a zero-sum game, but instead as a win-win situation.

Moreover, the case of the Village Redevelopment Program shakes one of the most common conceptualisations of hierarchical relations in the Chinese political system—the paradigm of principal–agent relations.[11] As a top-down approach, a main assumption of this model is that successful implementation of a policy is dependent on the ability of the principal to control his/her agent. However, the Village Redevelopment Program presents a very different situation. Choosing the better off first, thereby sabotaging the original goal of the policy, was not a consequence of the principal's inability to control the agent. Grassroots officials did not shun their superiors' understanding and operationalisation of the policy in either county. On the contrary. Officials in both Chenggu and Beian were obedient and loyal to their superiors' commands and expectations. The problem was that the principal himself issued governing directives that significantly narrowed the prospects of local officials meeting the BNSC policy's original goals in one of its most central aspects. The understanding that superiors, at all levels of the political system, have the power not only to decide a policy but also to sabotage it and reduce its prospects of success by their own commands and governing principles provides an alternative, yet complementary, understanding of state capacity in post-Mao China. Indeed, when this happens, even in cases of popular policies in which all players share the will for success, there is very little that implementers can do to change the fate of the policy.

So what are China's prospects of succeeding ultimately in its ambitious project of village redevelopment and in decreasing social disparity and inequality? On the one hand, this book is optimistic. No doubt, by announcing the BNSC program, China has entered a new stage of state–society relations. This is a stage in which the state, at its highest levels, is willing to take responsibility for rural areas and to allocate significant amounts of resources to support rural problems.

---

10 I thank Professor Li Lianjiang for highlighting this point.
11 The principal–agent relations framework is discussed in Chapter 1.

The sense of urgency in decreasing rural–urban disparities and improving rural wellbeing has continued under the current leadership of Xi Jinping and Li Keqiang, with an ambitious goal of completely eradicating absolute poverty in rural areas[12] and establishing a 'moderately prosperous society' (*xiaokang shehui* 小康社会) by 2020. New national policies were announced to further guide rural development nationwide, including (to note a few examples) policies of constructing 'beautiful villages' (*meili xiangcun* 美丽乡村),[13] 'rural vitalization'[14] (*xiangcun zhenxing* 乡村振兴) and the 'three clean-ups (*san qing* 三清), three transformations (*san gai* 三改), three constructions (*san jian* 三建) and "three-isations"' (*san hua* 三化).[15] Meanwhile, the BNSC ostensibly began losing momentum.[16] Yet, a close observation of these (and other) recent policies reveals many similarities in their vision of a developed Chinese countryside in the twenty-first century. Policies have continued along the lines introduced and developed under the BNSC paradigm, including rural urbanisation, urban–rural integration, rural inhabitants' relocation, improving rural infrastructure and social services, ecological and environmental protection, improving the local rural economy and fiscal government prioritisation.[17]

This paradigmatic continuity at the national level was reflected in continued efforts to redevelop villages in Chenggu and Beian.[18] In Chenggu, a new policy called *san hua* (三化, the three-isations) was introduced to guide villages' redevelopment, focusing on three large areas of improvement:

---

12 Eradication of absolute poverty refers to guaranteeing the population of China's poorer rural areas with food, clothing, safe housing, free education and basic medical care. See, for example, 'China Near to Eliminating Poverty', *China Daily*, 27 December 2019, www.chinadaily.com.cn/a/201912/27/WS5 e04ebbaa310cf3e35580e33.html, accessed 31 October 2021. Some have criticised the CCP for ignoring urban poverty and for targeting only low standards of wellbeing in the rural areas. See, for example, Westcott and Wang, 'Xi Jinping Is Determined'.

13 This policy has gained momentum, particularly since 2014, under the guidance of the Ministry of Agriculture.

14 See, for example, Li, 'Road to Rural Vitalization', 18–20.

15 The three 'isations' refer to: 1) greening (*lühua*), 2) lightening (*lianghua*) and 3) beautifying the villages (*meihua*). For more detail on the policy see, for example, zgxncw.cn/News/n3292.html, accessed 21 October 2021.

16 Ahlers, *Rural Policy Implementation*, 216.

17 'The "Three Cleansing, Three Reforming, Three Building and Three Modernization" Plans in Rural Areas Will Help the Construction of New Rural Areas and Develop Beautiful New Villages!', Yuwei Life Encyclopedia, 24 July 2019, www.360kuai.com/pc/9dedb52c96d79d2d5?cota=3&kuai_so=1&sign=360 _7bc3b157, accessed 31 October 2022. On the central authorities' perception of the construction of rural communities under the leadership of Xi Jinping and their implementation at the grassroots levels, see Meyer-Clement, 'Rural Urbanization', 187–207.

18 As noted in Chapter 1, since I left Beian and Chenggu I lost my contacts in both counties due to personnel transitions and I have not been able to return. The following is based mainly on available written resources.

paving (or hardening) additional roads, sanitation and beautifying the villages. According to local sources, a sense of competitiveness and a will to excel in implementation has guided the Chenggu government, which, in 2015, became the first county in the prefecture to implement basic standards of the *san hua* in its villages.

Side by side with the implementation of the *san hua* policy, the prefecture has continued to promote and regulate the 'advanced' redevelopment policy of restructuring villages into new 'rural communities' (*nongcun shequ* 农村社区). In 2016, the prefecture announced an ambitious goal to have more than 500 'well-constructed' and 'fully functioning' 'service centres' (*nongcun shequ fuwu zhongxin* 农村社区服务中心) within its jurisdiction by 2018 to facilitate accessibility and consumption of basic services by rural residents.[19] To support this goal, the prefecture earmarked RMB6 million and, in 2017, conducted inspections of entire counties and districts to investigate the implementation and progress of this project.[20] A local document published by the prefecture that year described the importance of the construction of rural communities:

> With the acceleration of new (*xinxing* 新型) industrialisation, informatisation (*xinxihua* 信息化), urbanisation, and agricultural modernisation, rural society is undergoing profound changes while traditional villages are 'disappearing' one after another and the villagers' networks of daily life are breaking down. In this process, many new situations and problems in grassroots social governance are slowly surfacing. The rural community is the basic unit of rural social and governance services. Construction of rural communities is constructive not only for promoting integration and interaction between government administrative management, public services and villagers' self- management and self-services, but also for enhancing the rural communities' autonomy and service (provision) capacity, laying solid foundations for farmers' wellbeing, sustainable agricultural development and rural harmony and stability.

In Chenggu, where construction of new rural communities had gained high support all along, new land use policies have continued to be implemented, such as the policy of 'linking increases and decreases of urban and rural construction land' (*chengxiang jianshe yongdi zengjian guagou* 城乡建设

---

19   Service centres are compulsory institutions that the central authorities (most notably the Ministry of Civil Affairs) demand to be constructed in each 'rural community'.

20   Unfortunately, the inspection's outcomes were not published publicly.

用地增减挂钩). [21] This further increases local governments' motivation to restructure the countryside, as a means to facilitate land transfers between rural and urban settlements, to further consolidate rural–urban integration and development of the county's rural towns.[22] According to local documents, 90 rural communities involving 136 villages and almost 600 rural service points (*nongcun shequ fuwu wangdian* 农村社区服务网点) were already under construction by 2014, and the total accumulative investment exceeded RMB4 billion. Twenty-thousand rural households had already moved into new residences by that time.

In 2017, Chenggu gained an important achievement with the inclusion of Village A4—one of Chenggu's most prosperous villages and a shining exemplar for the construction of new rural communities—in a national list compiled by the Ministry of Civil Affairs of the 100 most successful demonstration villages. By 2020, projects to relocate villagers into new rural communities had expanded to nearly all townships, including the previously excluded rural ones (though still on a minor scale compared to the county's industrialised and urban centres).

Endeavours to redevelop villages have also continued in Beian. In 2014, the policy of constructing 'beautiful villages' was announced in Beian as a comprehensive framework to guide rural development in the county. Village redevelopment, as before, included better sanitation; paving rural roads; beautifying villages; constructing sporting, cultural and leisure facilities; and renovating service-provision infrastructures etc. Yet, unlike in prosperous Chenggu, where redevelopment (either the 'simple' model of redeveloping villages individually or the more 'advanced' model of merged rural communities) has affected practically all villages in the county, in Beian, implementation has occurred much more slowly and has continued to affect mainly the central hamlets (*zhongxin cun* 中心村) of administrative villages in the county hinterland.

Apart from poorer economic conditions, a main reason for Beian's slower pace of implementation was a significant change in the county's interpretation of the redevelopment program in terms of the 'beautiful villages' policy. The emphasis shifted from simple improvement of the physical living environment within villages to a more comprehensive integration of physical redevelopment with broader aspects of 'rural

---

21   This policy is discussed in Chapter 3.
22   Chenggu was selected as an experimental site for this policy by the Shandong provincial government.

ecology, environmental protection, and improvement of agriculture and the local rural economy'. In many villages, this translated into projects of rural eco-tourism (*shengtai lüyou* 生态旅游), for example: developing ecological agriculture (particularly blueberries, strawberries and plum blossom, for self-picking and sightseeing); establishing 'leisure tourism villages' (*meili xiuxian lüyou xiangcun* 美丽休闲旅游乡村); building fishing centres; organising festivals during the fruit picking months; and organising sports activities and competitions. To support this positioning of the county as a tourist centre, the prefecture and provincial governments held several conferences in the county on issues such as fitness and rural leisure.

Yet, despite its claims of shaping a *new* countryside, village redevelopment has failed to break the most basic rules of the system that supports the perpetuation of inequality and disparity. A decade and a half of implementation has resulted in significantly more villages enjoying the benefits of rural redevelopment in industrialised Chenggu than in agricultural Beian. In both counties, the villages that were already prosperous remain the program's main beneficiaries. Ironically, it seems that the redevelopment program has turned into another state mechanism to support and benefit the better located and better off rural areas over the 'periphery' (the agricultural, remote and poor rural areas).

The discriminatory nature of this is demonstrated by another model of implementation I encountered when I researched South Field, a rural community in a recently urbanised district north of Qingdao City, Shandong Province, in 2016. At the heart of this model, which mostly prevails in rural areas with lucrative land and developed local real estate markets (usually due to urbanisation and industrialisation and/or commercialisation), are contracts signed with construction companies in exchange for construction rights in 'development zones' (*kaifa qu* 开发区). In South Field, construction of a new rural community began in 2008 and was completed within a year and a half. A construction company was contracted to build the entire new community: six-storey apartment buildings, public buildings, recreation areas and infrastructure. In return, the company received construction rights on more than 6.5 hectares of the village's land and built multistorey buildings of up to 16 storeys, which it sold at market prices. As part of the deal, each of South Field's households were allocated two to three apartments within the new community[23] in exchange for their old village houses and tiny agricultural plots (less than 1 mu per household).

The contrast between South Field, Beian and Chenggu is telling: in agricultural Beian, even 'simple' redevelopment had to rely on villagers' investment; in richer Chenggu, villagers were expected to buy their new residences by themselves; yet villagers in South Field (who, despite their old village's underdevelopment enjoyed higher incomes than their counterparts in Chenggu and Beian due to their proximity to industrialised Qingdao's developed labour markets) [24] were completely exempt from any expense as part of their village reconstruction. So lucrative was the village land that the villagers could enjoy a well-constructed community (at higher standards than any new community I witnessed in Chenggu) and two or three apartments for free.[25]

Village redevelopment was announced as a central part of Chinese leaders' efforts to solve rural problems and decrease inequality and disparity. Yet, in reality, it achieved the opposite. The cases of Chenggu and Beian demonstrate not only that this is an outcome of divergence in local economic capacities but that it also reflects the fundamental failure of the entire political bureaucracy to adjust politics of command to varying social-political-economic circumstances at the local level. If China is to appropriately tackle rural problems, new priorities and new modus operandi are desperately needed. These can be introduced by only the highest levels of the political hierarchy. With very little leeway for genuine discretion, grassroots officials are simply too weak to do so.

---

23   Each household received two apartments. Those who had a son received a third apartment, to better ensure the son would reside within the community and support the parents.
24   According to local statistics, when the BNSC was announced average per capita rural incomes in the rural areas administered by Qingdao City were 80 per cent higher than the national rural average, compared with 46 per cent higher in Chenggu and only 11 per cent higher in Beian.
25   On this model, see, for example, Chung and Unger, 'The Guangdong Model', 33–41. This model often entailed additional financial benefits for the villages and its residents; however, a thorough discussion of this point exceeds the scope of this book.

References

Ahlers, Anna L., *Rural Policy Implementation in Contemporary China: New Socialist Countryside*. New York: Routledge, 2014, doi.org/10.4324/9781315869742.

Ahlers, Anna L. and Gunter Schubert, '"Building a New Socialist Countryside"—Only a Political Slogan?', *Journal of Current Chinese Affairs* 38, no. 4 (2009): 35–62, doi.org/10.1177/186810260903800403.

Ahlers, Anna L. and Gunter Schubert, 'Strategic Modelling: "Building a New Socialist Countryside" in Three Chinese Counties', *China Quarterly*, no. 216 (2013): 831–49, doi.org/10.1017/s0305741013001045.

Anagnost, Ann, 'The Corporeal Politics of Quality (Suzhi)', *Public Culture* 16, no. 2 (2004): 189–208, doi.org/10.1215/08992363-16-2-189.

Anhui Province Statistical Yearbook. Beijing: China Statistics Press (Zhongguo Tongji Chubanshe), various years.

Bakken, Børge, *The Exemplary Society: Human Improvement, Social Control, and the Dangers of Modernity in China*. New York: Oxford University Press Inc., 2000.

Beian County Statistical Yearbook. Beian: Beian Statistical Bureau, various years.

Bernstein, Thomas P., 'Unrest in Rural China: A 2003 Assessment', CSD Working Papers, Center of the Studies of Democracy, UC Irvine, 2004.

Bernstein, Thomas P. and Xiaobo Lü, *Taxation without Representation in Contemporary Rural China*. Cambridge: Cambridge University Press, 2003, doi.org/10.1017/s1537592704690694.

Bernstein, Thomas P. and Xiaobo Lü, 'Taxation without Representation: Peasants, the Central and the Local States in Reform China', *China Quarterly*, no. 163 (2000): 742–63, doi.org/10.1017/s0305741000014648.

Boisot, Max and John Child, 'The Iron Law of Fiefs: Bureaucratic Failure and the Problem of Governance in the Chinese Economic Reforms', *Administrative Science Quarterly* 33, no. 4 (1988): 507–27, doi.org/10.2307/2392641.

Bray, David, *Social Space and Governance in Urban China: The* Danwei *System from Origins to Reform*. Stanford: Stanford University Press, 2005, doi.org/10.1017/s0305741006260247.

Bray, David, 'Urban Planning Goes Rural: Conceptualizing the "New Village"', *China Perspectives*, no. 3 (2013): 53–62, doi.org/10.4000/chinaperspectives.6273.

Burch, Betty B., 'Models as Agents of Change in China'. In *Value Change in Chinese Society*, edited by Richard W. Wilson, Amy Auerbacher Wilson and Sidney L. Greenblatt, 122–36. New York: Praeger Publishers, 1979, doi.org/10.1017/s0305741000012492.

Cai, Yongshun, 'Between State and Peasant: Local Cadres and Statistical Reporting in Rural China', *China Quarterly*, no. 163 (2000): 783–805, doi.org/10.1017/s0305741000014661.

Cai, Yongshun, 'Irresponsible State: Local Cadres and Image-Building in China', *Journal of Communist Studies and Transition Politics* 20, no. 4 (2004): 20–41, doi.org/10.1080/1352327042000306039.

Cailliez, Charlotte, 'Nongcun weisheng zhidu de zhuangkuang' [The situation of the health system in the villages]. In *Jinru 21 shiji de Zhongguo nongcun* [Rural China enters the 21st century], edited by Jingming Xiong, 238–48. Beijing: Guangming Ribao Chubanshe, 2000.

Chen, Biding, 'Tuijin "dabaogan" xiang "zaibaogan" de xin fazhan' [The new development of shifting from a "household responsibility system" to a "new responsibility system"], *Zhongguo Jingji Shibao* [China economic times], 31 August 2009.

Chen, Guidi and Wu Chuntao, *Will the Boat Sink the Water?* New York: PublicAffairs, 2006.

Chen, Weixing, 'Politics and Paths of Rural Development in China: The Village Conglomerate in Shandong Province', *Pacific Affairs* 71, no. 1 (1998): 25–39, doi.org/10.2307/2760821.

Chenggu County Statistical Yearbook. Chenggu: Chenggu Statistical Bureau, various years.

China Labour Bulletin, 'Migrant Workers and Their Children', 4 May 2021, clb.org.hk/content/migrant-workers-and-their-children, accessed 21 October 2021.

China Statistical Yearbook. Beijing: China Statistics Press (Zhongguo Tongji Chubanshe), various years.

Chung, Him and Jonathan Unger, 'The Guangdong Model of Urbanization: Collective Village Land and the Making of a New Middle Class', *China Perspectives*, no. 3 (2013): 33–41.

Crissman, Lawrence W., 'G. William Skinner's Spatial Analysis of Complex Societies: Its Importance for Anthropology', *Taiwan Journal of Anthropology* 8, no. 1 (2010): 27–45.

Crouch, Colin, *Industrial Relations and European State Traditions*. Oxford: Clarendon Press, 1993.

Cummings, Sally N. and Ole Nørgaard, 'Conceptualizing State Capacity: Comparing Kazakhstan and Kyrgyzstan', *Political Studies* 52, no. 4 (2004): 685–708, doi.org/ 10.1111/j.1467-9248.2004.00503.x.

Dang, Guoying, 'Zhongguo de xin nongcun yinggai shi zheyang de' [China's new countryside must be this way], *Xuexi Shibao* [Study times], 20 October 2007.

Deininger, Klaus, Songqing Jin, Zude Xian and Scott Rozelle, 'Implementing China's New Land Law: Evidence and Policy Lessons', Stanford University, Working Paper, 2004, aparc.fsi.stanford.edu/publications/implementing_chinas_new_land _law_evidence_and_policy_lessons, accessed 20 October 2021.

Diamond, Norma, 'Model Villages and Village Realities', *Modern China* 9, no. 2 (1983): 163–81.

Edin, Maria, 'State Capacity and Local Agent Control in China: CCP Cadre Management from a Township Perspective', *China Quarterly*, no. 173 (2003): 35–52, doi.org/10.1017/s0009443903000044.

Fewsmith, Joseph, 'The Elusive Search for Effective Sub-County Governance'. In *Mao's Invisible Hand: The Political Foundations of Adaptive Governance in China*, edited by Sebastian Heilmann and Elizabeth J. Perry, 269–96. Cambridge: Harvard University Asia Center, 2011, doi.org/10.2307/j.ctt1sq5tc6.15.

Fock, Achim and Christine Wong, 'China: Public Services for Building the New Socialist Countryside'. Washington, DC: The World Bank, Report 40221-CN, 2007, documents.worldbank.org/curated/en/527001468218981236/pdf/ 402210CN.pdf, accessed 1 November 2022.

Fu, Ruren, Liexing Hui, Yuanheng Yang, Xuewu Wei, Daonian Su and Chaowei Yue, 'Shandong sheng shehuizhuyi xin nongcun jianshe xian ji fenlei zhibiao tixi yanjiu' [Research on Building a New Socialist Countryside's indicators at the county level in the province of Shandong]. In *Xin nongcun jianshe jiaqiang fenlei zhidao: yanjiu yu tansuo* [Strengthening guidance in Building the New Socialist Countryside: Research and exploration], edited by Ruren Fu, 37–54. Jinan: Huanghe Chubanshe, 2007.

Fu, Ruren, Xuewu Wei, Daonian Su, Chaowei Yue, Shanfeng Li, Yuanheng Yang and Min Song, 'Guanyu dui Shandong sheng shehuizhuyi xin nongcun jianshe jiaqiang fenlei zhidao de zonghe yanjiu baogao' [Integrated research about strengthening guidance in Building a New Socialist Countryside in Shandong Province]. In *Xin nongcun jianshe jiaqiang fenlei zhidao: yanjiu yu tansuo* [*Strengthening Guidance in Building the New Socialist Countryside: Research and Exploration*], edited by Ruren Fu, 3–34. Jinan: Huanghe Chubanshe, 2007.

Gao, Lingzhi, Hongbin Yang and Yanan Wang, 'Shandong liang xian hecun bingju ji nongcun shequ jianshe qingkuang diaocha' [Investigation of merging villages and rural community building in two counties, Shandong Province], *Zhongguo Fazhan* 11, no. 3 (2011): 53–60.

Gao, Mobo C. F., *Gao Village: A Portrait of Rural Life in Modern China*. London: Hurst & Company, 1999.

General Office of the CCP Central Committee and the General Office of the State Council, '*Guanyu shenru tuijin nongcun shequ jianshe shidian gongzuo de zhidao yijian*' [Instructions on further promoting the pilot work of constructing rural communities], 31 May 2015.

Göbel, Christian, *The Politics of Rural Reform in China: State Policy and Village Predicament in the Early 2000s*. New York: Routledge, 2010, doi.org/10.4324/9780203849767.

Greenhalgh, Susan and Edwin A. Winckler, *Governing China's Population: From Leninist to Neoliberal Biopolitics*. Stanford: Stanford University Press, 2005, doi.org/10.1111/j.1548-1425.2008.00073.x.

Grindle, Merilee S., 'Policy Content and Context in Implementation'. In *Politics and Policy Implementation in the Third World*, edited by in Merilee S. Grindle, 3–39. Princeton, New Jersey: Princeton University Press, 1980, doi.org/10.1002/pad.4230020308.

Guo, Xiaolin, 'Land Expropriation and Rural Conflicts in China', *China Quarterly*, no. 166 (2001): 422–39, doi.org/10.1017/s0009443901000201.

Guo, Yanan, 'Nongcun shequ jianshe zhong cunzai de wenti ji qi duice' [Problems and countermeasures during the construction of rural communities], *Zhongguo Fazhan Guancha*, no. 11 (2012), theory.people.com.cn/n/2012/1127/c40531-19715962.html, accessed 20 October 2021.

Guowuyuan fazhan yanjiu zhongxin [Development Research Centre of the State Council of the PRC], 'Xin nongcun diaocha: zoujin quanguo 2749 ge cunzhuang [Investigating the new countryside: Into 2749 villages nationwide'], 2007.

Han, Guoming and He Wang, 'Woguo gonggong zhengce zhixing de shifan fangshi shixiao fenxi: jiyu shifan cun jianshe ge'an de yanjiu' [Analysis of failures in the demonstration mode in China's public policy implementation: The case of constructing demonstration villages], *Zhongguo Xingzheng Guanli* [Chinese public administration], no. 4 (2012): 38–42.

Han, Seung-Mi, 'The New Community Movement: Park Chung Hee and the Making of State Populism in Korea', *Pacific Affairs* 77, no. 1 (2004): 69–93.

Harding, Harry, *Organizing China: The Problem of Bureaucracy 1949–1976*. Stanford: Stanford University Press, 1981, doi.org/10.1086/ahr/88.2.453.

Heberer, Thomas and Anja Senz, 'Streamlining Local Behaviour through Communication, Incentives and Control: A Case Study of Local Environmental Policies in China', *Journal of Current Chinese Affairs* 40, no. 3 (2011): 77–112, doi.org/10.1177/186810261104000304.

Heberer, Thomas and René Trappel, 'Evaluation Processes, Local Cadres' Behaviour and Local Development Processes', *Journal of Contemporary China* 22, no. 84 (2013): 1048–66, doi.org/10.1080/10670564.2013.795315.

Heilmann, Sebastian, 'From Local Experiments to National Policy: The Origins of China's Distinctive Policy Process', *China Journal*, no. 59 (2008): 1–30, doi.org/10.1086/tcj.59.20066378.

Heilmann, Sebastian, 'Policy-Making through Experimentation: The Formation of a Distinctive Policy Process'. In *Mao's Invisible Hand*, edited by Sebastian Heilmann and Elizabeth J. Perry, 62–101. Cambridge and London: Harvard University Press, 2011, doi.org/10.2307/j.ctt1sq5tc6.9.

Heilmann, Sebastian and Elizabeth J. Perry (eds), *Mao's Invisible Hand: The Political Foundations of Adaptive Governance in China*. Cambridge: Harvard University Asia Center, 2011, doi.org/10.3138/cjh.47.3.708.

Hillman, Ben, 'Factions and Spoils: Examining Political Behavior within the Local State in China', *China Journal*, no. 64 (2010): 1–18, doi.org/10.1086/tcj.64.20749244.

Hillman, Ben, *Patronage and Power: Local State Networks and Party-State Resilience in Rural China*. Stanford, California: Stanford University Press, 2014, doi.org/10.1017/s0305741015000508.

Ho, Samuel P. S., *Rural China in Transition: Non-Agricultural Development in Rural Jiangsu 1978–1990*. Oxford: Clarendon Press, 1994.

Huang, Yasheng, 'Central–Local Relations in China during the Reform Era: The Economic and Institutional Dimensions', *World Development* 24, no. 4 (1996): 655–72, doi.org/10.1016/0305-750x(95)00160-e.

Imai, Katsushi S., Xiaobing Wang and Woojin Kang, 'Poverty and Vulnerability in Rural China: Effects of Taxation', *Journal of Chinese Economic and Business Studies* 8, no. 4 (2010): 399–425, doi.org/10.1080/14765284.2010.513177.

Jia, Hao and Zhimin Lin, *Changing Central-Local Relations in China: Reform and State Capacity*. Boulder: Westview Press, 1994, doi.org/10.4324/9780429038761.

Jiang, Zhengmao, 'Shehuizhuyi xin nongcun "xin" zai nali?' [What is new in the new socialist countryside?], *Renmin Wang* [People network], 1 March 2006.

Kennedy, John James, 'State Capacity and Support for Village Institutions in Rural Shaanxi', *China Information* 23, no. 3 (2009): 383–410, doi.org/10.1177/0920203x09340941.

Kim, Hyung-A, *Korea's Development under Park Chung Hee*. New York: RoutledgeCurzon, 2004.

Kipnis, Andrew B., 'Audit Cultures: Neoliberal Governmentality, Socialist Legacy, or Technologies of Governing?', *American Ethnologist* 35, no. 2 (2008): 275–89, doi.org/10.1111/j.1548-1425.2008.00034.x.

Kipnis, Andrew, 'Neoliberalism Reified: Suzhi Discourse and Tropes of Neoliberalism in the People's Republic of China', *Journal of the Royal Anthropological Institute* 13, no. 2 (2007): 383–400, doi.org/10.1111/j.1467-9655.2007.00432.x.

Kipnis, Andrew B., *Producing Guanxi: Sentiments, Self and Subculture in a North China Village*. Durham: Duke University Press, 1997, doi.org/10.1017/s0305741000006044.

Kipnis, Andrew B., 'School Consolidation in Rural China', *Development Bulletin*, no. 70 (2006): 123–25.

Kipnis, Andrew, 'Suzhi: A Keyword Approach', *China Quarterly*, no. 186 (2006): 295–313, doi.org/10.1017/s0305741006000166.

Klotzbücher, Sascha, Peter Lässig, Jiangmei Qin and Susanne Weigelin-Schwiedrzik, 'What Is New in the "New Rural Co-operative Medical System"? An Assessment in One Kazak County of the Xinjiang Uyghur Autonomous Region', *China Quarterly*, no. 201 (2010): 38–57, doi.org/10.1017/s0305741009991068.

Kong, Sherry Tao and Jonathan Unger, 'Egalitarian Redistributions of Agricultural Land in China through Community Consensus: Findings from Two Surveys', *China Journal*, no. 69 (2013): 1–19, doi.org/10.1086/668808.

Kung, James, Yongshun Cai and Xiulin Sun, 'Rural Cadres and Governance in China: Incentive, Institution and Accountability', *China Journal*, no. 62 (2009): 61–77, doi.org/10.1086/tcj.62.20648114.

Lai, Lili, 'Discerning the Cultural: An Ethnography of China's Rural -Urban Divide'. PhD diss., The University of North Carolina, 2008.

Lampton, David M., 'The Implementation Problem in Post-Mao China'. In *Policy Implementation in Post-Mao China*, edited by David M. Lampton, 3–24. Berkeley: University of California Press, 1987, doi.org/10.2307/2057688.

Li, Chunling, 'Pinkun diqu jiaoyu' [Education in poverty-stricken areas]. In *Jinru 21 shiji de Zhongguo nongcun* [Rural China enters the 21st century], edited by Jingming Xiong, 228–37. Beijing: Guangming Ribao Chubanshe, 2000.

Li, Guoxiang, 'Road to Rural Vitalization', *China Pictorial*, no, 836 (February 2018): 18–20, china-pictorial.com.cn/media/1/Magazine_covers_and_PDF/2018-02.pdf, accessed 21 October 2021.

Li, Jing, 'Jianshe xin nongcun qieji "yi dao qie"' [Avoiding uniform implementation during the construction of a new socialist countryside], *Renmin Wang* [People network], 15 February 2006.

Li, Linda Chelan, 'Working for the Peasants? Strategic Interactions and Unintended Consequences in the Chinese Rural Tax Reform', *China Journal*, no. 57 (2007): 89–106, doi.org/10.1086/tcj.57.20066242.

Li, Xu, 'Xin nongcun jianshe 'xin' zai nali?' [What is new in building the new countryside?], *Sichuan Xinwen Wang* [Sichuan news network], 6 April 2010.

Li, Zuojun, *Zhongguo xin nongcun jianshe baogao* [A report on the building of a new countryside in China]. Beijing: Shehui Kexue Wenxian Chubanshe, 2006.

Lieberthal, Kenneth, 'China's Governing System and Its Impact on Environmental Policy Implementation', *China Environment Series*, no. 1 (1997): 3–8.

Lieberthal, Kenneth, *Governing China: From Revolution through Reform*. New York: W.W. Norton & Company, 2004 [1995].

Lin, Wanlong and Christine Wong, 'Are Beijing's Equalization Policies Reaching the Poor? An Analysis of Direct Subsidies under the "Three Rurals" (Sannong)', *China Journal*, no. 67 (2012): 23–45, doi.org/10.1086/665738.

Lipsky, Michael, *Street-Level Bureaucracy: Dilemmas of the Individual in Public Services*. New York: Russell Sage Foundation, 1980, doi.org/10.1177/00323 2928001000113.

Liu, Hongqiao, *China's Long March to Safe Drinking Water*, China Water Risk, 2015, translated by Hannah Short, s3.amazonaws.com/cd.live/uploads/content/file_en/8035/chinas-long-march-to-drinking-water-2015-en.pdf accessed 20 October 2021.

Liu, Mingxing, Juan Wang, Ran Tao and Rachel Murphy, 'The Political Economy of Earmarked Transfers in a State-Designated Poor County in Western China: Central Policies and Local Responses', *China Quarterly*, no. 200 (2009): 973–94, doi.org/10.1017/s0305741009990580.

Liu, Yigao, 'Xiaofei' [Expenses]. In *Jinru 21 shiji de Zhongguo nongcun* [Rural China enters the 21st century], edited by Jingming Xiong, 362–88. Beijing: Guangming Ribao Chubanshe, 2000.

Looney, Kristen E., 'China's Campaign to Build a New Socialist Countryside: Village Modernization, Peasant Councils, and the Ganzhou Model of Rural Development', *China Quarterly*, no. 224 (2015): 909–32, doi.org/10.1017/s0305741015001204.

Lu, Jie, *Varieties of Governance in China: Migration and Institutional Change in Chinese Villages*. Oxford: Oxford University Press, 2015.

Lü, Xiaobo, *Cadres and Corruption: The Organizational Involution of the Chinese Communist Party*. Stanford, California: Stanford University Press, 2000, doi.org/10.1017/s0003055400400602.

Manion, Melanie, 'Policy Implementation in the People's Republic of China: Authoritative Decisions versus Individual Interests', *Journal of Asian Studies* 50, no. 2 (1991): 253–79, doi.org/10.2307/2057208.

Meyer-Clement, Elena, 'Rural Urbanization Under Xi Jinping: From Rapid Community Building to Steady Urbanization?', *China Information* 34, no. 2 (2020): 187–207, doi.org/10.1177/0920203x19875931.

Migdal, Joel S. (ed.), *Strong Societies and Weak States: State–Society Relations and State Capabilities in the Third World*. Princeton: Princeton University Press, 1988, doi.org/10.1017/s0017257x00016511.

Ministry of Agriculture and Rural Affairs of the People's Republic of China, *Nongyebu guanyu shishi 'jiu da xingdong' de yijian* [The Ministry of Agriculture's opinion on the implementation of 'the nine big actions'], 2006.

Ministry of Civil Affairs of the People's Republic of China, *Minzhengbu guanyu kaizhan 'nongcun shequ jianshe shiyan quan fugai' chuangjian huodong de tongzhi* [A notice by the Ministry of Civil Affairs on 'full coverage of experimenting construction of rural communities'], document no. 27, 2009.

Moore, Mick, 'Mobilization and Disillusion in Rural Korea: The Saemaul Movement in Retrospect', *Pacific Affairs* 57, no. 4 (1984–85): 577–98, doi.org/10.2307/2758710.

Munro, Donald J., 'The Chinese View of Modeling', *Human Development* 18, no. 5 (1975): 333–53.

Munro, Donald J., *The Concept of Man in Contemporary China*. Ann Arbor: University of Michigan Press, 1979.

Murphy, Rachel, 'Turning Peasants into Modern Chinese Citizens: "Population Quality" Discourse, Demographic Transition and Primary Education', *China Quarterly*, no. 177 (2004): 1–20, doi.org/10.1017/s0305741004000025.

O'Brien, Kevin J., 'Implementing Political Reform in China's Villages', *Australian Journal of Chinese Affairs*, no. 32 (1994): 33–59, doi.org/10.2307/2949826.

O'Brien, Kevin J. and Lianjiang Li, 'Accommodating "Democracy" in a One-Party State: Introducing Village Elections in China', *China Quarterly*, no. 162 (2000): 465–89, doi.org/10.1017/s0305741000008213.

O'Brien, Kevin J. and Lianjiang Li, *Rightful Resistance in Rural China*. New York: Cambridge University Press, 2006.

O'Brien, Kevin J. and Lianjiang Li, 'Selective Policy Implementation in Rural China', *Comparative Politics* 31, no. 2 (1999): 167–86.

Oi, Jean C., *Rural China Takes Off: Institutional Foundations of Economic Reform*. Berkeley: University of California Press, 1999.

Oi, Jean C., *State and Peasant in Contemporary China: The Political Economy of Village Government*. Berkeley: University of California Press, 1989.

Ong, Lynette H., 'State-Led Urbanization in China: Skyscrapers, Land Revenue and "Concentrated Villages"', *China Quarterly*, no. 217 (2014): 162–79, doi.org/10.1017/s0305741014000010.

Opertti, Renato and Daoyu Wang, 'China: Regional Preparatory Workshop on Inclusive Education', International Bureau of Education, UNESCO, 2007, ibe.unesco.org/fileadmin/user_upload/COPs/News_documents/2007/0711 Hanghzou/Final_Report_of_ICE_Workshop_East_Asia.pdf, accessed 21 October 2021.

Patton, Dominique and Kevin Yao, 'UPDATE 1-China to Allow Farmers to Use Land, Property as Loan Collateral', *Reuters*, 24 August 2015, www.reuters.com/article/china-land-loans-idUSL4N10Z1I320150824, accessed 20 October 2021.

Perry, Elizabeth J., 'From Mass Campaigns to Managed Campaigns: "Constructing a New Socialist Countryside"'. In *Mao's Invisible Hand*, edited by Elizabeth J. Perry and Sebastian Heilmann, 30–61. Cambridge: Harvard University Press, 2011, doi.org/10.2307/j.ctt1sq5tc6.8.

Qi, Ye, Mark Henderson, Ming Xu, Jin Chen, Peijun Shi, Chunyang He, and G. William Skinner, 'Evolving Core-Periphery Interactions in a Rapidly Expanding Urban Landscape: The Case of Beijing', *Landscape Ecology*, no. 19 (2004): 375–88, doi.org/10.1023/b:land.0000030415.33172.f5.

Ragin, Charles C., *The Comparative Method: Moving Beyond Qualitative and Quantitative Strategies*. Berkeley: University of California Press, 1987, doi.org/10.1353/jsh/25.3.627.

Robin, Françoise, 'The "Socialist New Villages" in the Tibetan Autonomous Region: Reshaping the Rural Landscape and Controlling Its Inhabitants', *China Perspectives*, no. 3 (2009): 56–64.

Rosen, Stanley, 'Restoring Key Secondary Schools in Post-Mao China: The Politics of Competition and Educational Quality'. In *Policy Implementation in Post-Mao China*, edited by David M. Lampton, 321–53. Berkeley: University of California Press, 1987, doi.org/10.2307/2057688.

Rosenberg, Lior, 'Urbanizing the Rural: Local Strategies for Creating "New Style" Communities in China', *China Perspectives*, no. 3 (2013): 63–71, doi.org/10.4000/chinaperspectives.6279.

Rosenberg, Lior, 'Why Do Local Officials Bet on the Strong? Drawing Lessons from the Case of the Village Redevelopment Program', *China Journal*, no. 74 (2015): 18–42, doi.org/10.1086/681812.

Sabatier, Paul A., 'Top-Down and Bottom-Up Approaches to Implementation Research: A Critical Analysis and Suggested Synthesis', *Journal of Public Policy* 6, no. 1 (1986): 21–48, doi.org/10.1017/s0143814x00003846.

Schubert, Gunter and Anna L. Ahlers, 'County and Township Cadres as a Strategic Group: "Building a New Socialist Countryside" in Three Provinces', *China Journal*, no. 67 (2012): 67–86, doi.org/10.1086/665740.

Shandong Sheng Fazhan he Gaige Weiyuanhui [Committee of Development and Reform of Shandong Province], 'Shandong sheng jianshe shehuizhuyi xin nongcun jianshe zonyi guihua, 2006-2020' [Building a New Socialist Countryside—an overall planning of the province of Shandong, 2006–2020], doi.org/10.21474/ijar01/2071.

Sicular, Terry, 'The Challenge of High Inequality in China', *Inequality in Focus* 2, no. 2 (2013): 1–5.

Skinner, G. William, 'Cities and the Hierarchy of Local Systems'. In *The City in Late Imperial* China, edited by G. William Skinner, 275–351. Stanford: Stanford University Press, 1977, doi.org/10.1017/s0305741000036316.

Skinner, G. William, 'Marketing and Social Structure in Rural China', *Journal of Asian Studies* 24, no. 1 (November 1964): 3–43.

Smith, Graeme, 'Political Machinations in a Rural County', *China Journal*, no. 62 (2009): 29–59.

Smith, Graeme, 'The Hollow State: Rural Governance in China', *China Quarterly*, no. 203 (2010): 601–18.

Song, Guiwu, 'Xin nongcun jianshe yao zhuzhong ruan jianshe' [Building a new countryside must pay attention to soft construction], 2008, songguiwu.blogchina.com/552827.html, accessed 21 October 2021.

Su, Minzi, *China's Rural Development Policy: Exploring the 'New Socialist Countryside'*. Boulder: FirstForumPress, 2009.

Sun, Zifeng, 'Zhufang cunzhuang jianshe' [Housing and village construction]. In *Jinru 21 shiji de Zhongguo nongcun* [Rural China enters the 21st century], edited by Jingming Xiong, 138–63. Beijing: Guangming Ribao Chubanshe, 2000.

Swanson, Kate E., Richard G. Kuhn and Wei Xu, 'Environmental Policy Implementation in Rural China: A Case Study of Yuhang, Zhejiang', *Environmental Management* 27, no. 4 (2001): 481–91, doi.org/10.1007/s00267 0010164.

Tao, Ran, Kaizhong Yang and Mingxing Liu, 'State Capacity, Local Fiscal Autonomy, and Urban–Rural Income Disparity in China', *China Information*, no. XXIII (2009): 355–81, doi.org/10.1177/0920203x09343975.

Thøgersen, Stig, 'Building a New Socialist Countryside: Model Villages in Hubei'. In *Politics and Markets in Rural China*, edited by Björn Alpermann, 172–86. London and New York: Routledge, 2011.

Thøgersen, Stig, 'Cultural Life and Cultural Control in China: Where Is the Party?', *China Journal*, no. 44 (2000): 129–41, doi.org/10.2307/2667479.

Tong, Zhihui, 'Xin nongcun jianshe bing bu biran zhuiqiu nongcun chengshihua' [Building a new countryside is not necessarily urbanizing the villages], *Sociology Perspective*, 11 October 2007.

Tsai, Lily L., *Accountability without Democracy*. New York: Cambridge University Press, 2007.

Unger, Jonathan, 'The Struggle to Dictate China's Administration: The Conflict of Branches vs Areas vs Reform', *Australian Journal of Chinese Affairs*, no. 18 (1987): 15–45, doi.org/10.2307/2158582.

Vilela, Andrea, 'Pension Coverage in China and the Expansion of the New Rural Social Pension', *HelpAge International, Briefing on Social Protection in Older Age*, no. 11 (2013), doi.org/10.1163/2210-7975_hrd-9997-3036.

Wang, Shaoguang, 'Learning through Practice and Experimentation: The Financing of Rural Health Care'. In *Mao's Invisible Hand: The Political Foundations of Adaptive Governance in China*, edited by Sebastian Heilmann and Elizabeth J. Perry, 102–37. Cambridge: Harvard University Asia Center, 2011, doi.org/10.2307/j.ctt1sq5tc6.10.

Wang, Shaoguang and Angang Hu, *The Chinese Economy in Crisis*. Armonk, New York: M.E. Sharp, 2001.

Wang, Xianfeng, 'Xin nongcun jianshe de Beijing he tiaojian' [The background and conditions of building the new countryside]. In *Zhongguo xin nongcun jianshe baogao* [A report on the building of a new countryside in China], edited by Zuojun Li, 27–39. Beijing: Shehui Kexue Wenxian Chubanshe, 2006.

Weigelin-Schwiedrzik, Susanne, 'The Distance between State and Rural Society in the PRC. Reading Document No 1 (February 2004)', *Journal of Environmental Managementent* 87, no. 2 (2008): 216–25, doi.org/10.1016/j.jenvman.2007.03.046.

Westcott, Ben and Serenitie Wang, 'Xi Jinping Is Determined to End All Poverty in China by 2020. Can He Do It?', *CNN*, 20 April 2019, edition.cnn.com/2019/04/19/asia/poverty-alleviation-2020-xi-jinping-intl/index.html, accessed 21 October 2021.

White, Tyrene, 'Implementing the 'One-Child-Per-Couple' Population Program in Rural China: National Goals and Local Politics'. In *Policy Implementation in Post-Mao China*, edited by David M. Lampton, 284–317. Berkeley: University of California Press, 1987.

Whiting, Susan H., *Power and Wealth in Rural China: The Political Economy of Institutional Change*. New York: Cambridge University Press, 2001.

Whyte, Martin King, 'China's Post-Socialist Inequality', *Current History* 111, no. 746 (September 2012): 229–34, doi.org/10.1525/curh.2012.111.746.229.

Whyte, Martin King, *Myth of the Social Volcano: Perceptions of Inequality and Distributive Injustice in Contemporary China*. Stanford: Stanford University Press, 2010, doi.org/10.1515/9780804774185.

Whyte, Martin King, 'The Paradoxes of Rural–Urban Inequality in Contemporary China'. In *One Country, Two Societies: Rural–Urban Inequality in Contemporary China*, edited by Martin King Whyte, 1–25. Cambridge, Massachusetts: Harvard University Press, 2010, doi.org/10.2307/j.ctt1sq5t74.4.

Whyte, Martin King and Dong-Kyun Im, 'Is the Social Volcano Still Dormant? Trends in Chinese Attitudes toward Inequality', *Social Science Research*, no. 48 (2014): 62–76, doi.org/10.1016/j.ssresearch.2014.05.008.

World Bank, *China to Improve Rural Roads and Highway Management with Help from World Bank*, Press Release, 31 March 2015, worldbank.org/en/news/press-release/2015/03/31/china-improve-rural-roads-highway-management-world-bank, accessed 21 October 2021.

World Bank, *China: World Bank to Support Rural Roads in Guiyang*, Press Release, 6 March 2014.

Wright, Tim, 'State Capacity in Contemporary China: "Closing the Pits and Reducing Coal Production"', *Journal of Contemporary China* 16, no. 51 (2007): 173–94, doi.org/10.1080/10670560701194392.

Xiao, Yun, Li Li and Zhao Liqiu, 'Education on the Cheap: The Long-Run Effects of a Free Compulsory Education Reform in Rural China', *Journal of Comparative Economics*, no. 45 (2017): 544–62, doi.org/10.1016/j.jce.2017.07.003.

Xiong, Jingming and Yang Wenliang, 'Nongmin fudan' [Peasants' burden]. In *Jinru 21 shiji de Zhongguo nongcun* [Rural China enters the 21st century], edited by Jingming Xiong, 467–77. Beijing: Guangming Ribao Chubanshe, 2000.

Xu, Jiang, '"Rich Brothers" and "Poor Cousins": The Political Economy of Post-Reform Rural Disparity in a Chinese Township', *Journal of Contemporary China* 13, no. 41 (2004): 801–17, doi.org/10.1080/1067056042000281495.

Xu, Jin, 'China's Rural Land Reform Will Go Much Deeper This Year', CGTN, 20 February 2019, news.cgtn.com/news/3d3d514d3549444f32457a6333566d54/index.html, accessed 20 October 2021.

Yang, Shisong, 'Dui xin nongcun shequ jianshe de tansuo' [Exploring the construction of new rural communities], *Juece Tansuo* [Policy research & exploration], December 2011.

Yep, Ray, 'Local Alliances in Rural Urbanization: Land Transfer in Contemporary China', *China Information* 34, no. 2 (2020): 168–86, doi.org/10.1177/0920203x19865978.

Yu, Guoan, Wen Xinsan, Li Haijun, Wang Yudong, Zhang Shaosheng, and Yang Xiaoli, 'Shandong sheng caizheng zhichi xin nongcun jianshe fenlei fuchi zhengce yanjiu' [Research on Shandong Province's financial policies for supporting the new socialist countryside]. In *Xin nongcun jianshe jiaqiang fenlei zhidao: yanjiu he tansuo* [Strengthening guidance in Building The New Socialist Countryside: Research and exploration], edited by Fu Ruren, 55–82. Jinan: Huanghe Chubanshe, 2007.

Zhang, Jing, 'Laodong mofan: zai daode yu quanli zhijian—cong shehuixue de shijiao kan yi zhong daode jiaoyu zhidu' [Model workers: Between morality and power—a sociological perspective on moral education system], *Kaifang Shidai* [Open times], no. 2 (2007): 107–23.

Zhang, Linxiu, Renfu Luo, Chengfang Liu and Scott Rozelle, 'Investing in Rural China: Tracking China's Commitment to Modernization', *Chinese Economy* 39, no. 4 (2006): 57–84, doi.org/10.2753/ces1097-1475390404.

Zhang, Qian Forrest, 'Retreat from Equality or Advance toward Efficiency? Land Markets and Inequality in Rural Zhejiang', *China Quarterly*, no. 195 (2008): 535–57, doi.org/10.1017/s0305741008000763.

Zhang, Xin, Zeng Qingmin and Ruan Xianqiang, '*Miaozhun yiliu biaozhun gongjian xingfu jiayuan-Xianningshi zhashi tuijin nongcun shequ jianshe*' [Work together to build high standards happy homesteads: The city of Xianning soundly promotes construction of rural communities], *Zhongguo Shehui Bao*, 1 February 2019.

Zhao, Jijun and Jan Woudstra, '"In Agriculture, Learn from Dazhai": Mao Zedong's Revolutionary Model Village and the Battle against Nature', *Landscape Research* 32, no. 2 (2007): 171–205, doi.org/10.1080/01426390701231564.

Zhao, Shukai, 'The Accountability System of Township Governments', *Chinese Sociology and Anthropology* 39, no. 2 (Winter 2006–7): 64–73, doi.org/10.2753/csa0009-4625390207.

Zhao, Shukai, 'The Debt Chaos of Township Governments', *Chinese Sociology and Anthropology* 39, no. 2 (Winter 2006–7): 36–44, doi.org/10.2753/csa0009-4625390204.

Zhao, Shukai, 'Hard-Pressed Township Finances', *Chinese Sociology and Anthropology* 39, no. 2 (Winter 2006–7): 45–54, doi.org/10.2753/csa0009-4625390205.

Zhao, Shukai, 'Obligatory Interactions in the Affairs of Township Governments', *Chinese Sociology and Anthropology* 39, no. 2 (Winter 2006–7): 17–25, doi.org/10.2753/csa0009-4625390202.

Zhao, Shukai, 'The Power System of Township Governments', *Chinese Sociology and Anthropology* 39, no. 2 (Winter 2006–7): 8–16, doi.org/10.2753/csa0009-4625390201.

Zhao, Shukai, 'Township–Village Relations: Disconnection in the Midst of Control', *Chinese Sociology and Anthropology* 39, no. 2 (Winter 2006–7): 74–93, doi.org/10.2753/csa0009-4625390208.

Zhou, Xueguang, 'The Institutional Logic of Collusion among Local Governments in China', *Modern China* 36, no. 1 (2010): 47–78, doi.org/10.1177/00977 00409347970.

Zhou, Yingying, Han Hua and Stevan Harrell, 'From Labour to Capital: Intra-Village Inequality in Rural China, 1988–2006', *China Quarterly*, no. 195 (2008): 515–34, doi.org/10.1017/s0305741008000751.

Zweig, David, 'Context and Content in Policy Implementation: Household Contracts and Decollectivization, 1977–1983'. In *Policy Implementation in Post-Mao China*, edited by David M. Lampton, 255–83. Berkeley: University of California Press, 1987, doi.org/10.2307/2057688.

Appendix

Table A1: Building the New Socialist Countryside — Targets of the County and Two Townships

Eight new and one good	Specific targets	Township A	Township E
1. Creating a new industrial development structure (*dazao chanye fazhan xin geju* 打造产业发展新格局)	• Keep developing and extending industry as a key solution to rural (*sannong* 三农) problems	Yes	Yes
	• Develop secondary and tertiary industries to reach the ratio of 3:72:25 between 1st, 2nd and 3rd industries • Reach the ratio of 3:59:38 by 2015	Yes, to reach 3:72:25	Yes, to reach 5:70:25
	• Develop five main industries (*chanye* 产业): markets (*shichang* 市场), dining (*canyin* 餐饮), circulation of goods (*wuliu* 物流), real estate (*fangdichan* 房地产) and tourism (*lüyou* 旅游)	Yes, except for tourism	Yes, except for tourism
	• Develop services such as finance, insurance, information and consultation	No	No
	• Shift rural industry from villages to townships • Shift workers into non-agricultural sectors • Accelerate the pace of becoming a strong county that raises livestock (*xumu qiang xian* 畜牧强县) • Develop modernised and high-quality agriculture and recycled (*xunhuan* 循环) agriculture • Cultivate leading industries • Improve agricultural industry and its modernisation	Yes	Yes

Eight new and one good	Specific targets	Township A	Township E
2. Constructing a new unified countryside (*jianshe chengxiang yiti xin cunzhen* 建设城乡一体新村镇)	• Remove small and 'empty' villages • Move remote villages • Build central villages (*zhongxin cun* 中心村) • Develop villages with distinguishable features (*tese cun* 特色村) • Promote the establishment of residential communities (*juzhu shequhua* 居住社区化) according to local conditions to achieve changes in residential areas, industries and (rural) scenery • Prepare village plans and scientifically decide villages' construction orientation • Complete public facilities • Use resources efficiently • Create a beautiful living environment and a comfortable lifestyle • Ensure that new houses meet the people's needs and culture, are beautiful and incorporate different styles (not merely uniform)	Yes	Yes, except for the part of changing new housing, production and scenery
3. New living and production facilities (*wanshan shengchan shenghuo xin sheshi* 完善生产生活新设施)	• Annually increase the budget allocated by the government to support rural areas • Shift public resources into villages • Extend public facilities into villages • Increase the coverage of public services and their accessibility • Consistently improve undeveloped production conditions • Upgrade the level of agricultural mechanisation • Improve integrated agricultural production abilities • Upgrade agricultural machinery and professional equipment • Increase the scope and standardised methods of breeding livestock • Better usage of crop straws • Build methane gas pits • Improve ecological agriculture and recycling resources • Improve public goods and services such as roads, electricity, water and garbage disposal, education, hygiene, culture, communication and commerce • Continually improve the level of public services	Yes	Yes

Eight new and one good	Specific targets	Township A	Township E
4. Beautify the new environment in rural communities (*meihua nongcun shequ xin huanjing* 美化农村社区新环境)	• Create green, clean, bright and beautiful villages • Strengthen management of villages' environment • Optimise (*youhua* 优化) the environment for residences • Embrace the process of 'three and one' (*sangeyi* 三个一, i.e. every village should have a place to conduct public affairs, a model road and an activities courtyard) • Implement the 'three transformations, three cleanings and three constructions' (*san gai, san qing, san jian* 三改，三清，三建) process (i.e. transforming water, toilets and cooking ovens) • Clean up garbage, polluted water and useless old buildings • Construct waste pools, water ditches and facilities for garbage disposal) • 'Separating three areas' (refers to separating living areas, livestock areas and industrial areas) • Build facilities for central garbage collection • Thoroughly change the village environment and get rid of what is dirty (*zang* 脏), in disorder (*luan* 乱) and poor quality (*cha* 差) • Make the village greener • Reduce air pollution • Popularise the use of clean energies • Provide clean drinking water • Use hygienic toilets • Create blue skies and clear water (*lantian bishui* 蓝天碧水) • Create a happy and comfortable ecological environment	Yes	Yes

Eight new and one good	Specific targets	Township A	Township E
5. Establish a new social security system (*jianli shehui baozhang xin tixi* 建立社会保障新体系)	• Establish a secure employment system • Unblock information channels • Set up carrier services • Complete service networks • Encourage organised shifts of manpower and full employment • Build sound production and livelihood safeguards • Speed up the creation of a communal services centre and convenient supermarkets • Complete the creation of science and technology network services • Establish service organisations in the villages that are set up by the people, operated by the people and benefit the people • Handle practical affairs for the masses and solve difficult problems • Complete the welfare system • Commence rural pensions and develop an economic support system to assist peasants with difficulties • Popularise preschool education • Implement the policy of free education and 'two free, one subsidised' *liangmian yibu* 两免一补 (which refers to free tuition and textbooks and subsidised boarding) • Establish up-to-standard health clinics in the villages and ensure that all peasants participate in the new-style medical cooperative insurance • Build a system that prevents the spread of disease • Ensure a minimum standard of living • Assist the physically and mentally disabled, old party members and old people with difficulties • Compensate peasants who have lost their land • Provide the five guarantees to support old people (refers to food, shelter, clothing, medical treatment and burial expenses) • Solve the problem of housing • Provide temporary subsidies to families dragged into poverty due to illness, disaster or injury	Yes	Yes

Eight new and one good	Specific targets	Township A	Township E
6. Cultivate new peasants with modern consciousness (*peiyu xiandai yishi xin nongmin* 培育现代意识新农民)	• Set up a whole-life educational system • Cultivate new-style peasants who are civilised, understand technology and are capable of managing affairs • Provide professional training to foster new skilled professional workers with a focus on practical technology for the villages • Create new educated labour force	Yes	Yes
	• Technological training for existing workforce will not last less than 10 days per year	No	No
	• People of the appropriate age will become new-style peasants or industrial workers who will be skilled, of high quality and high employability • 75 per cent of labour force will move to secondary and tertiary industries	Yes	Yes
7. Advocating new fashion of healthy civilisation (*changdao jiankang wenming xin fengshang* 倡导健康文明新风尚)	Build villages with civilised spirit • Select honourable households who meet the five styles (refers to technology, virtue, law, sports and hygiene) and have leading people in science and technology, good mothers-in-law, good daughters-in-law, good neighbours etc. • Establish cultural activities for the people • Organise daily sports and recreation activities that are rich, colourful and healthy • Lead and educate the people to obey and act according to laws and regulations • Raise the level of self-cultivation • Change existing habits and create new healthy habits • Extend and improve the people's civilised and moral thinking	Yes	Yes
8. Implementing new standards for work in townships and villages (*luoshi zhencun gongzuo xin guifan* 落实镇村工作新规范)	• Implement the '*siwei yiti* 四位一体' (refers to integrating economic construction, political construction, cultural construction and social construction) • Support the 'four democracies and two transparencies' (*si minzhu, liang gongkai* 四民主两公开, refers to elections, decision-making, management and supervision, public affairs and finances) • Develop the activity of 'democratic politics day' (*minzhu yizheng ri* 民主议政日) • Deepen the building of safe villages • Strengthen public order and governance • Complete the creation of a mediation system to resolve disputes, protect social stability	Yes	Yes

Eight new and one good	Specific targets	Township A	Township E
9. Building a group of 'two highs and two strongs' (*jianshe shuang gao shuang qiang hao banzi* 建设双高双强好班子)	• Continue creating advanced party and village organisations to foster 'two highs and two strongs' village officials (refers to high-quality politics, high prestige in the eyes of the masses, a strong ability to get rich and a strong ability to lead others to become rich) • Measure the organisation and the implementation of Building the New Socialist Countryside according to its accomplishments • Cadres to operate according to a standard • Change cadres' (low) abilities and working methods • Strengthen the abilities of village groups to govern and to build a socialist harmonious society • Improve coordination between village groups • Improve the level and ability of managing services and assistance to raise people's income • Strengthen the village party corps • Ensure that party members have tasks, posts, responsibilities, take action and lead effectively • Strengthen the reserves of cadres in the villages	Yes	Yes

Translated by the author.

Index

Note: Page numbers in italics indicate illustrations or maps. Page numbers with 'n' indicate footnotes.